THE PUBLIC AFFAIRS
GUIDE TO WESTMINSTER

The Handbook of Effective and Ethical Lobbying

Robert McGeachy

welsh academic press

Published in Wales by Welsh Academic Press, an imprint of
Ashley Drake Publishing Ltd
PO Box 733
Cardiff
CF14 7ZY

www.welsh-academic-press.wales

First Edition - 2019

ISBN
Paperback - 978 1 86057 1343

© Ashley Drake Publishing Ltd 2019
Text © Robert McGeachy 2019

British Library Cataloguing-in-Publication Data.
A CIP catalogue for this book is available from the British Library.

Typeset by Prepress Plus, India (www.prepressplus.in)
Cover design by Siôn Ilar, Welsh Books Council, Aberystwyth

Contents

Acknowledgements   *v*
Glossary   *ix*
Foreword   *xv*
Introduction   *xvii*

1. The Westminster Dynamic   1
2. Developing a Public Affairs Strategy   8
3. The Impact of Devolution   26
4. Exploiting Parliamentary Monitoring and Political
    Intelligence Gathering   40
5. Influencing Key Policy Makers   60
6. Engaging with MPs and Peers   78
7. Influencing the Political Parties   87
8. Making the Most of Consultation Responses   101
9. Engaging with Parliamentary Committees   111
10. Legislation: Influencing the Pre-legislative Stage   129
11. Legislation: Overview of the Parliamentary Process   142
12. Legislation: Influencing the Parliamentary Process   158
13. Private Members' Bills   184
14. Parliamentary Questions   193
15. Parliamentary Debates   203
16. Early Day Motions   217
17. Petitions   229
18. All-Party Parliamentary Groups   238
19. Maximising the Impact of Parliamentary Events   247
20. Making the Most of Party Conferences   257
21. Developing Effective Partnership Working   277
22. Maximising Media Impact   288

Conclusions   301
Bibliography   303
Index   305

In memory of:
Lord Harry Ewing of Kirkford,
Lord Neil Carmichael of Kelvingrove, and
Lord Donald Macaulay of Bragar

Acknowledgements

Working in the House of Lords for the Labour Party between 1989 and 1997 was a tremendous honour and privilege. I worked for distinguished leaders and Chief Whips, initially Lord Cledwyn of Penrhos and Lord Ponsonby of Shulbrede, followed by Lord Richard of Ammanford and Lord Graham of Edmonton, all of whom made a significant contribution to the Labour Party, and to British politics.

The late Lord Cledwyn of Penrhos and Lord Ponsonby of Shulbrede were an astute, highly respected and accomplished team. Their tactical expertise ensured that the Labour Party in the House of Lords was effective, able to consistently put the Conservative Government under significant pressure in the Upper House and to secure important concessions on major legislation. Lord Richard and Lord Graham were also a formidable team, and deserve great credit for maintaining the pressure on the Conservative Government through their vision, parliamentary expertise and effective strategy, which regularly inflicted defeats upon the Government on key legislation in the House of Lords.

As well as Leaders and Chief Whips of note, the Labour Party also had the benefit of being able to rely on distinguished, multi-talented frontbench spokespersons in the House of Lords. The members of the Labour Party's frontbench in the House of Lords were highly skilled and effective parliamentarians, and made an invaluable contribution to the Labour Party. They were a truly remarkable group, and I am not alone in holding them in the highest esteem for their individual and collective achievements.

It was also the Labour Party's good fortune that it could draw upon the tremendous support of the backbench Labour Peers, all of whom had made a major contribution to the Labour movement, and continued to represent the Labour Party with distinction. They included, to name but a few: Lord Peter Archer of Sandwell, Lord John Ardwick, Baroness Alma Birk, Lord Billy Blease, Lord Terry Boston, Lord Arthur Bottomley, Lord Donald Bruce of Donnington, Lord Callaghan of Cardiff, Lord Michael Cocks, Baroness Nora David, Lord Joe Dean of Beswick, Lord Jack Dormand of Easington, Lord

David Ennals, Baroness Doris Fisher, Lord John Gallacher, Lord Myer Galpern, Baroness Joyce Gould of Potternewton, Lord Glenamara, Lord Dennis Healey, Baroness Jenny Hilton, Lord Clive Hollick, Lord Houghton of Sowerby, Lord Bill Hughes of Hawkhill, Lord Johnny Jacques, Baroness Lena Jeger, Lord Jenkins of Putney, Lord Kennet, Lord Kirkhill, Lord Leatherland, Baroness Pat Llewelyn-Davies, Lord Peter Lovell-Davis, Baroness Betty Lockwood, Lord John Mackie, Lord Roy Mason, Lord Merlyn-Rees, Lord Mishcon, Lord Len Murray, Baroness Wendy Nicol, Lord Bert Oram, Lord David Pitt of Hampstead, Lord Nick Rea, Lord Bill Sefton of Garston, Baroness Bea Serota, Lord Shackleton, Lord Malcolm Shepherd, Lord Donald Soper, Lord Stoddart of Swindon, Lord Jock Stallard, Lord Strabolgi, Lord Tom Taylor of Gryffe, Lord Reg Underhill, Baroness Eirene White, Lord Ted Willis and Lord Wilson of Rievaulx.

I would like to express my deep gratitude to Lord Graham of Edmonton and to Lord Clinton-Davis for their unfailing kindness and generosity, and for their support, which is much appreciated.

The Labour Peers were supported by excellent staff in the House of Lords under the wise guidance of Mrs Shirley Shepherd. They included Jess Bawden-Bouche, Elizabeth Gardiner, Jane Jonas, David Melhuish, Marianne Morris, Katharine Quarmby and Natalka Znak. The staff also included the late Clare Cozens who made such an important contribution to the work of the Labour Peers on parliamentary legislation, latterly as a special adviser to Baroness Jay of Paddington and as an adviser on the equalities legislation until her sad and untimely death. It was an honour and privilege to work with all of my former colleagues in the Opposition Whips' Office in the House of Lords, as well as with colleagues from the wider Parliamentary Labour Party including, to name but a few: Rowan Andrews, Josh Arnold-Foster, Dan Corry, David Clark, Jon Cruddus, Julian Eccles, Mick Fisher, Tye Goddard, Joanne Goodwin, Catherine Jarman, Kirti Ambasna-Jones, John Ludlow, Tom Lynes, Jim Mahon, David Miliband, Joe McCrae, Pat McFadden, Cathy McGlynn, Ian MacKenzie, John McTernan, Nick Pecorelli, Siôn Simon, Nigel Stanley, Stephen Tindale, Roy Trivedy, Helen Walters, Sheila Watson, Larry and Angela Whitty and John Lumsden.

During the period I worked in the House of Lords I was deeply impressed by the professionalism, dedication and expertise of the staff who worked in the Upper House including, to name but a few: Simon Burton, Mark Cooper, John Breslin, the staff in Black Rod's office, the Committee staff, the *Hansard* staff, the House of Lords library staff, Margaret Pironi, Brendan Keith, Bob Jolly, Richard Jolly, 'Taff' Evans and all the post room staff, George Martin and Mick Skelton and all the door keepers, the police and security staff, Tom Mohan, Geoffrey Newsome, Ted Norris, Ed Ollard, Mary Ollard, and the staff in the Printed Paper Office, Chris Boulton and the information team, and Edward Wells.

My time in London was enriched by the company of good friends including Sam Rush, Mike Mulvihill, Duncan Adamson, Caroline and Adam Bray, Ewan and Claire Cameron, Richard Chambers, Robyn Cornford, Simon and Janet Crawford, Lesley Farrell, Colin Galloway, Brian Gardner, Veronique Gerber, David Gray, Mike Hewitt, Frankie and Sandra Houston, Dominic Judge, Alex Leitch, George and Natalie McPhee, Jason Phelps, Jasna Suzic, Dr J.D. Young and Mrs Lorna Young, and Carolyn Woodger. I was also privileged to be a member of Breens FC during its ascent through the various divisions of the Enfield and Edmonton Sunday Football League, along with John King, Tommy Breen Jnr., Steve Breen, Paul Gray, Eric Stuart, Brian Gardner, Chris Thomas, Terry Norman, Matt Stubbins, John Downes, Chris Francis, Paul Lowen, Roy Ephgrave, Chris Coles, Peter Howarth, Graham Kingsbury, Karl Harrington, Christian Blunkle, Keith Dodds, Phil McMurdie and Neil McHugh. Special mentions to Dave Jones and to the late Tom Breen Snr., who lit up the dressing room with their wit and banter – win, lose or draw.

Special thanks go to Jonathan and Juliet Buchan, and Cairns Leslie and Alison Kirkwood, for their kindness, encouragement and good humour, which is deeply appreciated as always. I would also like to thank Alex Cole-Hamilton MSP, Sam Ghibaldan, Mark Ballard, Chris Donnelly, Steven Livingstone, Gareth Brown, Mandy Rhodes at *Holyrood Magazine*, and Martin Dewar at Staybright Digital for their support along the way.

I would also like to pay tribute to the skills and best practice of Bill Scott, Andrew Strong, Gareth Jones, Craig Wilson, Marion Davies and Satwat Rehman, all of whom have made a significant contribution to helping to shape policy development and legislation in their respective policy areas.

I am very grateful to Michael Clancy OBE, Director of Law Reform at the Law Society of Scotland, for providing the Foreword to this book. Michael has a distinguished track record in shaping and influencing legislation in the Scottish Parliament, and in both Houses of the UK Parliament. No-one has been more effective than Michael in these areas, and his impact upon legislation in the Scottish Parliament and in the UK Parliament is second to none. I was also delighted that Michael agreed to provide comments on the early drafts of this book, given his encyclopaedic knowledge of how Westminster works, and unrivalled mastery of the legislative processes in both Houses. His comments were invaluable, and have greatly strengthened the book.

I am also very grateful to Michael Clancy OBE for his generous Foreword, as well as to Brendan O'Hara MP for his support and kind words.

I would like to thank Ashley Drake, Managing Director of Welsh Academic Press, for publishing *The Public Affairs Guide to Westminster - The Handbook of Effective and Ethical Lobbying*, and for all of his support and advice which is deeply appreciated. My thanks also go to the production team at Welsh Academic Press for the excellent job they have done in publishing this book.

I would like to express my deep appreciation for the knowledge and expertise of the staff of the House of Commons Information Office, of the House of Commons Library, of the House of Lords Information Office and of the House of Lords Library. Their excellent and highly informative publications, including web based material, have been an invaluable resource in writing this book. I would also like to thank the House of Commons Enquiry Service for providing information which I have used in this book. Their efficient, thorough and expert service has been immensely helpful.

My biggest thanks, however, go to my wife Sandy, and to our children James, Eve and Olivia, to whom I am deeply indebted for all of their support and encouragement, and without which I could not have written this book.

Robert McGeachy
Edinburgh
July 2019

Glossary[1]

Act of Parliament	After a Bill has been passed by both Houses of Parliament it receives Royal Assent, and becomes an Act of Parliament and part of UK law.
Adjournment debate	Short debates taken at close of business in the House of Commons.
Affirmative procedure	Statutory instruments subject to the affirmative procedure must be expressly approved by both Houses of Parliament.
Amendments	Changes to a Bill, or a Motion, proposed by an MP or Peer. They can be used to add text to a Bill, or to delete text from the legislation, or to repeal provisions in other legislation.
All-Party Parliamentary Groups (APPGs)	Informal, cross-party parliamentary groups, consisting of MPs and Peers. APPGs focus on specific policy issues, or regions or countries.
Assembly Member (AM)	Member of the National Assembly for Wales, to be renamed the Senedd (Members of the Senedd) under the terms of The Senedd and Elections (Wales) Bill.
Backbenchers	MPs or Peers who do not hold ministerial office, or serve as front bench spokespersons for an opposition party.
Bill	A proposal for a new law, or a proposal to amend or repeal an existing law, that is presented to Parliament. Once the Bill has been passed by both Houses, and has received Royal Assent, it becomes an Act of the UK Parliament and part of UK law.
By-elections	Elections which occur when a seat becomes vacant between General Elections.
Cabinet	The group of Government ministers appointed by the Prime Minister to lead on, and to oversee, specific policy areas.
Committee Stage	The stage of a Bill which follows Second Reading. The Committee Stage focuses on the line by line scrutiny of the Bill.
CBI	Confederation of British Industry
Consultations	Government departments, and other agencies, use consultations to seek the views of stakeholders on various policy areas and issues.
Crossbench Peers	Peers who are non-party political.

---

1 Some of the explanations used in the glossary draw upon information available on the UK Parliament's website, www.parliament.uk.

Delegated legislation (also known as secondary legislation)	Acts of Parliament (primary legislation) often contain provisions which enable ministers to introduce delegated/secondary legislation, usually by statutory instrument. The aim of the secondary legislation is to add greater detail to the primary legislation, and often to add provisions which were considered too complex or detailed to be included in the primary legislation.
Devolved and reserved matters	Devolved matters are policy and legislative areas and issues that fall within the powers of the Scottish Parliament, the Northern Ireland Assembly and the National Assembly for Wales. Reserved matters are policy and legislative areas that fall within the powers of the UK Parliament.
Divisions	These are used to count who is for or against a Motion when there is a vote in the House of Commons or in the House of Lords, and the members go into the Division lobbies to be counted.
Draft Bills	Bills circulated for consultation prior to the Government finalising its legislative proposals, and introducing a final version of the Bill in Parliament.
Early Day Motions ("EDMs")	Formal Motions for debate used to highlight policy issues, or campaigns or developments, although it is rare for EDMs to lead to a debate.
Electorate	Those members of the population eligible to vote in elections to Parliament.
English Votes for English Laws ("EVEL")	EVEL refers to the English Votes for English Laws process.
First Reading	First Reading marks the formal introduction of a Bill in either House of Parliament.
'Flagship' Bill	A high profile Government Bill.
Government	The Government is in charge of the United Kingdom. It is usually formed by the party with the largest number of seats in the House of Commons. The Government is led by the Prime Minister, who appoints his or her ministers. The latter are accountable to Parliament. The Government is responsible for UK-wide policies that are not devolved to the Scottish Parliament or to the Northern Ireland Assembly or to the National Assembly for Wales. Its duties include introducing new laws.
Green Papers	These are Government discussion papers which outline draft proposals for policy changes, as well as options for progressing these changes. The Government consults on the proposals contained in Green Papers.

Groupings	Confirm the order in which amendments to a Bill will be debated, and which amendments will be debated together.
Hansard	*Hansard* (the Official Report) is the daily report of parliamentary sitting days in both the House of Commons and the House of Lords.
Legislative Consent Motion	Motion passed by a devolved body to allow the UK Parliament to legislate on a matter normally devolved to the devolved body.
Marshalled List	List of amendments tabled for debate on a Bill.
Member of the Legislative Assembly (MLA)	Member of the Northern Ireland Legislative Assembly
Member of Parliament ("MP")	A person elected by the electorate in a parliamentary constituency to sit as an MP in the House of Commons.
Member of the Scottish Parliament ("MSP")	A person elected by the electorate in a parliamentary constituency to sit as a Member of the Scottish Parliament.
Ministers	These are the MPs and Peers appointed by the Prime Minister to serve as Government spokespersons on, and to oversee, specific policy areas.
NHS	National Health Service
Negative procedure	Statutory instruments subject to the negative procedure will automatically become law without debate unless there is an objection from either House, i.e. an MP or Peer lodges a Motion to Annul (known as a 'Prayer') within 40 days of the statutory instrument being laid objecting to the statutory instrument and requiring that it be annulled.
The Opposition (HM Official Opposition)	The party with the next most seats in the House of Commons after the party of Government. The leader of this party is known as the Leader of the Opposition.
Opposition parties	Parties that are not in Government are described as opposition parties.
Parliamentary Questions	Parliamentary questions or PQs are questions put formally by MPs or Peers to Government ministers either orally or in writing about matters over which the latter have responsibility.
Parliamentary session	A parliamentary session lasts a year, and will usually commence in Spring with the State Opening of Parliament, and end with Prorogation when Parliament rises. Each Parliament generally consists of five sessions.

The Party Whip	The Party Whip is a circular sent by each party to its MPs or Peers outlining forthcoming parliamentary business, and instructing its members on how to vote on particular Divisions in debates or legislation. The Whip is 'underlined', with a 'three-line' Whip being the most important.
Party Whips	The whips are MPs or Peers appointed by their party to help organise its response to parliamentary business. Their key duties include mobilising their party's MPs or Peers to vote in Divisions and to vote in accordance with the Party's Whip, and acting as Tellers during Divisions.
Peer	A member of the House of Lords.
Policy Asks	The specific actions or steps you wish a policy maker, or groups of policy makers, to take on your behalf in relation to influencing policy development and legislation.
Pre-legislative scrutiny	The consideration of a draft Bill by a select committee prior to its provisions being finalised by the Government.
Prime Minister	The leader of the Government.
Prime Minister's Question Time	Prime Minister's Question Time, or PMQs, are oral questions from MPs answered by the Prime Minister in the House of Commons every Wednesday between 12 noon and 12.30pm.
Private Members' Bills	Private Members' Bills are a type of public bill, which can be introduced by backbench MPs and Peers (who do not hold ministerial responsibilities), to propose new laws, or to repeal or facilitate changes to existing laws.
Public Bills	Public Bills refer to the Parliamentary Bills introduced by the Government, or by individual MPs or Peers as Private Members' Bills, which seek changes to the law on matters applying to the whole population.
Public Bill Committees	Public Bill Committees are appointed by the House of Commons to scrutinise specific Bills. All Bills, except Money Bills, are automatically sent to a Public Bill Committee in the House of Commons, after their Second Reading, unless they are to be dealt with by a Committee of the Whole House.
PLC	Public Limited Company
Queen's Speech	Speech made by the Queen in the House of Lords at the State Opening of Parliament to outline the Government's programme for the Parliament.
Report Stage	The Report Stage follows the Committee Stage of a Bill, and permits scrutiny by the whole House (either the House of Commons or the House of Lords) of the Bill as amended at Committee Stage.

Royal Assent	After both Houses have agreed the content of a Bill, it can then be presented to the Monarch for final approval known as Royal Assent. This approval is required to enable the Bill to become an Act of the UK Parliament, and part of UK law.
Second Reading stage	The Second Reading stage of a Bill gives either House an opportunity to debate the principles and provisions of a Bill. If the Bill passes its Second Reading, it then enters its Committee Stage.
Speaker	The Speaker is an MP elected by MPs to chair debates in the House of Commons, and to maintain order in the Chamber.
Special advisers	Political appointees made by political parties, usually the Government, to advise on matters of policy and strategy.
Standing Orders	Written rules governing the regulation of proceedings in the House of Commons and in the House of Lords.
Starred Questions	Oral questions in the House of Lords.
Statutory Guidance	Statutory guidance is guidance introduced by the Government through duties placed on it under specific Acts of Parliament. It generally provides guidance on aspects of the legislation.
Super-affirmative procedure	Orders subject to the super-affirmative procedure require the minister to have regard to "representations, House of Commons and House of Lords resolutions, and Committee recommendations that are made within 60 days of laying, in order to decide whether to proceed with the order and (if so) whether to do so as presented or in an amended form."[2]
Third Reading	Final opportunity for both Houses to decide whether or not to pass or to reject a Bill.
Usual Channels	The behind the scenes negotiations involving the leaders and Chief Whips of the respective parties about the management of parliamentary business.
Westminster Hall	A lot of important parliamentary business is taken in Westminster Hall, which takes place in a room off Westminster Hall rather than in the main Commons Chamber.
White Papers	Policy statements issued by the Government for consideration by a wide range of policy makers including the opposition parties, and individual MPs and Peers as well as by other stakeholders including organisations with an interest in the subject matter and issues raised in the White Paper. These publications often build upon proposals initially set out in Government Green Papers, and confirm how these proposals will be progressed, including through legislation.

---

2   UK Parliament, 'Legislative Reform Orders', UK Parliament website, www. parliament.uk

Foreword

In these uncertain political times, particularly in the light of the continuing turmoil resulting from the 2016 Brexit referendum, it is vital for those working in public affairs to have a solid and reliable guide they can depend on, and Robert McGeachy has performed a great service to those who needing to operate within with the political structures at Westminster.

His *Public Affairs Guide to Westminster – The Handbook of Effective and Ethical Lobbying* is just such a guide. It is an essential tool for anyone who wishes to lobby the UK Parliament in a cogent and successful way. This comprehensive book covers it all. Robert explains, in an easy to understand way, how to develop a public affairs strategy, how to monitor Parliament and gather political intelligence and how to influence key policymakers.

In terms of Parliamentary procedure, notwithstanding recent innovations (which some might consider to be particular to the Brexit issue) Robert shows his mastery of procedure in both the House of Commons and the House of Lords. He explains how to deal with committees, and various other mechanisms for catching attention and developing the political campaign to a successful conclusion. His analysis of Private Members' bills, Parliamentary questions and debates, Early Day Motions and Petitions confirms how comprehensive a work this is.

Robert has drawn on his long Parliamentary experience to produce a fascinating book full of insight. The helpful summary of key points at the end of each chapter is a useful reminder of what should be done when engaging with Parliament. For those unfamiliar with devolution his chapter on this is extremely helpful.

Although he is too modest to take any credit, if one studies the analysis of changes made to the Welfare Reform Bill one can see how effective Robert's expertise can be.

Reading this book will help any campaigning organisation or individual to emulate that example.

Michael P Clancy OBE
July 2019

Introduction

The UK Parliament is one of the oldest parliaments in the world. Over the centuries it has experienced many changes, as its membership, structures and processes have adapted to reflect political and socio-economic developments in our society. Some of the most notable changes in recent years have been associated with the devolution arrangements for Scotland, Northern Ireland, and Wales. These individual settlements have each, in their own right, been significant, and have resulted in a wide range of policy and legislative areas being transferred from the UK Parliament to the Scottish Parliament, to the Northern Ireland Assembly, and to the National Assembly for Wales respectively. The policy and legislative areas falling within the remit of the UK Parliament, and those falling within the remit of the Scottish Parliament, of the Northern Ireland Assembly, and of the National Assembly for Wales are considered in more detail in Chapter 3.

Despite the impact of devolution, however, Parliament continues to be responsible for major areas of policy and legislation affecting people, institutions and laws across the UK. It is not surprising then that, on a daily basis, large numbers of organisations and individuals continue to approach the Government, the opposition parties at Westminster, as well as individual MPs and Peers, seeking to influence policy development and legislation at Government level, and in both Houses of Parliament. The outcomes achievable through such approaches can be far reaching. Approaching the Government could, for example, potentially secure a visit by the Prime Minister to your business, or to the public body or charity you work for or have an association with. This would offer significant benefits in terms of influencing opportunities, and in raising the profile of your organisation. It could also generate a meeting with a Government minister to discuss a concern you wish to raise in a specific policy area, or enlist the minister's support for your business in policy areas to promote the growth of your business or the sector in which it operates. Other outcomes might include persuading an MP or Peer to table amendments to a Bill introduced by the Government or to introduce a Private Member's Bill on your behalf, or to raise issues in a debate or to ask a written or oral question for your organisation. These would all represent positive outcomes, although an organisation's capacity to deliver such outcomes will depend upon a number of factors. In this respect, the organisation's connections across the political spectrum of parties and groupings represented in both Houses of Parliament would be important factors, as would its knowledge of the political landscape, the effectiveness of its public affairs strategy (if one is in place), and the organisation's capacity to undertake public affairs work.

The success of such approaches has varied enormously, with each new parliamentary session providing examples of best practice in public affairs work, as well as examples of ineffective public affairs strategies that have failed to deliver tangible results. Indeed, while certain organisations and individuals have enjoyed major success in influencing the Government and policy development and legislation in Parliament, many others have struggled to achieve the same impact. Significantly, some organisations will identify issues on which they wish to engage with leading policy makers, and policy areas and legislation that they would like to help shape and influence, but feel unable to actively contribute in these areas due to a sense that such activity is simply beyond their knowledge and expertise. This is often due to capacity issues within organisations, and a lack of resources and staff to get involved in activities beyond the core tasks of keeping their business on track, or of delivering key services.

This guide seeks to help overcome these barriers by providing organisations with the information and guidance they will require to develop an effective public affairs strategy, or to strengthen their existing public affairs strategy. Following the advice in this guide will assist organisations to maximise the impact of their public affairs strategy, and to ensure that this strategy is best equipped to deliver tangible outcomes. In particular, it provides insights and recommendations, based on successful best practice, which will enable organisations across the private sector, the public sector and the third sector to help shape and influence policy development and legislation at Government level, and key parliamentary business in both Houses of Parliament. Furthermore, it can support organisations to raise their profile with the Government, with the opposition parties, and with individual MPs and Peers.

The guide will be of equal interest and relevance to organisations in different sectors, including the private sector, the public sector and the third sector. With careful adaptation to suit particular circumstances, the advice and recommendations in this guide can be developed, and used, by organisations in all of these sectors. The term 'organisation' is, therefore, used throughout the guide to refer to businesses, to statutory bodies and agencies, and to charities and voluntary organisations including community groups. The guide will also be invaluable to individuals seeking information about, and strategies on, how they can influence the Government, and other key policymakers in Parliament.

The aim of this guide is to strengthen the public affairs capacity and knowledge base of organisations, and to support them to undertake public affairs work effectively or more efficiently, and with confidence or greater confidence. By following the advice in this guide, public affairs work can become much more accessible to organisations seeking to engage with, and to influence, Government (ministers and civil servants), the opposition parties, as well as individual MPs and Peers on specific policy issues or areas, or on particular parliamentary business such as Public Bills. This guide seeks to empower such organisations to feel confident and able to undertake public affairs work, where it will be advantageous to their organisation to do so. Furthermore, it provides advice on how to progress public affairs work, and to do it well, even where organisations' resources are strictly limited. The guide also offers new insights and strategies, based on successful best practice, which will strike a chord with the more seasoned public affairs professionals.

It does not provide detailed information about the history and functions of Parliament or of Government, or about the legislative processes in Parliament. The guide focuses, instead, on how best to develop public affairs strategies to influence policy makers up to ministerial level, as well as engaging with the opposition parties, and with individual MPs and Peers. It offers insights into the full range of activities which organisations should consider undertaking as part of the process of developing, and delivering, effective public affairs strategies to influence national policy developments and legislation.

The guide will be an invaluable source of information for organisations seeking to develop their public affairs work, and to strengthen their capacity in this area. It offers clear advice on how organisations can develop their public affairs strategies, and on ways in which these strategies can be successfully progressed and implemented. Chapters have been structured to provide sound guidance and advice on specific types, and areas, of public affairs work, which organisations can use to engage with Government, with the opposition parties and political groupings and with individual politicians. It will be an essential resource for organisations wishing to become active in public affairs work to raise the profile of their organisation, but lacking the skills and knowledge to do so and looking for support on how to develop their work in this area. The guide will also be a useful source for organisations which are already involved in public affairs work, and are seeking new perspectives into specific areas of public affairs work such as, for example, how to influence the legislative process in the House of Commons or in the House of Lords.

Applying the advice and guidance in this guide will provide your organisation with the knowledge and insights necessary to engage with politicians on a more confident basis, and in ways which are more guaranteed to deliver success. With careful thought and application, the guide can have a positive impact on your organisation's public affairs work and strategy, and raise its involvement in these areas to a much higher and more effective level. It will help to ensure that your organisation's public affairs strategy influences key policy makers, and delivers tangible outcomes which raise the profile of your organisation and enable it to shape relevant policy development and legislation at a national level. These are major outcomes, and ones which are achievable by the vast majority of organisations. This guide will help to maximise your organisation's opportunities of successfully doing so, and of influencing key policy debates and developments at a national level.

Finally, before engaging with Government Representatives (Government Ministers and senior civil servants) it is vital that you first consider the guidance provided by the Registrar of Consultant Lobbyists to determine if you are carrying out the business of consultant lobbying, i.e. paid lobbying on behalf of a client, in which case you will need to join the Register of Consultant Lobbyists. On the other hand, those falling within one of the exemptions outlined in the Transparency of Lobbying, Non-Party Campaigning and Trade Union Administration Act 2014 are not required to join the Register of Consultant Lobbyists.

Robert McGeachy
July 2019

1

The Westminster Dynamic

For organisations seeking to influence policy makers and policy development at Government level, and the legislative processes within Parliament, it is vital to be aware of the unique dynamics of the Westminster system. This includes the interface between the Government and Whitehall departments which help to drive forward the Government's policy development and legislative proposals. This is one of the areas looked at in more detail in Chapter 10. It also embraces the relationship, and interaction, between both Houses of Parliament. The devolution arrangements with Scotland, Northern Ireland and Wales are another factor to be considered. These are all part of the political landscape which your organisation will need to take into account when developing its public affairs strategy. Further details about the devolution arrangements can be found in Chapter 3.

A key part of the Westminster dynamic which your organisation will need to weigh up in assessing how best to influence leading policy makers is the bicameral structure of the UK political system based on the House of Commons and on the House of Lords. In this respect, it is vital that your organisation does not lose sight of the fact that potentially there could be strategic opportunities to influence senior policy makers, policy development and parliamentary legislation in both the House of Commons and in the House of Lords. The benefits for your organisation, if it follows the advice in this guide on how to develop an effective public affairs strategy, will be considerable. Your organisation should also remember that the two Houses each have their own distinct traditions, character and processes, and that these will be important factors in terms of how your organisation seeks to develop and progress its influencing strategy in the House of Commons and in the House of Lords.

Need for a 'Two Chambers' approach

There is a wide range of public affairs activities focusing on the House of Commons and on the House of Lords, which your organisation may wish to consider undertaking to develop its relations with key policy makers, whether in support of a campaign it is launching, or to engage in dialogue on specific policy issues of mutual interest. Once your organisation has established that the issues on which it is focusing definitely fall within the legislative competence of Parliament, it must consider how best to take these issues forward with the Government at ministerial level, as well as with the Government's civil servants and special advisers. Your organisation should also give thought to how to engage on these issues with the spokespersons of the Official Opposition party, with the other opposition parties' spokespersons, as well as with individuals MPs and Peers. It is recommended that your organisation, in shaping its strategy, focuses on the bicameral structure of the UK parliamentary system, and develops a strategic 'Two Chambers' approach. This will ensure your organisation is best placed to make the most of opportunities to engage on these issues with, and to influence, politicians in the House of Commons and in the House of Lords up to ministerial level. Such an approach will support your organisation to increase its chances of having a tangible impact upon parliamentary business in both Houses.

Against this background, it is strongly recommended that your organisation develops a public affairs strategy featuring activities in the House of Commons and in the House of Lords, and which is linked to the key parliamentary business relevant to your organisation and its interests in the respective Houses. An important part of your organisation's work in this area will be to ensure that it monitors, and tracks, any parliamentary business in both Houses that is relevant to your organisation and its work. Significantly, both Houses of the UK Parliament feature similar types of parliamentary business including Parliamentary Questions, debates, Government statements, and parliamentary legislation which is often the main daily business in Parliament. Your organisation should, therefore, be prepared to take, and develop, a flexible approach which can switch, where necessary, between business in the House of Commons and in the House of Lords with equal effectiveness and dexterity. This should not be too onerous if your organisation prioritises parliamentary business according to the significance of its impact upon your organisation and its interests. By doing so, you will be able to ensure that such switches actually help your organisation to efficiently achieve its strategic aims, rather than to weaken the overall strategic focus of its public affairs strategy.

Another area where your organisation should consider developing its public affairs strategy is the relations between the House of Commons and the House of Lords. These can sometimes give rise to tensions, where the two Houses are controlled by different political parties, or if the political will and vision of the governing party in the House of Commons is not shared by the House of Lords, including elements within its own party in the Upper House. The latter scenario can mean Government defeats in the House of Lords, particularly on Divisions, i.e. votes, on key provisions in Bills or on Orders or on other forms of delegated legislation. Such defeats can occur even where the party of Government is nominally the largest party in the Lords. The reasons for these defeats can be attributed to the facts that the Government of the day does not have an overall majority in the House of Lords, and that there are a large number of crossbench Peers who will often vote for or against measures on their merits, and without regard to party politics. Furthermore, although the parties will all whip their members, i.e. provide instructions to vote in a particular way on specific measures in the House of Lords, there is often a willingness by Peers of all parties, and on all sides of the House, to approach issues in the House of Lords on a cross-party basis, and objectively on their merits. This sometimes extends to a willingness by some Peers to vote against their own Party's Whip, where they disagree with their party's position on a particular issue or Bill. The incidence of this practice in the House of Lords will depend upon factors such as the specific policy issues under consideration, and the political landscape at the time of the vote. What is clear is that MPs in the House of Commons generally do not take a cross-party approach on policy issues, unless instructed to do so by the Party Whip. Indeed, when backbench MPs do take such an approach in the House of Commons, and act against the instructions of The Party Whip, it will often be presented in the media as a 'backbench rebellion'. These key characteristics of the House of Lords can potentially provide organisations with significant scope to build up cross-party alliances in support of their policy positions, or campaigns or proposed amendments to legislation. This issue is considered in more detail in Chapters 11 and 12 below.

The challenges of working in the bicameral system, as well as of utilising the opportunities it may present, can best be illustrated by reference to the legislative processes in both Houses. By way of a quick overview, a Public Bill will complete all of its stages in the House of Commons, and will then be transferred to the House of Lords where it will go through similar stages or vice versa. The start of this process will depend upon whether or not the Bill is a 'House of Commons Bill' or a 'House of Lords Bill', i.e. whether it was commenced in the House of Commons or in the House of Lords. If the legislation raises issues for your organisation, the legislative process may require you to put in place a strategy which will respond to the legislation as it progresses through each House, unless, of course, your organisation is able to secure its influencing objectives as a result of concessions made by the Government in the House where the Bill is first introduced.

This is not as difficult as it may sound, and Chapters 11 and 12 provide clear advice and guidance, based on successful best practice, on how your organisation can help to shape and influence legislation in both Houses. Preparing a public affairs strategy for both Houses, in response to a Public Bill, is the recommended approach even if there is a strong chance you might secure your influencing objectives at an early stage in the legislative process. Significantly, governments are not always willing to make early concessions on their Parliamentary Bills. Furthermore, it should be recognised that it usually takes time for organisations to build up support from MPs and Peers in favour of a particular amendment proposed by a Government minister, or MP or Peer. On that basis, your organisation should start from the assumption that it may require public affairs activities in both Houses to achieve its aims and objectives. Taking this approach will ensure that your organisation's public affairs strategy, in response to the legislation, is focused and well structured, and helps to influence the legislation. It will also place your organisation in the best possible position to raise its profile with Government ministers, the opposition parties, MPs and Peers, and to ensure that its public affairs strategy achieves tangible outcomes in response to the legislation.

Many of the same considerations would apply for organisations with an interest in progressing a Private Member's Bill in either the House of Commons or the House of Lords. Private Members' Bills are dealt with in Chapter 13. These Bills offer organisations important opportunities to potentially change the law. They can also offer organisations a strong focus for a campaign, which can be progressed on a short-, or medium- or long-term basis. For a Private Member's Bill to become law, however, it will need to successfully navigate its way through the legislative processes in both Houses. Only a small minority are able to do so. Your organisation will increase the chances of its Private Member's Bill becoming law, and of achieving the above outcomes, therefore, if you have developed and progressed a public affairs strategy in support of the legislation in both Houses. The influencing opportunities in the House of Commons and in the House of Lords, presented by a Private Member's Bill, can be significant. Organisations which remain focused on the need for a 'Two Chambers' approach will be best placed to secure tangible outcomes around a campaign focusing on a Private Member's Bill.

It is recommended that you also adopt such an approach with regard to other types of parliamentary business such as debates, and Parliamentary Questions. Briefing MPs for a debate in the House of Commons, for example, could offer your organisation an excellent opportunity to raise its profile, and to engage on key policy issues, with the Government, with the opposition parties and with MPs. It is also more likely, subject to the policy areas being addressed in the debate, that there will be media interest in a debate in the House of Commons. While a debate in the House of Lords will, depending upon the subject matter, generally attract less media interest, it will still present significant influencing opportunities, and should not be neglected. A House of Lords debate will potentially offer important chances to influence the Government, and to raise the profile of your organisation's policy positions on particular issues. Significantly, if the debate is focusing on issues which will subsequently be revisited during the course of parliamentary legislation it could also lay the foundations of a public affairs strategy which will enable your organisation to brief Peers when the relevant Parliamentary Bill reaches the House of Lords, and to persuade Peers to subsequently vote against and potentially defeat the Government on key amendments to the Bill reflecting these issues.

Using the 'Two Chambers' approach is also helpful if you are seeking to put pressure on the Government on a particular policy issue or area, and to continue to exert that pressure until your organisation has secured concessions on the issue or has otherwise achieved its aims and objectives. This can be illustrated by reference to the potential use of Parliamentary Questions in both Houses. Where your organisation is seeking to raise an issue with the Government, options would include approaching an MP or Peer to lodge an oral or written question in the House of Commons or in the House of Lords. Apart from securing potentially significant information which your organisation could use to inform its public affairs strategy, this option would help your organisation to increase the profile of the issues it is seeking to raise.

This could be particularly effective if you are seeking to exert some pressure on the Government on a specific policy issue. Raising the questions in the House of Commons, supported by a media strategy, would be a high profile way of putting the Government under pressure where your organisation's previous engagement with the latter has proved ineffective or reached an impasse. In this respect, you could also approach a Peer to lodge similar questions in the House of Lords to further raise the profile of the issues you are raising, and to keep the Government under pressure. Alternatively, your organisation could use information obtained by your organisation through an oral or written question in one House, to support, and strengthen your policy position, for the questions you will then raise in 'Another Place' or the 'Other Place'.[1] Organisations can use this technique to build up the momentum behind a policy issue, and as a means of raising the profile of issues and to try and exert pressure on the Government to make concessions in a particular policy area.

---

1   MPs and Peers by Convention will not refer to the other House in Parliament when speaking in the Chamber. An MP or Peer will instead refer to events in 'Another Place' or in the 'Other Place'.

Summary of key points

The key points from this chapter can be summarised as follows:

- Organisations seeking to influence policy makers, policy development and the legislative processes in both Houses of Parliament must develop public affairs strategies, which take into account, and reflect, the unique dynamics of Westminster.
- Successful public affairs strategies are most likely to include activities to exploit strategic opportunities to influence senior policy makers, policy development and parliamentary legislation in both the House of Commons and in the House of Lords.
- Taking a 'Two Chambers' approach to public affairs will help organisations to maximise the impact of their strategy at Westminster.

2

Developing a Public Affairs Strategy

There is often a lot of discussion and debate within different sectors about what is meant by the term 'public affairs' and the activities it embraces, and about the interface between 'public affairs' and parliamentary work and lobbying. Such terms are fairly synonymous in practice, and you should avoid getting bogged down in semantics. 'Public affairs' defines and includes the full range of activities which organisations use to influence politicians from backbench MPs and Peers up to the level of the Prime Minister and Government ministers on policy and legislative issues. Given the importance of the local government community in decision-making affecting numerous policy areas and issues, this would also include activities to engage and influence key figures within the local government community, from senior officials and local councillors up to council leadership level.[1] 'Public affairs' will also include any media work your organisation undertakes in support of its parliamentary and governmental engagement to influence policy makers.

Are public affairs campaigns always necessary?

For some organisations, especially local authorities and other public sector bodies and agencies, and businesses and companies in the private sector, the main focus of their public affairs activity will normally be developing and maintaining their relationships with key policy makers up to ministerial level. These organisations often have good, close relationships with senior policy makers, and will be well positioned to try and influence public policy through their usual course of formal and informal contacts with Government ministers and their

---

1 This would include council leaders and lead spokespersons, and elected mayors.

special advisers and senior civil servants, MPs, Peers and members of the local government community up to council leadership level. Where an organisation enjoys such relationships with senior policy makers, it may find that it never needs to launch a high profile public affairs campaign. Indeed, for some organisations such a course of action might not be appropriate or strategically advantageous. A large PLC, for example, would generally be more likely to rely on meetings with the Prime Minister and Government ministers, and with senior decision makers in the opposition parties, to influence their policies in particular areas, rather than to launch a high profile public affairs campaign.

These are factors which your organisation should address at the beginning of planning its influencing strategy. Will it be able to achieve its objectives without undertaking a public affairs campaign, simply by requesting and securing a meeting with the Prime Minister or with the relevant Government minister and/or with their special advisers and officials, or with an opposition party spokesperson, or with an MP or Peer or with local councillors and with other senior policy makers in the local government community? At such meetings your organisation would raise its concerns, or share details of an initiative, with the national and/or local politician, and if the meeting is positive you might secure all or at least some of your main objectives, and 'policy asks', i.e. the specific actions or steps you wish the policy maker to take on your behalf. Perhaps you might influence a Government policy strategy with your input and proposals, or gain acceptance for an amendment you are proposing to a Bill in Parliament, or secure invaluable support and/or funding for your business or for one of your projects or services. These scenarios sometimes occur, but for many organisations they will often, unfortunately, be very rare, and more likely to be the exception rather than the rule.

As a starting point in developing your organisation's public affairs strategy, it is recommended that you contact the Prime Minister, or the relevant Government minister's office, or your local MP or a sympathetic Peer, or local councillors or other senior members of the local government community to raise your organisation's issues and concerns, and to request a meeting before undertaking a public affairs campaign. This might resolve the concerns you are seeking to raise, or help your organisation to secure the opportunities it has identified and, if it does so, this will save your organisation a lot of time, effort and money. You should note, however, that in many cases obtaining a meeting with the Prime Minister or with the relevant Government minister will not be possible, given the demands on their time. It is, therefore, recommended that you undertake a realistic assessment of which politicians to approach. In this respect, it is vital that you clearly identify the problem you wish to raise or the opportunity you want to secure, the required solution, and which policy maker is best placed to deliver the solution. These are the type of factors that will determine which policy maker your organisation should decide to engage with before developing a more extensive public affairs campaign.

Organisations developing a public affairs strategy should also give careful consideration to ways in which they can use their character, image and reputations to best effect in helping to maximise the impact of such strategies. To put this in perspective, community and voluntary sector organisations play a key role in many local communities across the UK, and are an important part of the fabric of our society. These organisations have a breadth of knowledge and experience, and deliver a wide range of excellent services. Community and voluntary organisations often have good stories to share. For such organisations the secret is to make sure that the right politicians are aware of their successes, and of the important work the organisation undertakes. Significantly, the same type of opportunities will often potentially arise equally for organisations in the public sector and in the private sector. Organisations across the different sectors should, therefore, not be shy about raising policy issues with the Prime Minister or a Government minister, or an MP, or Peer, or a key policy maker in the local government community up to council leadership level. In many cases they will be only too willing to engage with you, and to consider the issues you are raising on their merits.

One little tip to mention – and ignore it at your peril – is that if your organisation does decide to write to a Government minister make sure that you send the letter by post and by e-mail to their ministerial postal and e-mail addresses. Please note that using the postal address for their constituency office or their 'MP' e-mail address could result in significant delays in the time it takes to receive a response. This could prove costly if you are trying to engage the minister on a matter of the greatest importance and urgency. The ministerial postal and e-mail addresses can be obtained from the Government's website, or by telephoning the Government's central switchboard. Contact details for MPs are available on the Parliament's website, and those of local council leaders, elected mayors and local councillors on the website for the relevant local authority.

If, however, your approach on a policy matter to the Prime Minister or to a Government minister, or to the relevant spokespersons of the different opposition parties, or to an MP or Peer, or to a key figure within the local government community draws a blank, your organisation should then review its public affairs activities, and consider if it would be appropriate and advantageous to run a public affairs campaign. In this respect, your organisation would need to consider what type of public affairs campaign it should run, the strategic aims and objectives of the campaign, its key messages and the 'policy asks' on which it will focus. It would also need to decide upon the length of the campaign, its major milestones and the outcomes you are hoping the campaign will deliver. Consideration should also be given to the 'outputs' of the campaign, i.e. the public affairs activities which will be necessary to progress the campaign, and to ensure it delivers the desired outcomes.

Aims and objectives

Key considerations for your organisation, in developing a public affairs campaign or initiative as part of its public affairs strategy, must be collectively considering why it is seeking to undertake public affairs activities in the first place? What is your organisation hoping to achieve? What are its 'policy asks'? Does it have specific goals it is seeking to attain in relation to influencing policy development and parliamentary business, or is it more about generally raising your organisation's profile? If it is the latter, why does your organisation need a high public profile, or a higher public affairs profile? Where does your organisation stand in terms of its public profile? Where does it want to be, and how does it get there?

The answers to these questions will depend to a great extent on the type of organisation concerned, and its overall aims and objectives. Is your organisation, for example:

- a PLC with business interests across the UK?
- a public sector body such as a local authority, or an NHS Trust?
- a membership organisation (sometimes referred to as an umbrella organisation) such as the CBI, or a professional body or a trade

union campaigning, and speaking out, on behalf of its members, or otherwise representing its members' interests?

- a large UK-wide charity campaigning to, for example, tackle poverty, or to protect the environment?
- a local community-based organisation or campaign focusing on health issues?

These are just a few examples of the type of organisations or campaigns which will benefit from a public affairs strategy mapping out the range of activities to deliver key campaigns or initiatives. Some of the above organisations will have very different aims and objectives from each other, but others will reflect a close synergy in aspects of their public affairs work, or in the areas in which their public affairs activities should focus.

The type of organisation or campaign, and their key aims and objectives, will generally help to shape and inform the kind, and range, of public affairs activity undertaken. Another important factor is that the above organisations or campaigns will generally have varying levels of expertise, experience and resources with which to deliver effective public affairs strategies and activities. This will also have a significant bearing on the sort of public affairs campaign or initiative adopted and progressed.

It is recommended that your organisation should, before launching its public affairs campaign or initiative, define and agree very clear aims and objectives, and 'policy asks', for the work you will be undertaking in this area. These potential aims and objectives could include, for example:

- raising your organisation's profile with the Prime Minister, with Government ministers, with the opposition parties, with individual MPs of all parties, with Peers and with local councils;
- shaping and influencing key Government legislation or policy initiatives or strategies likely to impact upon your organisation and its work, and/or on those you work with/for, and/or on the policy issues on which you campaign or have an interest;
- securing cross-party support for a 'policy ask' or initiative your organisation has developed, and wishes to progress;
- undertaking a range of public affairs activities to secure cross-party support to help safeguard funding for your organisation, or for one of your services/projects, or to protect your core business; and

- securing representation on high profile Government working groups.

It may be that the aims and objectives of your public affairs initiative or campaign will include some or all of the above. Indeed, many of the above aims and objectives would be complementary to each other.

Developing key messages

Before launching a public affairs campaign or initiative, your organisation must also ensure that it has got the right key messages and 'policy asks', and has sufficiently risk-assessed and 'road-tested' them to withstand the most robust scrutiny. This might appear self-evident, but it is surprising the number of public affairs strategies and campaigns which rely on a 'scatter-gun' approach, and would appear to have been launched simply hoping for the best.

Your organisation will generally stand a much better chance of achieving its public policy aims and objectives if it spends a bit of time, before launching a public affairs campaign or initiative, on developing and fine tuning the messages and 'policy asks' on which it wishes to focus. Part of this process should involve identifying the evidence and best practice that will underpin, and support, these messages and 'policy asks'. You should also invest some time anticipating any criticism your organisation's headline messages may attract, or potential weaknesses in the underlying detail. Addressing these factors before you go public with your headline themes, messages and 'policy asks' will help to strengthen the impact of your campaign.

Your organisation also needs to be very clear about the messages it wishes to convey to the policy makers, and it is advised that you should try and keep things as simple as possible. Admittedly, this is not always easy when the issues are often complex, but you need to boil things down to clear, concise messages as much as possible, and to concentrate your campaign or initiative on these key themes and messages. Maintaining a clear focus will be critical throughout all stages of your organisation's public affairs strategy, including any campaigns or initiatives within this strategy. Furthermore, your organisation should apply this standard in progressing any public affairs campaign or initiative, whether or not it is trying to persuade a

Government minister to visit one of its services to find out more about its best practice or to secure the latter's support for a particular policy position. Similarly, the same factors should be taken into account when trying to persuade members of a parliamentary Public Bill committee to support an amendment lodged on your organisation's behalf by the local MP or by a Peer, on legislation likely to impact upon your organisation and its work. Keeping your main messages simple will help to maximise the chances of your public affairs campaign or initiative being successful, and of delivering lasting benefits to your organisation, and to its work.

Playing to your strengths

It is recommended that organisations should always bear in mind, when developing their key themes and messages, the need to make sure they play to their strengths. Many organisations fail to do so, or do so ineffectively and, as a result, their engagement with politicians often does not deliver the positive outcomes and rewards which their best practice and excellent businesses or services merit and demand. This, in turn, limits the impact of their public affairs strategy or activities.

Government ministers, the opposition parties, individual MPs and Peers, and senior members of the local government community are more likely to respond positively to the issues your organisation is raising if these issues are based on the proven best practice of its business or services, and upon persuasive evidence. If possible, and if your organisation has the resources, you should back up your key messages with best practice and evidence from your organisation, and its services which have been externally evaluated. Being able to draw upon an external evaluation report, compiled by an independent organisation or agency, will potentially strengthen your organisation's policy position and increase its persuasiveness with the politicians you are seeking to influence.

Many community and voluntary organisations will be unable to afford external evaluations of their work to underpin and strengthen their headline messages. If your organisation falls into this category, you should consider other ways of presenting the best practice and evidence from your work to make it as attractive and persuasive as possible to Government ministers, to the opposition parties, to MPs of all parties, to Peers and to key figures in the local government community. When doing so your organisation needs to highlight its strengths, and how it can contribute to specific areas of policy development, and to current policy debates.

The aim of any public affairs campaign or activities should be to persuade the Government, the opposition parties, individual MPs, Peers and leading members of the local government community that the specific objectives you have set for the campaign or activities, and the issues your organisation is raising, are compelling, and are based on successful practice, and on strong qualitative and/or quantitative evidence. In this respect, if your organisation provides services then you should, for example, consider undertaking a survey of service users/customers where there are high levels of service user/customer satisfaction. You should then present the findings of the survey, along with any quotes from service users/customers which demonstrate their satisfaction with the services received, and/or emphasise the concerns you are raising on their behalf. This will help to reinforce your organisation's headline messages, and demonstrate to the policy makers that these messages are based upon proven experience and expertise, including best practice of what works.

Providing genuine case studies is another good way of helping to illustrate, and strengthen, your main themes and messages. Case studies are particularly useful if your organisation is briefing MPs or Peers for a debate in Parliament, or if it is seeking support from members of a key parliamentary committee for amendments to a piece of legislation. Again, using case studies helps to demonstrate to the policy makers that your headline messages have been developed on the back of effective practice, and from experience of what works.

For many policy makers, a short bullet-point case study is worth a thousand words of briefing. It helps them to quickly drill down to the main issues, and to get a better understanding of the issues you are raising. Remember you need to remain sensitive to the fact that the minister or MP or Peer might not have much time to intervene in the debate or during the Public Bill committee's consideration of amendments, so it is recommended that you present your organisation's briefing material in ways which will best support the minister's or the MP's or the Peer's intervention. You might, for example, draft the MP's speaking notes for the debate, or in support of your amendment, to ensure that they raise the issues you wish to prioritise, and in the way that your organisation will find most beneficial.

Understand the context

Another important factor for your organisation to get right at the beginning of planning its public affairs strategy, including campaigns or initiatives, is the political, public policy and legislative context. These are all inter-related, but you need to give them all careful thought before the launch of your campaign or public affairs initiative to maximise the chances of it delivering success and tangible outcomes for your organisation.

A key development in shaping the political context will be the Government's announcement of its priorities in the Queen's Speech at the start of each new session of Parliament, and also any subsequent statements made by the Government about its business programme. These statements will give your organisation an insight into the legislation, policy initiatives and strategies which the Government will be introducing, and the timescales involved. It will also confirm which policy areas the Government will be prioritising for the duration of the parliamentary session, i.e. the parliamentary year, and for the overall parliamentary term of five years.[2] Other major areas for your organisation could be the fiscal environment, and in particular Government announcements in the Budget Autumn Statement. Policy changes and discussions associated with the UK's vote to leave the European Union will also exert a powerful influence for many organisations and sectors.

Your organisation should familiarise itself with the Government's programme, and keep itself updated on any related Government statements made about this programme, or arising from other key aspects of the political context. Doing so will provide your organisation with a strong lead in terms of knowing which Government legislation, policy initiatives and strategies are likely to impact upon your work.

---

2   Under the Fixed-Term Parliaments Act 2011 General Elections are normally held every five years, unless there is a vote of 'no-confidence' in the Government, or a Motion for an earlier election is supported by two-thirds of the seats in the House of Commons (434 out of 650); UK Parliament, 'General Elections', UK Parliament website, www.parliament.uk.

It will also give your organisation an indication of the timescales involved, and a sense of what time will be available to plan and develop your organisation's public affairs strategies in response. Your organisation should then decide which Government policy and legislative business you will prioritise, and also the interface between this business and any proactive public affairs and initiatives your organisation might already be progressing.

Once the Government has outlined its policy priorities, and your organisation has identified the headline themes, issues, and 'policy asks' you will be progressing in response, you will be in a strong position to begin planning a public affairs campaign or initiative. Rather than risking a 'scatter-gun' approach to your organisation's attempts to influence Government ministers, the opposition parties, individual MPs and Peers and senior members of the local government community, you should try, as much as possible, to frame any approaches you make to these groups in the context of the relevant key Government and parliamentary business. Making the connection between a particular Government policy initiative and your work in this area is much more likely to help your organisation to secure, for example, a ministerial visit to one of its projects or businesses, than a general invite to Government ministers to visit its projects or businesses. Government ministers, the opposition parties' spokespersons and MPs probably get hundreds of general invites each week. The secret is to make your organisation's invite relevant, and to stand out for the right reasons. Demonstrating how your organisation's projects or services interact with, and complement, the Government's policy and legislative priorities will help in engaging with the Government. Alternatively, the opposition parties may be interested in your organisation's projects or services if they are successful, and complement their policies or demonstrate weaknesses in the Government's policies or approaches. Highlighting the innovative and successful approach of your organisation will increase the relevance of its invite to policy makers generally.

Another important consideration is to analyse, and to take on board, the political make-up of the Parliament, and which party or parties have formed the Government, including the political representation and balance within key parliamentary committees. It is vital that you take this into account when developing and progressing your organisation's public affairs strategy, including any specific campaigns or initiatives. Against this background, your organisation should consider, when developing its public affairs strategy, how to use the pre-legislative and consultative stages of legislation to the best advantage, and to engage early with key policy makers to raise issues and to share concerns and to try and secure concessions during these stages. This is considered in more detail in Chapter 10.

Your organisation should also weigh-up the advantages of working in alliance with other like-minded organisations on particular issues. Taking a partnership approach is not always appropriate, but it should at least be considered on its merits on a case-by-case basis, especially when you are seeking to respond to legislation that will impact on other organisations in the sector or sectors in which your organisation predominantly operates. In this respect, partnership working will demonstrate to the Government, to the opposition parties and to individual MPs and Peers that it is not just 'special pleading' by your organisation on particular policy issues, but that you are raising issues which are supported by a range of organisations. Demonstrating such support could make it more likely that your public affairs campaign or initiative will deliver successful outcomes, rather than going it alone. A lot will depend, however, on the issues you are raising with the policy makers, and the action you are calling for through this engagement.

Furthermore, your organisation should bear in mind that any partnership campaigns or initiatives must not be allowed to significantly dilute your organisation's own profile, particularly if it has taken the lead in raising the issues in the first place, and has done much, if not all, of the developmental legwork. This underlines the need for your organisation to take an integrated approach internally in progressing a public affairs campaign or initiative. Close co-operation between your senior management team, and colleagues working in public affairs and policy and in media, can help to minimise these risks, and to ensure that any initiatives to work on a partnership basis with other organisations are carefully considered, and subject to appropriate risk assessments at a senior level in your organisation. Taking such an approach will make it more likely that your organisation's experience of partnership working is positive, and that your organisation does not miss out on the benefits arising from the outcomes delivered through a specific partnership or joint venture.

Public affairs activities

Once your organisation has addressed the issues outlined above in shaping and developing its public affairs strategy, it can then start planning specific activities and initiatives for this strategy. Outlined below you will find a list of the type of activities which would fall within the scope of public affairs activities, and which have been successfully used as part of public affairs strategies. This list is by no means exhaustive, but it will at least give you a sense of the range of activities which can be involved in public affairs work. It is recommended that you look at the list below, and assess which of these activities would work best for your organisation to help deliver its public affairs strategy's aims and objectives. It may be that your organisation will find it most effective to take one or two of the activities from the list below, and to then build up its strategy around these activities, drawing upon, and weaving in, its own proposals for public affairs activities as appropriate.

Examples of typical public affairs activities include:

	Public Affairs Activities
1.	[For an organisation relying on local authority funding or considering a business start-up in the local authority area] Request a meeting with a member of the council's leadership, including the council leader or elected mayor or local councillor or officer with lead responsibility within the council for the policy/service areas covering your organisation's work. If relevant, this could be an invite to the council leader or elected mayor or lead spokesperson to visit one of your organisation's projects or services.
2	With regard to engaging with key policy makers at the national level, write to the following requesting meetings to brief them on your organisation's work, and to discuss issues of mutual interest including any concerns: • the Prime Minister; • Government ministers with portfolios relevant to your organisation's work; • the relevant spokespersons of the Official Opposition party; • the spokespersons of the other opposition parties with portfolios relevant to your organisation's work; • the chairs of parliamentary committees relevant to your organisation's work; • individual MPs; and • individual Peers

	Which of the above policy makers your organisation contacts will depend upon the aims and objectives of your approach, the concern or opportunity you have identified, the solution and your view of which policy maker can best deliver the solution.
3.	Write to the leaders of all the political parties represented in Parliament requesting meetings to brief them about your organisation's work, and to discuss the synergy between their policies or a particular policy position, and the work of your organisation and its policy positions including campaigns.
4.	Develop a programme of high profile visits to your organisation's projects/ services for Government ministers. Ministers should also be invited to launch new projects and services, and to give the keynote speech at celebration events at projects/services, e.g. events to open new premises, to launch new businesses or to celebrate a landmark anniversary, or specific achievements, of a project/service.
5.	Develop a programme of high profile visits to your organisation's projects/services for the spokespersons of the Opposition, and of the other opposition parties, with portfolios relevant to your organisation's work.
6.	Develop a programme of high profile visits to your organisation's projects/ services for MPs and Peers.
7.	Brief MPs/Peers, and submit written evidence, for key inquiries and debates in Parliament on issues relevant to your organisation.
8.	Respond to key legislation relevant to your organisation, and to its work, as follows: **Second Reading** Prepare briefing for the Second Reading debate. **Committee Stage** Draft amendments on key issues/concerns. **Report Stage** Progress key amendments not accepted during the Committee Stage. **Third Reading** In your Third Reading briefing prepared for the Government, the opposition parties and groupings and for individual MPs and Peers as appropriate, highlight issues overlooked, or which your organisation believes were dealt with unsatisfactorily, during the previous stages of the Bill.
9.	Respond to key Government consultations, and to consultations launched by other agencies, on issues relevant to your organisation and its work.

10.	Approach an MP or Peer to sponsor a members' debate on a subject area relevant to your organisation.
11.	Work with an MP or Peer on a Private Member's Bill focusing on an issue relevant to your organisation.
12.	Draft an e-petition to Parliament.
13.	Develop your organisation's involvement and participation in All-Party Parliamentary Groups relevant to its work
14.	Hold a parliamentary reception/briefing event on a key theme/issue relevant to your organisation
15.	Attend the political parties' spring and/or autumn conferences, and deliver a programme of activities at these conferences.

Now that we have considered some examples of the type of activities which contribute to a public affairs strategy, it is time to look at how these activities can be used to develop strategies that are successful, and deliver tangible outcomes.

To put this in perspective, the public affairs activities outlined above are revisited, and this time you will find included the aims and objectives or outcomes which it is advised you should be seeking to achieve through each activity. This list is not exhaustive. It should at least, however, give you some insight into the type of outcomes you should be looking to achieve through the activities your organisation decides to adopt and progress in its public affairs strategy.

	Activity	Aims and objectives
1.	[For an organisation relying on local authority funding or considering a business start-up in the local authority area] Request a meeting with a member of the council's leadership, including the council leader or elected mayor or local councillor or officer with lead responsibility within the council for the policy/service areas covering your organisation's work. If relevant, this could be an invite to the council leader or elected mayor or lead spokesperson to visit one of your organisation's projects or services.	To update local politicians about your work, and to secure recognition and/or support/funding for your work/business.

	Activity	Aims and objectives
2.	With regard to engaging with key policy makers at the national level write to the following requesting meetings to brief them on your organisation's work, and to discuss issues of mutual interest including any concerns: • the Prime Minister; • Government ministers with portfolios relevant to your organisation's work; • the relevant spokespersons of the Official Opposition party; • the spokespersons of the other opposition parties with portfolios relevant to your organisation's work; • the chairs of parliamentary committees relevant to your organisation's work; • to MPs; and • to Peers Which of the above policy makers your organisation contacts will depend upon the aims and objectives of your approach, the concern or opportunity you have identified, the solution and your view of which policy maker can best deliver the solution.	To raise key issues with lead policy makers, and to raise your organisation's profile, and to influence policy development and legislation.
3.	Write to the leaders of all the political parties represented in Parliament requesting meetings to brief them about your organisation's work.	To raise key issues with leading policy makers on a cross-party basis, and to raise your organisation's profile, and to influence policy development and legislation.
4.	Develop a programme of high profile visits to your organisation's projects/services for Government ministers. Ministers should also be invited to launch new projects and services, and to give the keynote speech at celebration events at projects/services, e.g. events to open new premises, to launch new businesses or to celebrate the 10th anniversary of a project/service	To develop relationships with Government ministers, and to showcase the success and best practice of your organisation. This would potentially offer important opportunities for media coverage, both in the national media and in social media.
5.	Develop a programme of high profile visits to your organisation's projects/services for opposition spokespersons with portfolios relevant to your organisation's work.	To develop relationships with the opposition parties, and to showcase the achievements and best practice of your organisation. This would

	Activity	Aims and objectives
		potentially offer important opportunities for media coverage, both in the national media and in social media.
6.	Develop a programme of high profile visits to your organisation's projects/services for MPs and Peers.	To encourage local MPs and Peers to become local champions for your organisation and its work in the local areas/their constituency. This would potentially offer important opportunities for media coverage, both in the national and/or local media and in social media.
7.	Brief MPs/Peers, and submit written evidence, for key inquiries and debates in Parliament on issues relevant to your organisation.	To raise key issues on a cross-party basis, and to raise the profile of your organisation.
8.	Respond to key legislation relevant to your organisation, and to its work, as follows: **Second Reading** Prepare briefing for the Second Reading debate. **Committee Stage** Draft amendments on key issues/concerns. **Report Stage** Progress key amendments not accepted during the Committee Stage. **Third Reading** In your Third Reading briefing prepared for the Government, the opposition parties and groupings and for individual MPs and Peers as appropriate, highlight issues overlooked, or which your organisation believes were dealt with unsatisfactorily, during the previous stages of the Bill.	To raise key issues on a cross-party basis to try and shape and influence key legislation, and to raise the profile of your organisation.

	Activity	Aims and objectives
9.	Respond to key Government consultations, and to consultations launched by other agencies, on issues relevant to your organisation and its work.	To raise key issues on a cross-party basis, to raise the profile of your organisation, and to influence policy development and legislation.
10.	Approach an MP or Peer to sponsor a private members' debate on a subject area relevant to your organisation.	To raise key issues on a cross-party basis, and to raise the profile of your organisation.
11.	Work with an MP or Peer on a Private Members' Bill focusing on an issue relevant to your organisation.	To raise key issues on a cross-party basis, to secure a significant change to the law, and to raise the profile of your organisation.
12.	Draft an e-petition to Parliament.	To raise a key issues relevant to your organisation, to secure changes in public policy and legislation and to raise the profile of your organisation.
13.	Develop your organisation's involvement and participation in All-Party Parliamentary Groups relevant to its work	To raise key issues relevant to your organisation. It would also raise the profile of your organisation, and potentially strengthen its parliamentary networks.
14.	Hold a parliamentary reception/briefing event on a key theme/issue relevant to your organisation	To raise key issues/themes relevant to your organisation, and to raise the profile of your organisation and to potentially strengthen its parliamentary networks.
15.	Attend the political parties' spring and/ or autumn conferences, and deliver a programme of activities at these conferences.	To raise key issues relevant to your organisation, and to raise the profile of your organisation. It will also help to strengthen your relationships with politicians in all of the parties represented at Westminster.

Summary of key points

The key points from this chapter can be summarised as follows:

- Before launching a public affairs campaign or initiative, ensure that your aims and objectives, and 'policy asks' will be supported by strong key messages underpinned by robust evidence and best practice.
- Set clear aims, objectives, and 'policy asks' for your organisation's public affairs strategy, including campaigns and activities, to maximise their impact.
- Frame any approaches made by your organisation to the Government, to the opposition parties, and to individual MPs and Peers in the context of relevant key Government and parliamentary business.
- Consideration should be given by your organisation to the advantages of working in alliance with like-minded organisations on specific issues and legislation.

3

The Impact of Devolution

The UK Government and the UK Parliament have responsibility for a wide range of policy and legislative areas, which affect the UK economy, the environment and communities and people across the UK. There are, however, certain factors which limit the UK Government's, and the UK Parliament's, powers and responsibilities in these areas. One of the key factors setting the limits of the UK Government's, and the UK Parliament's, powers and responsibilities has been the influence of EU law and policy development, an area outside this guide. This will, however, change with the UK's vote to leave the EU.[1] Another major factor limiting the powers and responsibilities of the UK Government, and of the UK Parliament, has been the impact of devolution in Scotland, in Northern Ireland and in Wales. Devolution has given the Scottish Parliament and the Scottish Government, the Northern Ireland Assembly and the Northern Ireland Executive, and the National Assembly for Wales and the Welsh Government significant powers and responsibilities in various policy and legislative areas.[2]

---

1   This is an ongoing process, and its impact upon Parliament's consideration of parliamentary business, and on parliamentary procedure, will be considered in future editions of this guide.

2   The framework governing the relations between the UK Government and the devolved administrations in Scotland, Northern Ireland and Wales are outlined in the 2012 *Memorandum of Understanding and Supplementary Agreements Between the United Kingdom Government, the Scottish Ministers, the Welsh Ministers, and the Northern Ireland Executive Committee*. This Memorandum outlines the principles underpinning relations between the administrations, highlighting the importance of good communication, consultation and co-operation, and outlining procedures for avoiding and resolving disputes. The Memorandum also established the Joint Ministerial Committee, and introduced concordat arrangements in relation "to the co-ordination of EU policy and implementation; financial assistance to industry; and international relations touching on the responsibilities

It is vital that your organisation, when developing its policy and public affairs strategy, takes into account the influence exerted by these factors in limiting the UK Parliament's, and the UK Government's, role in policy and legislative areas falling within the powers of the devolved administrations.[3] Against this background, one of the fundamental issues your organisation must address, as part of the process of developing its public affairs strategy, is whether or not the issues it wishes to focus on fall within the reserved powers of the UK Parliament and of the UK Government. Alternatively, are the issues under consideration devolved to the Scottish Parliament and to the Scottish Government? Or to the Northern Ireland Assembly and the Northern Ireland Executive? Or to the National Assembly for Wales and the Welsh Government?

Another important factor for your organisation to bear in mind, in the context of seeking to influence Government legislation, is whether or not the legislation impacts on England only, and/or on England and Wales. This would have a major bearing on which policy makers your organisation should seek to influence because legislation falling into these categories would be subject to the English Votes for English Laws ('EVEL') process. This applies to all Public Bills with the exception of Consolidation Bills, certain Financial Resolutions and the Consideration of Lords' Amendments. It does not apply to Private Members' Bills, or to Bills certified as 'Scottish' or falling within the remit of the Northern Ireland and Welsh Grand Committees. Under the EVEL process the Speaker will give a Public Bill a Speaker's Certificate if the Government Bill or parts of the Bill or amendments

---

of the devolved administrations". In addition, UK Government Departments have established bilateral concordat arrangements with their counterparts in the devolved administrations; *Memorandum of Understanding and Supplementary Agreements Between the United Kingdom Government, the Scottish Ministers, the Welsh Ministers, and the Northern Ireland Executive Committee*, UK Government website, www.gov.uk.

3   It is important to emphasise, however, that the UK Parliament remains sovereign, that all law making remains within its competence and that it still holds the powers to amend the Devolution Acts or to introduce legislation on devolved matters. Significantly, the UK Government has highlighted that it will only legislate on a devolved matter with the approval of the relevant devolved legislature, which would require a legislative consent Motion; UK Government, 'Guidance: Devolution of powers to Scotland, Wales and Northern Ireland', UK Government website, www. gov.uk.

to the Bill should be subject to the EVEL process.[4] This is considered in more detail in Chapter 11.

These will be major considerations for your organisation and would, for example, determine where you concentrate your organisation's policy and public affairs activities. In particular it will influence which government or executive or parliament or assembly as appropriate, and politicians, you need to influence to secure your objectives, and the procedure you will need to follow in the relevant parliament or assembly. Getting these issues right, in the initial stages of developing your organisation's public affairs strategy, will help to maximise the impact of this strategy. It will also spare your organisation any potential embarrassment arising from approaching the UK Government and the UK Parliament on a matter which actually falls within the remit and legislative competence of, for example, the Scottish Government and the Scottish Parliament.

It is strongly recommended that your organisation double checks that the policy and legislative areas on which your organisation is seeking to influence government and politicians are dealt with by the UK Government and by the UK Parliament. The need for such an approach is underlined by the fact that the devolution arrangements for Scotland, Northern Ireland, and Wales vary in each nation. This has given rise to political frameworks in Scotland, Northern Ireland, and Wales, in which different policy and legislative areas are sometimes devolved in each nation. In Northern Ireland, for example, benefits and welfare reform are devolved to the Northern Ireland Assembly and to the Northern Ireland Executive. By contrast, in Wales these policy and legislative areas are reserved/excepted to the UK Parliament and to the UK Government. While in Scotland aspects of certain benefits such as, for example, Disability Living Allowance, Personal Independent Payment and Carer's Allowance have been devolved under the Scotland Act 2016 to the Scottish Parliament and to the Scottish Government.

This chapter provides an overview of the devolution arrangements in Scotland, in Northern Ireland, and in Wales. It also offers summaries of the policy and legislative areas devolved by the UK Parliament to these nations, and which fall within the remit and legislative

---

4   UK Parliament, 'English votes for English laws: House of Commons bill procedure', UK Parliament website, www.parliament.uk.

competence of the Scottish Parliament and the Scottish Government, of the Northern Ireland Assembly and the Northern Ireland Executive, and of the National Assembly for Wales and of the Welsh Government. In addition, it gives advice on how best to engage with the Secretaries of State for Scotland, for Northern Ireland, and for Wales on policies and legislation reserved/excepted to the UK Parliament impacting upon either or all of these nations. This chapter includes tips for organisations based in Scotland, in Northern Ireland, or in Wales seeking to influence MPs representing constituencies in Scotland, in Northern Ireland, or in Wales on reserved policies and/or legislation impacting upon one/ or all of these nations. It also gives advice to UK wide organisations seeking to influence MPs and Peers on reserved policy areas and/or legislation impacting on the UK as a whole. This will provide your organisation with clarity going forward about the policy and legislative areas in which it should seek to influence the devolved administrations, and the UK Government and the UK Parliament, respectively.

The devolution arrangements for Scotland

The overarching devolution arrangements for Scotland can be found in the Scotland Act 1998. The Scottish Parliament and the Scottish Government subsequently gained legislative control over additional policy issues and areas under the Scotland Act 2012, and the Scotland Act 2016. Under the terms of the devolution arrangements, the Scottish Parliament and the Scottish Government have full legislative control over matters held to be 'devolved matters' for the purpose of the Scotland Act 1998 (as amended by the Scotland Act 2012 and by the Scotland Act 2016). Policy issues and areas over which the UK Parliament and the UK Government retain full legislative and executive control are known as 'reserved matters'.

The following policy issues and areas are devolved matters under the devolution arrangements for Scotland:

• Health and social work;
• Education and training;
• Local government and housing;
• Justice and policing;
• Agriculture, forestry and fisheries;

- The environment;
- Tourism, sport and heritage; and
- Economic development and internal transport.

In addition to the devolution of aspects of certain social security benefits referred to above, the Scotland Act 2016 also devolved powers to the Scottish Government and to the Scottish Parliament in the following areas:

- Setting the rates and bands of income tax, air passenger duty and the aggregates levy;
- The assignment of VAT revenues;
- Consumer advocacy and advice;
- Road signs and speed limits;
- Onshore gas and oil extraction; and
- Design over schemes relating to energy efficiency and fuel poverty.[5]

The policy issues and areas that remain reserved matters under the devolution arrangements include:

- The constitution;
- Foreign affairs;
- Defence;
- International development;
- The Civil Service;
- Financial and economic matters;
- Immigration and nationality;
- Misuse of drugs;
- Trade and industry;
- Parts of energy regulation;
- Parts of transport;
- Employment;
- Social security;
- Abortion, genetics, surrogacy, medicines;

5   A full summary of the powers devolved to the Scottish Parliament and to the Scottish Government can be found in the Explanatory Notes accompanying the Scotland Act 2016; Scotland Act 2016, Explanatory Notes, www.legislation.gov.uk website delivered by The National Archives.

- Broadcasting; and
- Equal opportunities.[6]

Significantly, the Scottish Parliament cannot legislate on reserved matters. Furthermore, the Scotland Act 2016 provided that, although the UK Parliament's sovereignty remains unaltered by the Scottish Parliament's legislative competence, "it is recognised that the Parliament of the United Kingdom will not normally legislate with regard to devolved matters without the consent of the Scottish Parliament".[7] Where the UK Government seeks to legislate on a matter which is devolved to the Scottish Parliament, to enable it do so, the Scottish Parliament would first have to pass a Legislative Consent Motion to enable the UK Parliament to legislate on a devolved matter. Similar processes apply in the Northern Ireland Assembly, and in the National Assembly for Wales.

The devolution arrangements for Northern Ireland

The devolution settlement and framework for Northern Ireland were largely established by the Good Friday Agreement 1998, and by the Northern Ireland Act 1998. Under the Northern Ireland devolution arrangements, the Northern Ireland Assembly was given full legislative control over certain policy areas, which are called 'transferred matters'. Policy areas over which the UK Government and the UK Parliament retain control are known as 'excepted matters' which fall outside the legislative competence of the Northern Ireland Assembly. A third category of policy and legislative areas are the 'reserved matters'. These are generally UK-wide, and fall within the legislative control of the UK Government and the UK Parliament, unless the Secretary of State for Northern Ireland gives consent for the Northern Ireland Assembly to legislate on these matters. Further guidance about the Northern Ireland devolution settlement can be found in the UK

---

6   UK Government, 'UK Government – Guidance, Devolution Settlement: Scotland', UK Government website, www.gov.uk.
7   Scotland Act 2016, Explanatory Notes, www.legislation.gov.ukwebsite delivered by The National Archives.

Government's *Guidance on the Devolution Settlement in Northern Ireland.*[8]

This guidance confirms that the following policy issues and areas are 'transferred matters':

- Health and social services;
- Education;
- Employment and skills;
- Agriculture;
- Social security;
- Pensions and child support;
- Housing;
- Economic development;
- Local government;
- Environmental issues, including planning;
- Transport;
- Culture and sport;
- The Northern Ireland Civil Service;
- Equal opportunities; and
- Justice and policing.

The following policy issues and areas are 'excepted matters', which fall within the legislative control of the UK Government and of the UK Parliament:

- The constitution;
- Royal succession;
- International relations;
- Defence and armed forces;
- Nationality, immigration and asylum;
- Elections;
- National security;
- Nuclear energy;
- UK-wide taxation;
- Currency;
- Conferring of honours; and

---

8   UK Government, 'UK Government – Guidance, Devolution Settlement: Northern Ireland', UK Government website, www.gov.uk.

- International treaties.

The UK Government's *Guidance on the Devolution Settlement in Northern Ireland* confirms that the following policy issues and areas generally fall within the legislative control of the UK Government and the UK Parliament, unless the Secretary of State for Northern Ireland gives their permission for the Northern Ireland Assembly to legislate on specific 'reserved matters':

- Firearms and explosives;
- Financial services and pensions regulation;
- Broadcasting;
- Import and export controls;
- Navigation and civil aviation;
- International trade and financial markets;
- Telecommunications and postage;
- The foreshore and seabed;
- Disqualification from Assembly membership;
- Consumer safety; and
- Intellectual property.[9]

The devolution arrangements for Wales

The devolution arrangements for Wales are set out in the Government of Wales Act 1998, and in the Government of Wales Act 2006. Under this settlement the National Assembly for Wales has legislative competence to make Assembly Acts in areas ('subjects') where the Welsh Ministers enjoy legislative control. Under Schedule 7 of the Government of Wales Act 2006 these subjects are:

- Agriculture, fisheries, forestry and rural development;
- Ancient monuments and historic buildings;
- Culture;
- Economic development;
- Education and training;
- Environment;

---

9   UK Government, 'UK Government – Guidance, Devolution Settlement: Northern Ireland', UK Government website, www.gov.uk.

- Fire and rescue services and promotion of fire safety;
- Food;
- Health and health services;
- Highways and transport;
- Housing;
- Local government;
- National Assembly for Wales;
- Public administration;
- Social welfare;
- Sport and recreation;
- Tourism;
- Town and country planning;
- Water and flood defence; and
- Welsh language.[10]

Under the Wales Act 2014, powers over landfill taxes, stamp duty and the aggregate levy were also devolved, along with the power to vary income tax subject to a referendum.[11]

The non-devolved matters over which the UK Government and the UK Parliament retain legislative control are any policy issues and areas not included in Schedule 7 of the Government of Wales Act 2006. These include, for example:

- Policing and criminal justice;
- Foreign affairs, defence and security issues;
- Welfare, benefits and social security;
- Taxation (with the exception of the powers to set council tax and business rates);
- Fiscal and macroeconomic policy; and
- Public expenditure allocation across the UK.[12]

---

10 UK Government, 'UK Government, Guidance: Devolution Settlement – Wales', UK Government website, www.gov.uk.

11 A summary of the key provisions in the Wales Act 2014 can be found in the Explanatory Notes accompanying the legislation; UK Government, Wales Act 2014, Explanatory Notes, www.legislation.gov.uk website delivered by The National Archives.

12 National Assembly for Wales, 'Governance of Wales: Who is responsible for what?', National Assembly for Wales website, www.assembly.wales.

The Wales Act 2017 has provided a clearer separation of reserved and devolved powers, and further increased the powers devolved to Wales in a number of areas. These new powers will give the Assembly greater powers to manage its own affairs. The legislation also gives the Assembly control over ports policy, speed limits, bus registration, taxi regulation, Local government elections, sewerage and energy consents up to 350MW. It also devolved responsibility to the Welsh Ministers for areas such as marine licensing and conservation, energy consents in relation to the Welsh offshore region and powers for the licensing of onshore oil and gas extraction.[13]

Influencing UK-wide policy development and legislation

Once your organisation has established that the policy issue and/ or legislation it is seeking to engage on fall within the reserved powers of the UK Parliament and the UK Government, you can then develop your influencing strategy focusing on key policy makers at UK Government level, and in both Houses of the UK Parliament. If your organisation is based in Scotland, or Northern Ireland, or Wales and wants to engage with key policy makers on UK-wide policy issues or legislation, and to ensure they take into account the context and conditions where your organisation operates, there are certain categories of policy makers whom you should prioritise. When doing so it is important to bear in mind that there could be tensions between the UK Government and the devolved administrations on specific policy issues and/or legislation. Where this is a factor or likely to be a factor, your organisation should engage sensitively and carefully with key policy makers in the UK Government, and in the devolved nation where it is based. This approach is vital if your organisation wishes to successfully influence how the UK-wide policy and/or legislation will impact where you are based. The same considerations would apply for UK-wide organisations seeking to ensure that the impact of the policy and/or legislation is better understood across the four nations.

One of these areas is engaging with the Secretary of State for

---

13 UK Parliament, 'Wales Bill: Explanatory Notes', UK Parliament website, www. parliament.uk.

Scotland or with the Secretary of State for Northern Ireland, or with the Secretary of State for Wales as appropriate. Engaging with the relevant Secretary of State will give your organisation an opportunity to raise concerns and issues about how a specific policy, strategy or initiative or Parliamentary Bill will affect your organisation, and its work. Given that so many policy issues and legislative areas have been devolved, you may find that the Secretary of State will be receptive to your organisation's approach, and will be keen to address any issues you raise to help safeguard the UK Government's influence and support in the relevant nation. In this context, UK Government Ministers may consider that there could be strategic and electoral advantages in being seen to draw upon issues raised across the four nations, or within specific nations. The Government may also find it advantageous to take a 'four nations' approach to ensure that the policy or legislation is as strong as possible, and has suitable relevance and application across the four nations. In certain cases, your organisation will be unaware of how politically important these considerations will be to the UK Government until such times as you start the process of engaging.

Your organisation should also ensure that it does not ignore MPs with constituencies in Northern Ireland, or Scotland or Wales as appropriate, or Peers with strong associations with a particular nation. This is vital if your organisation is keen to highlight the likely effects of a UK-wide policy, and/or piece of legislation, in a particular nation. To take an example, when the UK Welfare Reform Bill, which applied mainly to England, Scotland and Wales, was introduced in the UK Parliament in 2011, a wide range of stakeholders across the UK were interested in its effects. These included third sector organisations, the local government community, the advice sector and the health sector, the trade unions, as well as interest from individual claimants. Various alliances were formed across different sectors to influence the legislation, and to mitigate the effects of aspects of the legislation.

One of these alliances was established and led by Action for Children Scotland and by One Parent Families Scotland. It involved organisations across the UK such as Barnardo's, Citizens Advice Scotland, trade unions and church groups. The alliance focused on issues such as the sanctions regime, and in particular the need to ensure that claimants with children did not face sanctions because they were unable to access work due to a lack of availability of affordable, flexible childcare. The alliance highlighted the likely UK-wide impact of this issue on large numbers of claimants, while paying particular attention to the potential effects on single parent families in Scotland. MPs with Scottish constituencies were approached to lodge amendments at Committee and Report stages in the House of Commons to ensure that claimants did not face sanctions in these circumstances. The alliance also engaged with the UK Government, and with MPs on a cross-party basis, to try and secure their support for the amendments. During this process the alliance took steps to ensure that the Scottish Government, and MSPs in the Scottish Parliament, were kept fully updated.

Initially, the UK Government refused to make any concessions in response to the amendments when they were debated in the House of Commons. The alliance, therefore, approached Peers in the House of Lords and built up cross-party support for the amendments. This secured a concession from the UK Government at Report Stage of the legislation in the House of Lords. In response to amendments lodged on behalf of the alliance, the Government gave a commitment that the statutory guidance accompanying the legislation would explicitly confirm that claimants would not face sanctions where they were unable to access work due to a lack of affordable, flexible childcare. This significant concession demonstrates one way in which organisations can use the impact of a UK-wide policy and/or legislation in nations across the UK to help shape and influence the policy and/or legislation in question by drawing upon the sometimes different evidence bases and experience across the four nations.

Engaging with relevant committees

Organisations with a focus on Scotland, or on Northern Ireland or on Wales, as well as those organisations with a 'four nations' focus should also ensure that they engage with the House of Commons' Scottish Affairs Committee and/or the Northern Ireland Affairs Committee, and/or the Welsh Affairs Committee as appropriate. The main role of the House of Commons' Scottish Affairs Committee is to scrutinise the expenditure and work of the Scotland Office, and also considers the latter's relations with the Scottish Parliament. The Northern Ireland Affairs Committee has a similar role in relation to the Northern Ireland Office. The Welsh Affairs Committee focuses on policies and legislation falling within the remit of the Secretary of State for Wales, and also examines the latter's relations with the National Assembly for Wales. These committees generally consider the impact of UK Government policies in Scotland, Northern Ireland, and Wales respectively.

Conducting inquiries is a major part of each committee's work. The committees choose the subject matter and policy areas for such inquiries. They conduct the inquiries by taking oral evidence from a wide range of witnesses, and by seeking written evidence from individuals, agencies and organisations with an interest in the policy issues being addressed in the inquiries. The Scottish Affairs Committee, the Northern Ireland Affairs Committee, and the Welsh Affairs Committee all publish reports of their inquiries. These include recommendations to the UK Government, which it is generally obliged to respond to within two months.

These committees offer significant opportunities for organisations to influence policy and legislation generally falling within the legislative competence of the UK Government and the UK Parliament, which affects Scotland, Northern Ireland, and Wales. It is recommended that your organisation monitors the work of these committees to identify opportunities to contribute to their work, and in particular to give oral and written evidence to their inquiries. Once you are aware that one of these committees is undertaking an inquiry relevant to your organisation's work, you should contact the chair of the committee, and the clerking team, to confirm your organisation's interest in giving oral evidence to the committee. This will offer a high profile opportunity to engage with the committee, and to raise issues and concerns on behalf of your organisation around the subject matter of the inquiry.

You should consider ways in which your organisation can maximise the impact of any media opportunities around giving evidence as a witness. Where appropriate your organisation should also consider inviting the committee to visit its business, or services or projects if this would help to inform the committee members' understanding of the policies and issues they are investigating. Careful thought should also be given to how your organisation presents its written evidence, as submissions which are well argued and supported by strong evidence and best practice are most likely to feature prominently in the committee's final report. It is also recommended that you send a copy of your organisation's written evidence to the relevant UK Government minister, and to the relevant spokespersons of the opposition parties. By doing so, you will strengthen your organisation's position for engaging with the UK Government, and with the opposition parties, on issues around the inquiry.

Summary of key points

The key points from this chapter can be summarised as follows:

- To avoid embarrassment, make sure you seek to influence UK Government Ministers, the opposition parties, MPs and Peers on parliamentary business and legislation which falls within the legislative competence of the UK Parliament.
- Where your organisation is seeking to influence key policy makers on issues around the impact of UK Government policies on Northern Ireland, Scotland and Wales respectively, priority should be given to engaging with the relevant Secretary of State.
- Organisations should also seek to influence MPs with constituencies in Northern Ireland, Scotland and Wales as appropriate, and Peers with a strong association to a particular nation.
- They should also closely monitor the business of the Scottish Affairs Committee, the Northern Ireland Affairs Committee and the Welsh Affairs Committee as appropriate, and seek to influence their work including committee inquiries.

4

Exploiting Parliamentary Monitoring and Political Intelligence Gathering

The success of your organisation's public affairs strategy in Parliament will rely heavily on developing good relations with Government Ministers, civil servants and special advisers, as well as with the opposition parties and with individual MPs and Peers. This, amongst other things, will improve the chances that your organisation will receive early warning of parliamentary business likely to impact upon its interests. It will also depend upon the quality and effectiveness of its monitoring of business in both Houses of Parliament, and on its overall political intelligence gathering. Identifying key parliamentary business early, and tracking its progress, will be essential if your organisation wishes to make the most of the opportunities presented by relevant parliamentary business as it arises, and to influence key policy makers. It will also help your organisation to respond promptly to any parliamentary developments which could potentially have an adverse impact upon your organisation's interests.

This chapter outlines some of the basic factors you should consider when deciding the best approach for your organisation to take to parliamentary monitoring, and to political intelligence gathering. It also provides advice and guidance on how to successfully undertake parliamentary monitoring and intelligence gathering in the House of Commons, and in the House of Lords. This will help to maximise the impact of your organisation's public affairs strategy by ensuring that it is informed by the best available political intelligence drawn from highly effective parliamentary monitoring.

Parliamentary monitoring services

Different options are available for organisations wishing to monitor parliamentary business in Parliament, and to gather the type of political intelligence which will be most beneficial to their interests. One option is for organisations to subscribe to the parliamentary monitoring services provided by various specialist providers. These services can offer regular updates about key developments in Parliament impacting upon your organisation, its business, the sector or sectors in which it operates and, as appropriate, upon those interests or on whose behalf your organisation works. Many of the organisations choosing this option will also want to be updated on key political developments, and on the legislation and policy areas most relevant to their organisation. These subscriptions can be expensive, and organisations will usually find that the more tailored the services they require, the more expensive it is likely to be. For organisations already subscribing to such services, or considering this option, careful thought should be given to the type of areas on which you wish the parliamentary monitoring service to focus.

Where organisations wish to subscribe to such services, but only have a limited budget, you will need to strictly prioritise those areas most relevant to your organisation, to its core functions and to its interests for monitoring purposes. The type of policy areas and legislation relevant to your organisation will often be reasonably clear. A pharmaceutical company, for example, will generally be most interested in parliamentary business focusing on references to the company itself, to the pharmaceutical industry, to specific medicines, to the licensing of new medicines, to the NHS and to the health sector. By contrast, a third sector organisation campaigning on environmental issues would be likely to have a wide interest in parliamentary business relating to the environment, to the policies of the Government and other agencies in relation to environmental protection and to sustainable development. Such organisations may also want to track parliamentary business relevant to specific threats to the environment, including pollution caused by oil spills.

Deciding which types of parliamentary business should be monitored under the parliamentary monitoring service will also require careful consideration. In this respect, your organisation must decide on the range of parliamentary business it wishes the service to track. Is it your organisation's expectation that the parliamentary monitoring service will be comprehensive, and identify all parliamentary business relevant to your organisation in either House, or both Houses, of Parliament? This level of service would focus on all aspects of parliamentary business, including answers to written Parliamentary Questions. These answers, although less high profile than other types of parliamentary business, often yield significant parliamentary intelligence. The ways in which organisations can then use this information to exploit opportunities presented by parliamentary business, or to provide early responses to threats posed by such business, are considered in Chapter 14. Alternatively, does your organisation wish to monitor the key, headline parliamentary business itself, and only require the monitoring service to track specific areas of parliamentary business such as the progress of parliamentary legislation relevant to its interests?

Once your organisation has decided upon the type and level of service it requires from the parliamentary monitoring service, it should work closely with the service provider to identify the key words and references that will underpin the searches (usually daily during the parliamentary session) undertaken by the monitoring service on behalf of your organisation. Agreeing the main searches will enable the parliamentary monitoring service to take a more tailored approach to delivering your service, and will help to ensure that major parliamentary business impacting upon your organisation is not missed. This is essential if your organisation is to make the most of the service it is paying for, and to ensure that the service provider is delivering the best possible service for your organisation.

Undertaking your own parliamentary monitoring

Another option is for organisations to undertake their own parliamentary monitoring. For organisations taking this approach, it is important that a specific member of your staff is appointed to undertake the parliamentary monitoring. Furthermore, it is vital that this member of staff has been given clear guidance by the organisation about the policy areas, and about the types of parliamentary business, on which the organisation's parliamentary monitoring should concentrate. Ideally, your organisation should seek to assign someone to the task of parliamentary monitoring who knows the organisation well, understands its interests and can identify parliamentary business relevant to the organisation. The person appointed should be able to work with colleagues to exploit the potential opportunities for your organisation presented by specific parliamentary business, and who can also support the organisation to respond to any threats or risks arising from this business.

Many organisations will, however, simply want a designated colleague to identify parliamentary business relevant to the organisation and to its interests, and to update the organisation on this business as appropriate. It then becomes the responsibility of other colleagues within the organisation – usually senior managers – to determine whether or not there are any potential opportunities or risks in any of the items of parliamentary business identified by the colleague responsible for monitoring parliamentary business. How organisations respond to such business will then be critical to the overall effectiveness of their public affairs strategies. If your organisation is committed to progressing a proactive public affairs strategy, and to responding to relevant parliamentary business, it is essential that it has the capacity and commitment to respond to such business. This means ensuring that your organisation fully engages with key policy makers as soon as it becomes aware, through its parliamentary monitoring and political intelligence gathering, of parliamentary business relevant to its work and interests.

Key factors in monitoring

It is strongly recommended that your organisation monitors parliamentary business in both Houses of Parliament, either by subscribing to a parliamentary monitoring service or by undertaking its own parliamentary monitoring. Either way, it is vital that your organisation receives regular updates about parliamentary business relevant to its interests. Such information can identify both opportunities and threats for your organisation. The main thing is that you identify the parliamentary business early, and are able to put in place strategies to capitalise on such opportunities, or to respond effectively to any inherent threats, presented by the business. Effective parliamentary monitoring can put your organisation in that position, and at least give it a chance to try and shape and influence parliamentary developments which may impact upon its interests.

Missing out on opportunities, or failing to respond quickly enough to threats, raised by parliamentary business can be extremely costly for organisations, both financially and in reputational terms. Keeping on top of parliamentary monitoring, and ensuring your organisation receives good political intelligence through monitoring, will help to minimise such risks. Against this background, it is recommended that your organisation puts in place sound, effective internal systems which will enable it to capitalise on political intelligence identified through its relations with key political contacts and/or parliamentary monitoring. In this context, your organisation should consider how it will respond when parliamentary business is identified that may have an impact upon its interests and business. Are your organisation's internal processes and procedures strong enough to ensure that appropriate action is taken as soon as the opportunity or risk presented by the parliamentary business has been identified? If not, your organisation should address this potential weakness as a matter of urgency, and strengthen its internal systems to ensure that, from the point of relevant parliamentary business being identified, the organisation's response is quick, strategic and effective where the business merits further action. The next sections provide advice and guidance on how to monitor parliamentary business in the House of Commons and in the House of Lords, and on how to get the best results for your organisation through parliamentary monitoring.

Monitoring business in the House of Commons

The main documents for monitoring business in the House of Commons are as follows:

- Summary Agenda and Order of Business;
- Future Business;
- *Hansard*, i.e the official report of proceedings in the Chambers and Committees in both Houses;
- Private Business;
- Votes and Proceedings;
- The Early Day Motions database;
- The Questions Book;
- Deferred Divisions;
- European Business;

- The Public Bill List;
- Deposited Papers;
- List of Statutory Instruments;
- The Private Bill List; and
- The List of Legislative Reform Orders

All of the above documents can be accessed on the 'Parliamentary Business: Publications and Records – Business papers – House of Commons section of the Parliament's website.[1] Many of the above documents will be referred to in more detail in other chapters of this book. For the purpose of the current chapter, the focus will be on the House of Commons' Summary Agenda and Order of Business, and Future Business. These documents provide an overview of current and future business in the House of Commons, and are the ones which will provide you with the basic information necessary to help your organisation to develop its parliamentary influencing strategy.

The Summary Agenda for the House of Commons provides an overview of each sitting day's Order Paper. It provides a brief, daily summary of all business in the House of Commons' Chamber, and in Westminster Hall. This includes details of oral questions, debates, legislation, ministerial statements and business Motions. The Order of Business, on the other hand, provides a more detailed look at the business in the House of Commons on each sitting day. The Order of Business confirms which oral questions will be asked in the Chamber, and which Government ministers will respond. It also specifies the time when any 'urgent questions' and ministerial statements will be taken by the House. In addition, the Order of Business sets out any legislation that the House of Commons will consider, and at which stage of the legislative process. It also features details of any Motions proposing changes in membership of committees, as well as details of any adjournment debates including debates to be held in Westminster Hall. Other business featured in the Order of Business includes details of written statements, full details of business in the Delegated Legislation Committees and in the Select Committees and of reports published by parliamentary committees. Organisations undertaking effective parliamentary monitoring, or receiving an efficient service

---

1   www.parliament.uk.

from a parliamentary monitoring provider, will normally already be fully aware of any relevant business in the House of Commons' Summary Agenda and Order of Business. Such organisations will generally only have to refer to these documents to confirm the order of business for a particular day, and to make sure that there have been no last minute changes to key business.

For organisations which do not find themselves in this enviable position, it is strongly recommended that you either subscribe to a parliamentary monitoring service to ensure that you are updated on any relevant business in the House of Commons' Summary Agenda and Order of Business, or take responsibility for checking these documents on a daily basis. Please note, however, that although these documents are significant they will usually only give your organisation part of the political intelligence it will require if it is to respond effectively to parliamentary business relevant to its work. Relying on the Summary Agenda and the Order of Business on their own will often, for example, only give your organisation limited time to try and respond once it has been made aware of relevant parliamentary business through the monitoring service, or through its own parliamentary monitoring.

In this context, you might only find out about the business on the very day it is due to be considered by the House, or in the worst case scenario find out after the event. An organisation which discovers it only has a couple of hours to respond to relevant parliamentary business, will generally find that its opportunities to shape and influence this business become limited if not non-existent. Organisations which find themselves in this position could contact the relevant minister, and MPs including their local MP before the business is taken. The likelihood of success will, however, depend upon a number of factors, not least of which will be the closeness of the pre-existing ties between the organisation and the minister and/or MPs. The disadvantage of a last minute approach to a minister and/or MPs is that it runs the risk of creating a negative impression. It will also, in many cases, make it more difficult for the minister and/or MPs to respond positively, regardless of how much goodwill they bear your organisation. In some cases, where your organisation identifies an item of parliamentary business late in the day, it might be more effective to pick up with the minister and/or with MPs after the business has actually been considered by the House, and to base your organisation's engagement with the minister and/or with the MPs on concerns which remain outstanding in relation to the parliamentary business. This will have to be a judgment call made by your organisation after weighing up the specific circumstances of the case. The nature of the parliamentary business, its urgency and its importance to your organisation, will all be major factors in your decision making around which approach to take.

Against this background, it is advised that your organisation should, in order to increase its opportunities for influencing key policy makers at Westminster, adopt a strategy for parliamentary monitoring, and for building up political intelligence, based on early, regular scanning of the political landscape. It is vital that your organisation, to ensure it identifies early any major parliamentary business relevant to your organisation and its interests, focuses on monitoring future business in the House of Commons to maximise the time available for your organisation to engage with policy makers about this business. The 'Summary Agenda and Order of Business – Future Business' section of the House of Commons section of the Parliament's website will be a key source of information for your organisation in developing its public affairs strategy. This section has a Calendar of Business, which sets out the future business for each day in the Chamber, and in Westminster Hall. This includes details of oral questions, debates, legislation, ministerial statements and business Motions. It also includes a 'Remaining Orders and Notices' section, which outlines business that has still to be allocated a specific date in the parliamentary timetable.

Using House of Commons' Future Business to maximise influence

This section offers advice on how to use the 'Summary Agenda and Order of Business – Future Business' section of the Parliament's website to increase the effectiveness of your organisation's public affairs strategy, and to ensure that its engagement with key policy makers delivers tangible outcomes. Outlined below are the main sections of the Future Business section, with guidance on the type of action and activities your organisation should consider taking under each specific section, or in response to business which appears in these sections. Many of these actions and activities are considered in more detail in future chapters, especially in terms of the type of proactive steps your organisation can take in these areas. The purpose

of the table below is to briefly illustrate how you can use the House
of Commons' Future Business section to maximise opportunities for
your organisation, including responding early to any potential threats or
risks posed by parliamentary business which appears in this document.

House of Commons' Future Business	
Calendar of Business	
Oral Questions	Persuading MPs to table oral questions can provide significant opportunities to highlight issues and concerns on behalf of your organisation. This can help to raise the profile of these issues, and of your organisation, with key policy makers. This is considered in more detail in Chapter 14 below.
	Where an oral question appears in the House of Commons' Future Business section which is relevant to your organisation, and to its interests, you should consider engaging with MPs with a view to persuading them to intervene in the short question and answer session that the tabled oral question will generate. The first thing your organisation should do in these circumstances is to contact the office of the MP who has tabled the question. The purpose of this approach would be to find out more about why the MP is asking the question (if this is not obvious from the question, and from recent political developments), and to get a sense of the issues they are seeking to raise in their supplementary question to the minister. You should also flag up your organisation's interest in the issues being highlighted, and offer to provide a briefing to the MP and their colleagues if they are interested in the issues your organisation is seeking to raise in response to the oral question.
	It may be that the MP has tabled the question in reaction to concerns expressed by constituents or by another organisation, in which case they might not require additional briefing. A more productive route in these circumstances might, therefore, be to approach your local MP and/or MPs with whom your organisation already enjoys strong links. You should use this contact to outline the issues you are seeking to raise, and to find out if the MP would be willing to raise these issues during the question and answer session generated by the tabled oral question.
	If you are seeking to regularly brief MPs for oral questions it is recommended that your organisation should develop a 'bank' of standard briefings about your organisation, its business, its aims and objectives, key policy issues and areas etc. These documents can then be quickly and easily adapted for your briefing in response to the tabled oral question. Suggesting potential supplementary questions is also recommended, as it

House of Commons' Future Business	
	will help to highlight the key issues to the MP and, as a result, save them time. Where your organisation is seeking to brief MPs on a specific question, it is strongly advised that you send a copy of any briefing to the relevant Government minister to ensure that the minister has as much information as possible to provide a detailed response if an MP does raise issues on behalf of your organisation. You should also send a copy of the briefing to the relevant opposition parties' front bench spokespersons to provide that the short debate around the tabled question is as informed and wide ranging as possible.
Debates	The House of Commons' Future Business section contains full details of Government, and opposition parties', Motions for debates. It also includes details of Motions lodged by MPs for adjournment debates in the Chamber, and also in Westminster Hall. Using debates effectively as part of your organisation's public affairs strategy is considered in more detail in Chapter 15. Where Motions for debate appear in the Future Business section of the House of Commons section of the Parliament's website that are relevant to your organisation and its work, it is recommended that you take action to brief MPs for the debate. This is another area where having a stock of 'off the shelf' briefings about your organisation and about key policy issues, which can be quickly and easily adapted as appropriate, will save time and strengthen your influencing work. As soon as your organisation has decided that it wishes to engage with key policy makers in a particular debate, you should contact the office of the relevant Government minister or ministers who will be speaking in the debate. You want to ensure that they receive a copy of your organisation's briefing, and are aware of the main issues you wish to raise in the debate. Similar approaches should be made to the spokespersons of the opposition parties who will be participating in the debate. Your organisation should also ensure that it briefs MPs for the debate, and it is strongly recommended that you do so on a cross-party basis.
Legislation	Details of the introduction of new legislation, and of the next parliamentary stages of existing legislation, can be found in the Future Business section of the House of Commons section of the Parliament's website. Regularly monitoring this section will enable your organisation to capitalise on any media opportunities around the introduction of new legislation. It will also enable you to track the remaining stages of the legislation in the House of Commons, and to put

House of Commons' Future Business	
	in place effective planning for responding to each stage of the legislation. The Future Business section of the House of Commons section of the Parliament's website will provide you with details of both Government legislation, and of Private Members' Bills. It also includes information about secondary legislation,[2] which although less high profile than Parliamentary Bills, can nevertheless introduce provisions which can have a significant impact upon your organisation and upon its interests. How to use the legislative process to secure significant outcomes for your organisation is considered in more detail in Chapters 10, 11 and 12.
Motions	The details of parliamentary Motions included in the Future Business section of the House of Commons section of the Parliament's website should not be overlooked as it can often be an invaluable source of political intelligence. This section provides full details of Business Motions which will be considered by the House. These can include Motions confirming the introduction of Private Members' Bills under the 'Ten Minute Rule' procedure, or Motions seeking approval to debate specific issues. Motions seeking approval for forthcoming business in the House, or allocating time or confirming an extension for proceedings, are also included in this section. This can be a useful source of information for confirming when business, in which your organisation has an interest, is scheduled to be considered by the House. This section can be used to help your organisation to identify key business early. You can then use this information to plan how you will seek to influence Government ministers, the opposition parties and individual MPs on significant parliamentary business relevant to your organisation and its interests.

---

2   Once a Bill has received Royal Assent, delegated (also known as secondary) legislation will often be introduced in Parliament relating to the implementation of different aspects of the primary legislation (also known as the 'Parent Act'). This secondary legislation (usually in the form of Statutory Instruments) will be introduced through the order making provisions in the primary legislation. The aim of the secondary legislation is to add greater detail to the legislation, and to often add provisions which were considered too complex to be included in the primary legislation.

House of Commons' Future Business	
Backbench Business	The Future Business section of the House of Commons section of the Parliament's website features Backbench Business, which includes details of parliamentary business introduced by backbench MPs. This is another 'early warning' source for major parliamentary information. Your organisation should utilise this section as part of its political horizon scanning to maximise the time available to influence policy makers on high level parliamentary business impacting upon your organisation, and its interests. In this respect, once you have identified Backbench Business relevant to your organisation and its interests in the Future Business section of the House of Commons section of the Parliament's website (if not before), you should plan your organisation's response. A key part of this response will be deciding which MPs to engage with, and how, if at all, this engagement will be different from your engagement with Government ministers, on the issues raised by this business.
Westminster Hall	A lot of important parliamentary business is taken in Westminster Hall, which takes place in a room off Westminster Hall rather than in the main Commons Chamber. This includes short debates on a wide range of policy areas, including debates on e-petitions. These debates can offer organisations useful opportunities to raise major issues, and to engage with Government ministers, and with MPs on a cross-party basis.
Remaining Orders and Notices	
Motions for debate, legislation, including secondary legislation	The Remaining Orders and Notices Section provides details of Motions for debate, and of business such as the introduction of new legislation or of the next stages of existing legislation, which have still to be allocated a specific date and time for consideration by the House. This will often be the first point at which organisations become aware that important parliamentary business impacting upon their interests could soon be allocated time in the parliamentary calendar. It is, therefore, advisable to keep a close eye on this section, and to track the allocation of parliamentary time to this business.

Monitoring business in the House of Lords

The Parliamentary Calendar, available on Parliament's website, provides an overview of business in both Houses of Parliament. This source features confirmation of forthcoming business in the House of Lords, including Parliamentary Questions, Debates, Legislation,

Government Statements and Business Motions. To ensure that your organisation does not miss important business in the House of Lords you should also track House of Lords' business through the Parliamentary Calendar, and through the House of Lords' Order Paper, and House of Lords Business Paper and Minutes of Proceedings ('the Business Paper'). These are all available on the House of Lords section of the Parliament's website.[3]

The Order Paper and the Business Paper are generally published daily (except during parliamentary recesses) on the 'House of Lords Business Papers – House of Lords Business' section of the House of Lords section of the Parliament's website. The Order Paper provides details of the House of Lords business for that day, while the Business Paper features the business of the day, and details of forthcoming business. Apart from giving details about oral questions (or 'Starred Questions' as they are called in the House of Lords), debates, legislation, Government statements and business Motions, the Business Paper includes information about the publication of Select Committee reports, Motions relating to delegated legislation, questions for short debate and questions for written answer. In addition, the House of Lords' Business Paper features information about written questions unanswered after ten working days, and about the progress of legislation including next stages. Its Statutory Instruments section outlines details about secondary legislation, i.e. generally statutory instruments in the form of orders and regulations introduced through the relevant primary legislation. This includes confirmation of whether or not the statutory instrument is an 'affirmative instrument' or a 'negative instrument'. The Business Paper also confirms forthcoming committee business in the House of Lords, and includes a minute of proceedings confirming the business considered in the previous sitting of the House.

Using the House of Lords' Business Paper to maximise influence

We have seen above how organisations can use political intelligence from monitoring the House of Commons' business documents on the Parliament's website to maximise the impact of their public affairs strategies. This section provides step-by-step guidance on how to use

---

3   www.parliament.uk.

the House of Lords' Business Paper to identify the type of parliamentary business which your organisation can best utilise to influence leading policy makers. The table below features the main types of parliamentary business outlined in the Business Paper, and provides advice on the action your organisation should take in response to this business to influence key policy makers. Following this advice will help to ensure that your organisation uses political intelligence from the House of Lords' Business Paper to develop a highly effective public affairs strategy. The proactive approach your organisation can take in the areas identified below is considered in more detail in other chapters. This table simply seeks to provide an overview of how you can use the House of Lords' Business Paper, available on the House of Lords section of the Parliament's website, to develop your organisation's influencing strategy, and to ensure that its strategy delivers tangible outcomes.

House of Lords' Business Paper	
Starred Questions	Detailed advice on how to use oral questions ('Starred Questions') in the House of Lords, by persuading a Peer to lodge a question on behalf of your organisation, is considered in Chapter 14.
	Where a Starred Question which is relevant to your organisation is tabled, and appears in the House of Lords' Business Paper, you should consider providing the sponsoring Peer with briefing material focusing on the key policy issues for your organisation raised by the Starred Question. Even if the Peer already has a well-developed approach to their question in mind, and to the issues it raises, they might find your briefing useful for the supplementary question they will be able to ask the minister after the latter's initial response.
	You should also send your briefing to the relevant minister who will be responding to the Starred Question, and also to any Peers with an interest in the relevant policy areas on which the Starred Question focuses. Following these steps will help your organisation to raise significant issues in the question and answer session generated by the tabled Starred Question. It will also increase the profile of these issues, and of your organisation, with the minister and with Peers. Questions are generally well attended, and the benefits of using these approaches should not be ignored.
Motions for Debates	The House of Lords' Business Paper features details of Motions for debate tabled by the Government, by the Opposition, by other parties, by Crossbench Peers and by

	House of Lords' Business Paper
	individual Peers. This includes details of the Questions for Short Debate, which usually last one to one and a half hours. Keeping an eye on this section will give you advanced warning of forthcoming debates in the House of Lords. Where the debate is likely to focus on issues relevant to your organisation, you should agree a strategy for briefing Peers. Time permitting, you should consider arranging meetings with Peers that have an interest in the issues you are seeking to highlight in the debate. If holding meetings is not a realistic option particularly in view of any time constraints, your organisation should send briefing material to the Minister and/ or to the Peer who has lodged the Motion for debate, as well as to the spokespersons for the different opposition parties and groupings which will be participating in the debate. You should also send your briefing to Peers with specific interests in the issues you are seeking to raise. Following these steps will help your organisation to ensure that its issues are featured in the debate. Engaging with Peers on debates will increase awareness of these issues, and of your 'policy asks' in relation to these issues, and raise your organisation's profile with Peers. Information gained from the debate will also help to inform your organisation's future influencing work.
Bills in Progress	The Bills in Progress section confirms the type of Bill, and whether it is Government legislation or a Private Member's Bill. It also provides details of the stage of the legislation 'to be considered'. Is the Bill, for example, due to be debated at its Second Reading, or has it been committed to a Grand Committee or to a Committee of the Whole House for its Committee Stage or is it scheduled for its Report Stage or Third Reading? If your organisation has an interest in a specific Parliamentary Bill in the House of Lords this section will confirm key dates, and give you an early indication of how much time you will have to try and influence the legislation. Where the legislation has been scheduled for its Second Reading debate, your organisation should take steps to brief Peers on the main issues raised by the legislation for your organisation. If the legislation has reached its Committee Stage, or the next stage to be considered is its Report Stage or Third Reading, your organisation should consider if it needs to approach Peers to table amendments to the legislation. This section will give your organisation a sense of how much time it will have to table the amendments.

House of Lords' Business Paper	
Secondary legislation	The House of Lords' Business Paper contains details of Secondary Legislation, and a Statutory Instruments in Progress section including, for example, Affirmative Instruments waiting for consideration by the Joint Committee on Statutory Instruments, Affirmative Instruments waiting for Affirmative Resolution and Negative Instruments. These instruments often contain provisions which can have a significant impact upon organisations, and on different sectors.
	If your organisation had an interest in the primary legislation through which the secondary legislation was introduced (usually in the form of orders or regulations introduced by statutory instrument) it would be advisable to pay particular attention to the Statutory Instruments in Progress section as the Government will often use secondary legislation to 'flesh-out' key aspects, and details, of the primary legislation. It is very easy for this to slip under organisations' radar, and it is, therefore, strongly advised that your organisation should keep an eye on these sections of the House of Lords' Business Paper to ensure it is not missing parliamentary business which could have a profound impact on your organisation, its business and interests and on the sector in which it operates.
	Parliament can accept or reject a piece of secondary legislation but cannot, subject to certain exceptions, amend the legislation.[4] Where your organisation identifies secondary legislation which is likely to impact upon its interests, you should engage with the relevant Government minister's civil servants to get a sense of what approach the Government will be taking to the secondary legislation, and to clarify its likely content. Bearing this in mind, if the secondary legislation raises concerns for your organisation you should also contact the relevant spokespersons of the Opposition and of the other opposition parties, as well as the crossbench Peers, to find out which Peers, if any, would be willing to raise your organisation's concerns when the secondary legislation is considered.
	With a negative instrument that would involve persuading the Peer to 'pray' against the instrument, and thereby require the House to approve the instrument. Without this, the instrument would be passed as a formality, or to use a colloquialism from the Government Whips' office and the Opposition Chief Whips' offices, it would be passed as 'a nod job'.

---

4   UK Parliament, 'Statutory Instruments', UK Parliament website, www.parliament. uk

House of Lords' Business Paper	
	Secondary legislation can sometimes focus on highly technical issues. In this respect, if the secondary legislation does raise issues and concerns for your organisation, you will need to be ready and able to brief Peers, and to make the briefing as persuasive as possible, particularly where the legislation raises technical issues. Without such briefing, Peers will be less willing to intervene and, in the case of negative instruments, this could be the difference between the instrument receiving detailed scrutiny, or being 'nodded' through. This could have important consequences for your organisation if you are unable to persuade Peers to apply that level of scrutiny to the instrument. Such factors underline the need to keep on top of these sections in the Business Paper, even if the content of secondary legislation sometimes feels a bit obscure. The 'devil is in the detail', and there may be occasions in which your organisation will ignore it at its peril.
Motions	The Business Motions section provides details of Motions relating to the business of the House, including how the business will be considered and when. Examples would include Motions relating to business statements, debates and delegated legislation. Tracking business in this section should be an important part of your organisation's political horizon scanning because it will often provide early warning that business of the House relevant to your organisation will shortly be considered by the House.
Questions for Written Answer	This section lists the questions tabled for written answer, confirms when they were tabled and when an answer is due. The information contained in answers to written questions in the House of Lords can potentially supply organisations with vital information. This can be used to support their policy positions and to influence key policy makers, to raise awareness of major issues and to enhance organisations' profiles.
Questions unanswered after ten working days	The Business Paper includes this section which confirms those House of Lords' written questions that remain unanswered after ten working days. It lists who tabled the question, when the question was tabled and provides a reference number. This section also gives a breakdown of the departments with responsibility for the questions that remains unanswered. The section will be of particular assistance to organisations in the invidious position of facing delays in receiving answers to written questions tabled on their behalf by Peers.

House of Lords' Business Paper	
Legislative Reform Order in Progress	This section provides details of draft orders reported from the Regulatory Reform Committee. It confirms the 'date of laying' of the order, and the 'parliamentary procedure' for its consideration. This section will give your organisation early warning of forthcoming orders that could impact upon its interests. As with the 'Statutory Instruments in Progress' section, where business is likely to impact upon your organisation you should engage with the minister's office and the relevant Government department to find out more about the order. This will give your organisation the information it will need to develop an influencing strategy in response to the order. The internal discussions around that strategy will include which Peers to approach to request they raise issues on your behalf in response to a legislative reform order.
Public Bodies Orders in Progress	The 'Public Bodies Orders in Progress' section sets out details of draft orders reported from the Secondary Legislation Scrutiny Committee. These details include when the scrutiny period for the orders expires, and when they are 'To be considered'. This is another section which your organisation should keep an eye on. While many of the orders will not be relevant to, or have a significant impact upon, your organisation, equally you do not want to miss key business. Where an order does appear that raises issues for your organisation, it is recommended that you take the same approach as the section immediately above.
Committees	The 'Committees Section' confirms when committees will meet, and where. Further details about committee meetings can be found in the House of Lords' Committees Weekly Bulletin. Advice on how your organisation can proactively engage with committees in the House of Lords, and to influence their business, is considered in Chapter 9 below. Where business appears in the Committees Section that is relevant to your organisation you should contact the clerks to the committee to obtain more information about the business, and also to discuss ways in which your organisation could contribute to the committee's scrutiny of the business. Subject to the nature of the business, and to the way in which the committee has agreed to deal with it, options would include seeking to give oral evidence to the committee, submitting written evidence and briefing individual Peers who are members of the committee.

House of Lords' Business Paper	
Minutes of Proceedings	This section provides the Minute of Proceedings for the previous sitting day in the House of Lords, including confirmation of any decisions taken by the House. The Minute of Proceedings section provides a summary of the business considered by the House of Lords during the previous sitting days, and records key decisions. This summary can be a helpful source of information, particularly if read in conjunction with the House of Lords' *Hansard* for that day. The section will give you an overview of the main decisions taken by the House on a specific sitting day, and will also assist you to focus on which parts of *Hansard* you need to concentrate your analysis on for that day. This should be an important part of your organisation's political intelligence gathering.
Select Committee Reports	Details of when Select Committee reports were published can be found in this section. The Select Committee reports section can be a useful source of information for organisations seeking to influence key policy makers in both Houses. The policy areas and topics covered by these reports are wide ranging, and can provide useful evidence and statistics to underpin and strengthen your organisation's influencing work. It should not be overlooked, particularly as the reports published by House of Lords' Select Committees are often highly influential.
Papers	This section confirms any Command Papers presented to the House by command of Her Majesty, and any Affirmative Instruments and/or Negative Instruments laid before the House. It is recommended that you keep track of new publications through this section, as it will give you early warning that the papers have been published and will soon be considered by the House.

Summary of key points

The key points from this chapter can be summarised as follows:

- The effectiveness of your organisation's parliamentary monitoring will have a direct bearing on the success of its public affairs strategy.
- Monitoring parliamentary business in both Houses of Parliament will support organisations to keep abreast of policy developments likely to impact upon their interests.
- Organisations should put in place internal processes and procedures strong enough to ensure that appropriate action is taken as soon as an opportunity or risk presented by a particular piece of parliamentary business has been identified.

5

Influencing Key Policy Makers

The ability of organisations to influence key policy makers will be critical to the effectiveness of their public affairs strategies. After all, the extent to which an organisation is able to secure such influence will determine the level of success it enjoys in shaping policy development and legislation at Government level, and in Parliament. Against this background, it is strongly recommended that your organisation prioritises influencing senior policy makers up to Prime Minister and Cabinet minister level in its public affairs strategy.

For many organisations, achieving the aims and objectives of their public affairs strategies will involve engagement with various policy makers. Indeed, these strategies will often require specific policy makers, or groups of policy makers, to be targeted at different stages of an organisation's public affairs strategy. Taking a strategic approach will help your organisation to maximise its influence with leading policy makers. As part of this process it is recommended that your organisation should identify, and map out, the main policy makers it will need to influence to achieve the aims and objectives, and 'policy asks' of its public affairs strategy, and the timescales for doing so, as well as the key stages and milestones in that influencing process.

It is also important that your organisation has a clear sense of the type of outcomes it is seeking to achieve by engaging with individual policy makers, and with particular groups of policy makers. Taking these steps will help your organisation to maximise the impact of its public affairs strategy. It will also support your organisation to monitor, record and evaluate the ways in which it has influenced key policy makers, and the outcomes such engagement has delivered. These will be essential factors in enabling your organisation to evaluate which types of approaches to policy makers have worked best for your organisation, those that have failed or disappointed, and the approaches which will need fine tuning if they are to fulfil their potential. It is recommended that evaluation should be ongoing, and that your organisation's public affairs strategy is flexible enough to adapt to meet the needs of different stages of that strategy, including the impact of any unforeseen and unexpected political developments. These factors should be an important part of your organisation's analysis of how to initiate, develop and progress its public affairs strategy to ensure it influences leading policy makers. Building upon the lessons of such evaluation will strengthen your organisation's public affairs strategy, and its capacity to consistently influence policy development and legislation.

Preliminary considerations

One of the main starting points for your organisation, in developing a public affairs strategy, will be to identify, and to review, the range of policy makers it is seeking to influence, and to keep this under review as different stages of the strategy develop and are progressed. This range could be quite diverse, and will potentially include the Prime Minister, Cabinet ministers and other Government ministers in both Houses of Parliament, as well as the different opposition parties' leaders and spokespersons, and individual MPs and Peers. Government special advisers, senior civil servants, MPs' and Peers' researchers and other parliamentary staff are also significant groups in policy development, and it is recommended that your organisation should reflect this in its public affairs strategy, and activities. To increase the chances of your organisation's strategy delivering successful outcomes, it is important that you take a flexible approach to the policy makers with whom you engage. The advantages of such an approach are underlined by the fact that, at separate stages in your organisation's public affairs strategy, you may have to target different policy makers, and that this could change with political, economic and other developments including the effects of media coverage, and as your organisation's strategy progresses.

Another important starting point will be your organisation's aims and objectives in approaching a specific policy maker or group of policy makers. In this respect, it is important that your organisation has a clear view of why it is approaching the policy maker or policy makers in question, and what it is hoping to achieve through such engagement. Is your organisation, for example, seeking to gain the Government's support for its 'policy asks' on a specific policy issue? Or is it trying to secure the Government's backing for amendments your organisation wishes to make to a Bill? Alternatively, is your organisation seeking to secure the participation of a Government minister or opposition party spokesperson as the keynote speaker at a parliamentary event? Or to invite a local MP to visit your organisation's business or services in their constituency? Or to persuade a Peer to table a Motion for debate in the House of Lords? Identifying and setting the aims and objectives of, and 'policy asks' for, your organisation engagement with specific policy makers, and groups of policy makers, will support your organisation to take a strategic approach, and to increase the effectiveness of its public affairs strategy.

Some organisations have developed close relations with senior policy makers up to Cabinet minister level, and with the leaders and main spokespersons of the different opposition parties. Organisations which enjoy such relationships will have regular contact with these policy makers, both formally and informally. This level of contact will often enable the organisations to have an important influence on policy development and legislation impacting upon their organisation, on their business or services and upon those on whose behalf the organisation works. One of the main challenges faced by such organisations will be to ensure that their existing, high level influence with key policy makers is sustainable and weathers any changes of government, Cabinet reshuffles or significant changes on the front benches of the different opposition parties. Organisations falling into this category should ensure their public affairs strategies are fine tuned to these developments, and include risk assessments, and early warning mechanisms, in part through regular contacts with Government Ministers, opposition spokespersons, MPs and special advisers, to ensure they are fully prepared to meet such contingencies. This will help to try and insulate their influence as much as possible against the risks posed by changes in the political landscape and environment as a result of these developments.

For the purpose of this chapter, however, it is assumed that your organisation does not have close ties with the Government or with the different opposition parties, and is seeking to develop its influence in what could be major areas of its public affairs strategy. In this respect, once your organisation has decided which policy maker or policy makers it wishes to influence, and why, it also needs to consider what will be the most effective form of engagement. Three of the main options for your organisation to influence leading policy makers are through correspondence, or seeking meetings with the policy makers or inviting them to visit your organisation or to attend its events. Engagement with policy makers through the media, including social media, is considered separately in Chapter 22 below.

Correspondence

In some cases it might be appropriate for an organisation to try and achieve the aims and objectives of a particular part of its public affairs strategy by writing to the Prime Minister, or to the relevant Government minister, or to the leader or spokesperson of the Official Opposition party or to the leader or relevant spokesperson of another one of the opposition parties, or to a specific MP or Peer. Where your organisation does decide to e-mail a policy maker or to write to them by letter it is important that you use their correct titles to avoid inadvertently causing offence, and use the appropriate e-mail and postal addresses. After all, you want the policy maker to respond quickly and positively to your letter. For completeness, you should send the letter by post and by e-mail, and follow up by telephone with their office to confirm safe receipt. If you are writing to a Government minister, for example, in their ministerial capacity rather than as a local MP, it is vital that you use their ministerial postal and e-mail addresses rather than their constituency address. If you are unsure of the minister's official address, check the website of their department or phone the inquiries section in the relevant department and ask them to confirm the correct address. If, on the other hand, you wish to contact the minister in their capacity as your organisation's local MP then you should address the correspondence to their House of Commons or constituency office as appropriate by using the contact details on the Parliament website. Getting these basic steps right will increase the chances that your organisation will receive a quick and positive response to its e-mail or letter.

The type of reply your e-mail/letter receives from the Prime Minister or Government minister or other key policy maker will, however, depend upon a number of factors. These would include the purpose of the e-mail/letter, the issues it raises and the 'policy asks' it contains. A major consideration will also be the strength of your organisation's existing relations with the policy maker. The scope of the policy maker to respond positively to your e-mail/letter will also depend upon the Government's and/or their own party's priorities and positions on particular policy issues, and on any constraints these may impose. E-mails/letters can be effective where your organisation is seeking to raise issues of a particularly complex nature, or if it is important to have clarification in writing from the Government on an issue, or if your organisation is seeking the policy maker's support for a specific campaign or for amendments to a Bill.

You can potentially increase the impact of your organisation's letter, especially if it is addressed to the Government or to an opposition party or parties, if you combine it with a news release. This could generate a wider public debate on the issues raised in your organisation's letter, and put the policy maker under pressure to accept your 'policy asks'. Alternatively, it could alienate the policy maker, and make them less likely to respond positively to your letter. In these circumstances it is advisable to fully risk assess the advantages and disadvantages of issuing a news release in support of a letter, and to consider if strategically such action is more or less likely to help your organisation to achieve its aims and objectives. The impact on your organisation's relations with the policy maker would, for many organisations, be a critical factor in determining how to proceed. The importance of these considerations are likely to vary from organisation to organisation, hence the need for a robust risk assessment before deciding if you will issue a news release in support of your organisation's letter.

In this context, if your letter is raising specific 'policy asks' it might be best to let the correspondence quietly take its course without media coverage. Ultimately, however, it will depend upon what policy demands you are making, and the point which has been reached in any previous engagement/negotiations with the policy maker. If matters have reached a deadlock, or the Government is refusing to compromise, then a news release in support of the letter is certainly something that should be looked at. As indicated above, it is recommended that a full risk assessment should be carried out before going down that route, especially if relations with the Government have reached a delicate stage, and if there is still scope for your organisation's negotiations with the Government to deliver significant, positive outcomes for your organisation.

It is important to recognise that correspondence will often be a limited way of engaging with policy makers, and that seeking meetings with them, or inviting them to attend your events, will potentially offer more effective and productive means of engagement, and of establishing new, or strengthening existing, relations with leading policy makers. It should also be recognised that correspondence will, in many cases, simply be the early stage of an organisation's engagement with policy makers, rather than an end in itself, and that your organisation's initial correspondence may, in certain situations, lead to a meeting with the policy maker even if that was not the original intention. The main factor, in this context, will be the outcomes your organisation is seeking to achieve through the different forms of engagement.

Meetings with Cabinet Ministers and other key policy makers

Meetings with key policy makers can provide organisations with major opportunities to raise their profile, to develop new, or strengthen existing, relationships with policy makers and to contribute to policy development, and to influence legislation, at the highest level. Significantly, these are the areas where your public affairs strategy can deliver important, tangible outcomes for your organisation. The circumstances in which organisations can secure such meetings vary. For high profile organisations, with sophisticated public affairs strategies, such meetings will generally be part and parcel of their regular, business as usual, interaction with senior policy makers. By contrast, meetings for organisations lacking this level of regular contact, and trying to build up their contacts with policy makers, will usually come about because the organisations have written to request a meeting about a major policy issue or development. Other scenarios could include where the organisation has had an initial contact with the policy maker and their staff at an event (possibly even at the national conference of the political party, which the policy maker represents), and have followed up with a meeting request.

An important issue which your organisation will need to address, in taking forward initiatives to meet with policy makers, is the purpose of such meetings. It is essential that your organisation has clear aims and objectives, and 'policy asks', in approaching a particular policy maker for a meeting. Demonstrating this in your meeting request by providing a clear agenda will increase the likelihood that the policy maker will agree to meet your organisation. In addition, it will give the meeting a stronger focus, and help to promote mutually beneficial outcomes. It will also have a direct bearing on which policy maker or policy makers your organisation approaches with a meeting request. Is your organisation, for example, seeking a meeting with the Prime Minister or a Government minister or an opposition party leader or spokesperson because it wishes to discuss the Government's strategic policies or a specific policy, and its impact upon your organisation and its business? Alternatively, are there local issues which your organisation wishes to raise with its constituency MP, or issues that you want the latter to raise on your behalf with the Prime Minister or with specific Government ministers? Or are you seeking a meeting to brief Peers about amendments your organisation is proposing to make to a Bill during its passage in the House of Lords? These are the type of factors that your organisation will need to weigh up in deciding which policy maker or policy makers to approach for a meeting.

If you are seeking to engage with the Government about national policy issues, then you should consider whether or not it makes most sense strategically to request a meeting with the Prime Minister or with a Cabinet minister or other Government minister. All of these policy makers are extremely busy, and have appointments diaries which will be filled up months in advance. The response your meeting request receives, therefore, will depend upon the issues you are attempting to discuss, and the synergies between the Government's priorities and the issues you are raising. Placing your request in the context of a specific Government policy or high level parliamentary business will help to increase the attractiveness of your meeting request to the Government. After all, you should consider the question of how a meeting could benefit the Government, because no doubt the Minister and their special advisers and senior civil servants will be doing the same upon receipt of your organisation's request. The secret to a successful approach is to leave the policy maker with the impression that meeting your organisation would have considerable advantages, as well as significant risks or missed opportunities if they decline to do so.

The strength of your ties with the Government, and the benefits in the Government's eyes of meeting your organisation will also be decisive factors. If you believe that only a meeting with the Prime Minister will meet your aims and objectives then you should pitch the meeting request to make it as attractive as possible to the Prime Minister to meet your organisation. You should also bear in mind that most organisations will generally struggle to secure a meeting with the Prime Minister due to the latter's many other commitments. If the Prime Minister is unable to meet your organisation due to other diary commitments, but is interested in the issues you are raising, particularly if there is a strong interface with Government policy and/or current parliamentary business, then they might offer a meeting with one of their ministers. Subject to your organisation's aims and objectives in making the meeting request to the Prime Minister, this would still be an excellent result.

It should be highlighted that, while meeting the Prime Minister would be a high profile influencing opportunity, it will often be the case that a meeting with one of the Government's ministers may actually offer more tangible outcomes for your organisation. This is something you should bear in mind when deciding which policy maker to approach for a meeting. Securing a meeting with a minister, instead of a meeting with the Prime Minister, will still provide your organisation with major opportunities to influence the Government. It is advised that your organisation should not lose sight of the substantial outcomes a ministerial meeting could potentially deliver, including media opportunities. Against this background, it is recommended that your organisation should give careful thought to the points it wishes to get across at the meeting, and to the outcomes it is hoping to achieve from the meeting.

Another factor to which your organisation should give careful consideration is the need to provide the minister with a briefing paper outlining the issues you wish to raise, and including the evidence and best practice that you are relying on in support of these issues, and your 'policy asks'. Where the meeting will focus on policy issues or areas in which your organisation is highlighting there are specific problems, the briefing should also outline your organisation's suggested solutions to the problems, and its 'policy asks'. Providing this briefing will, if pitched appropriately and persuasively, help your organisation to influence the Government, because after the meeting ministers will, no doubt, want to reflect with their civil servants and special advisers upon the issues which have emerged during the meeting. Producing an effective, well-argued briefing will help to inform that process, and increase the chances that the meeting will deliver positive outcomes and solutions for your organisation.

Apart from making meeting requests to the Prime Minister and to Government ministers, your organisation should also identify which special advisers and senior civil servants it would be advantageous to engage with as part of its public affairs strategy. Securing meetings with special advisers and civil servants should be an important part of building up your organisation's influence with the Government. Time invested in such meetings can pay significant dividends. Meetings with special advisers and senior officials will be particularly helpful if your organisation is seeking to influence a national policy debate or Bill. These meetings will give your organisation opportunities to outline in detail the issues, including any concerns, you wish to raise with the Government. By doing so, you will be giving the special advisers and/or senior civil servants vital information with which they can brief the Government on the policy pros and cons, and risks and opportunities of your policy demands. Potentially, the meeting could lead to recommendations being made by special advisers or officials which have a direct bearing on Government policy in a specific area. This could be a positive or negative result for your organisation, so it is essential that your organisation is well prepared for these meetings, and can present its top-line issues as persuasively as possible. Being able to draw upon robust evidence and best practice will be definite advantages in this regard.

You should also carefully consider your organisation's response to any difficult areas such as the likely cost of your organisation's 'policy asks'. In real terms you need to persuade the special advisers and senior civil servants that your 'policy asks' are realistic, cost effective, present a positive synergy with Government policy, and will not have any unintended consequences which could embarrass the Government further down the policy line. Providing reassurance on all of these areas will make it more likely that the special advisers and officials will report favourably on your meeting, and on your organisation's 'policy asks'. This, in turn, could help to ensure that your organisation receives a positive response from the minister.

Meetings with MPs and Peers

Your organisation's public affairs strategy should include a strong focus on securing meetings with MPs and Peers. This type of engagement can make an important contribution to supporting organisations to achieve the aims and objectives of their public affairs strategy. Meeting MPs is particularly important where your organisation is seeking to raise issues and/or concerns about matters or developments which relate to their local MP's constituency. Organisations' engagement with MPs and Peers on wider issues and policy areas is considered in more detail in Chapter 6. Where your organisation has 'local' issues it wants to raise, it should consider how the local MP can help to support this process. The local MP could be particularly helpful where issues have arisen in their constituency which impact upon your organisation, and which may require some sort of intervention from the Government. Examples could include where national policy or legislation is having unintended consequences for your organisation, and your organisation is seeking to enlist the support of its local MP to raise its concerns with the Government, and to persuade it to take remedial action.

As with meetings involving Cabinet ministers, it is important that your organisation is fully prepared for meetings with local MPs, and is represented by those within the organisation who are best qualified to outline the issues, and any potential solutions, as persuasively as possible. Being able to draw upon the best practice and evidence of your organisation, and its business or projects or services, will strengthen your organisation's capacity to persuade the MP to lend their support to your 'policy asks'. This, however, will depend upon a number of factors including whether or not the MP is a Government backbencher, and the interface between your organisation's 'policy asks' and Government policy. Electoral factors such as the size of the MP's majority, and the proximity of the next General Election, could also have a bearing. It will also depend upon the type of issues you are highlighting. If, for example, you are raising issues which could have an impact upon large numbers of people within the constituency, such as the loss of important services or businesses, this will have a direct bearing on the MP's response, and their willingness to help – even to the extent of cutting across their own political party's policy position on a particular area.

It also recommended that organisations should seek meetings with Peers, especially if it relates to issues arising in a particular local area or part of the UK. Enlisting Peers with specific geographical connections can be of major benefit if your organisation is seeking to raise issues relating to an area or country with which the Peer has a close association. If the issues you are raising strike a chord with the Peer, the latter may raise the issues in a Starred Question at Question Time in the House of Lords, or even seek a short debate. Other options would include tabling written questions if there were issues on which your organisation is seeking clarification. The Peer might also be persuaded to meet the minister on your behalf, or to meet the minister with representatives from your organisation, to discuss the issues in question. Against this background, it is recommended that your organisation should identify the Peers with particular geographical interests or associations relevant to your organisation. Another important factor to consider is to enlist the support of Peers with a long standing involvement in the policy issues you are raising, especially Peers who were formerly MPs and held ministerial office or other senior positions within government or in their party.

Developing a cross-party approach

Strategically, it is vital that your organisation bears in mind the need to take a cross-party approach. In this respect, while it is important to focus your organisation's public affairs strategy on influencing the Government, it is also crucial that your organisation does not lose sight of the significance and benefits of engaging with the opposition parties at a senior level. This approach will help to safeguard your organisation against accusations of political bias, which could have an adverse, long-term bearing on its relations with the different political parties. For some organisations this may be less of a concern than for others, especially where their aims and objectives are naturally more in synch with the policies of a specific political party or parties. By contrast, most organisations will want to engage on a cross-party basis, and to keep their channels of communication open with all of the political parties and groupings in both Houses of Parliament.

This approach will often be the one best suited to influence national policy development at Government level, and in Parliament. It is worth considering that, if your organisation is seeking to influence a particular policy decision by the Government, and can demonstrate that its policy position is supported by some/all of the opposition parties, this is more likely to persuade the Government to make concessions on the issue (if it is inclined to make any concessions). This will be particularly relevant where an MP or Peer has tabled amendments to a Bill on behalf of your organisation, and you are working with the MP or Peer to persuade the Government to accept the amendments. In this context, arranging meetings with all of the opposition parties and groupings should be a major, and necessary, part of your public affairs strategy.

The potential benefits of adopting a cross-party approach will be considerable in the House of Lords, where Peers are often more willing than MPs to consider policy issues on their merits, and even to vote against their own party's whip, on specific issues. There is also an influential crossbench grouping, the existence of which strengthens the House of Lords' willingness to take a cross-party approach on a wide range of issues. The dynamics within the House of Lords present major opportunities for organisations to have their policy demands examined on their merits, and to have a significant bearing upon national policy development and legislation, especially where the Government feels under pressure from a cross-party alliance and could face defeat on key votes in the House of Lords.

More fundamentally, ensuring your organisation takes a cross-party approach will help to ensure that its influencing of Government is sustainable, and that your organisation is in a strong position to influence key policy makers despite any changes of government. What you should avoid is investing so heavily, in policy terms, in the current party of Government that your organisation and its policies become too closely identified with that party, to the extent that you will be left exposed if that party loses the next General Election. In this respect, it is crucial that you ensure your high profile contacts with Government do not overnight become largely redundant, and your influence marginalised, due to a change of party in Government.

Taking a cross-party approach can help to reduce the risks of this occurring. It is, therefore, strongly recommended that, when your organisation is pursuing meeting requests with senior Government ministers about particular policy issues or legislation, you should target similar meetings with the leaders, or with the relevant policy spokespersons, of the opposition parties. Apart from building up a cross-party alliance which could potentially increase the chances of your organisation influencing national policy and legislation, it will also help to safeguard against changes of government having a disastrous impact upon your organisation's ability to influence policy makers.

Ministerial visits and other key visits

Inviting leading policy makers to visit your organisation, or to participate in events it is hosting, can offer significant opportunities to raise the profile of your organisation, to showcase its work and to share the best practice of its businesses or projects or services. Securing visits to your organisation from Government ministers, or from opposition parties' leaders or opposition parties' spokespersons on policy areas relevant to your organisation and its work, including attending events at your organisation, will potentially provide your organisation with excellent opportunities to influence national policy development and parliamentary legislation. These visits and events are likely to be high-profile occasions, and can offer major media opportunities to publicise your organisation and its work, including the chance to promote your organisation through social media.

To make the most of these visits, it is recommended that your organisation should take a strategic approach and develop a public affairs engagement programme targeting the Government ministers and other leading policy makers you wish to invite to visit your organisation, and to participate in your events. This can be put in perspective by considering that securing a ministerial visit will allow your organisation, in addition to attracting potentially significant levels of media coverage, a chance to raise issues with the Government and to feed into national policy debates. It will also support your organisation to develop its relationships with the Government ministers most relevant to its work, which will be invaluable in keeping your organisation on the Government's radar in terms of the latter's policy thinking and planning. Equally, these visits can afford high profile opportunities to engage with the opposition parties, and to influence their policy development on particular issues.

Your organisation, in developing its programme of visits from Government ministers and other leading policy makers, should consider which policy makers it wishes to invite to visit, and why. Part of this process should involve identifying the outcomes you are hoping each specific visit or event will achieve for your organisation. Priority should be given to inviting those Government ministers most relevant to your organisation's work, and you should keep a close eye on which ministers are responsible for the policy areas in which your organisation works or has an interest. The same considerations would apply for your organisation in inviting the leaders and relevant lead spokespersons of the opposition parties, especially in view of the advantages outlined above of adopting a cross-party approach to your engagement with key policy makers.

To persuade a Government minister to visit your organisation you need to make the invite as attractive as possible. Invites which seek to secure the attendance of a Government minister at a landmark event being held by your organisation will increase the chances that the minister will agree to your request. Examples include celebration events to mark an organisation's 50th anniversary or other major anniversary, or to recognise specific achievements of the organisation and its staff such as winning a national award. Other examples could include commemorations of events in the organisation's history, or to celebrate the opening of new premises. Inviting the minister to participate in this type of event could be an attractive option for the Minister, especially where you want them to give the keynote speech or undertake some other high profile role. These type of events often generate excellent levels of publicity, and are ideal for promoting your organisation through social media. This is a good starting point for the minister in terms of their initial assessment of the benefits of attending the event.

The minister's attendance is not, however, guaranteed, given the demands upon their time, and a range of factors will influence the minister's decision making when it comes to responding to your organisation's invite. The likelihood of securing the minister's participation will increase if there is a strong synergy between your organisation's work and the issues it is campaigning on, and with the Government's own policy priorities and/or with major parliamentary business. Other factors will be the strategic electoral importance to the Government of the constituency in which the event will take place, and the proximity of any major by-elections, and of the General Election. These are the type of factors which the minister and their special advisers and senior civil servants will weigh up in deciding whether or not to accept your organisation's invite.

Planning a ministerial visit

Your organisation should take the same approach to organising a ministerial visit to its business/services/project, as it would for organising a visit from another key policy maker such as the leader of one of the opposition parties. Indeed, developing a common approach to such events will help your organisation to fine tune the planning and delivery of the events, and to build up significant expertise in consistently hosting high quality events.

These are showcase events, and need to be planned efficiently and at all times with the aims of your organisation's overriding public affairs strategy in mind. Getting the organisation of these events right will enhance the reputation of your organisation, getting it wrong could risk reputational damage, which is something that should be avoided at all costs. To take the example of a ministerial visit, Government ministers are extremely busy, and ensuring your invite translates into a date in their appointments diary can be a major challenge. To ensure that your organisation's invite receives serious consideration you need to allow a minimum of three months between the invite being sent to the minister and the date of the event itself. You also need to ensure that you send the invite to the ministerial address, and send it by e-mail and by post. In addition, you should suggest potential dates for the event to the minister, because finding a convenient date for the minister will be essential if your organisation is to receive a positive response to its invite.

It is recommended that you also try and follow up with the minister's special advisers and senior civil servants to 'sell' the event, and to persuade them of the major benefits of the minister attending. At this stage you need to get across the important advantages to the

Government and to the minister which will arise from their attending the event, and giving the keynote speech. It is also advised that you highlight the potential synergy between the proposed ministerial visit and the Government's policy priorities and/or relevant parliamentary business. Emphasising the media opportunities, including the social media potential, would also be helpful, especially if you can suggest ways in which these areas could be exploited for the minister's visit. Getting these points across to the special advisers and to the senior civil servants will help to inform the discussions which the ministerial team will have about how to respond to the invite to the minister to attend your event.

When organising high profile events at which the minister has been invited to deliver the keynote speech, you also need to give careful consideration to which other policy makers need to be invited. Your aim should be to strengthen relationships with the minister and with other key policy makers, in order to raise the profile of your organisation and to influence policy development and legislation. It is, therefore, important that you take a strategic view on which policy makers should be targeted to attend the event, and what formal role, if any, they should have at the event. Major considerations in this area should be securing the attendance of the policy makers whose participation will deliver the best outcomes for your organisation. This needs to be balanced with other important considerations such as ensuring that your organisation does not inadvertently alienate any leading policy makers by failing to invite them.

Against this background, it is recommended that your organisation ensures it invites the local MP, and also decides what sort of role, if any, the latter should have at the event. This needs to be handled sensitively, particularly if the minister and the local MP belong to different political parties. If you do not intend to invite the local MP to have a formal role at the event, and to simply be one of the invited guests, you might want to let their office know in advance that the minister will be participating in an event in the MP's constituency. This will help your organisation to maintain good relations with its local MP. There is, however, a lot to weigh up, including the purpose of the event and the extent to which your organisation needs to take a cross-party approach, the advantages of a cross-party approach and the importance of developing good relations with the local MP. It is, therefore, recommended that you invite the local MP to provide the 'welcome' speech at the start of the event, or to provide a speech highlighting the important contribution that your organisation makes to the lives of people within their constituency.

It is also advised that, in order to maximise the advantages to your organisation of the minister's input, and of any input from the local MP, you work with their staff before the event to update them on the overriding aims of the event, the format of the event, and on the focus of the formal inputs. Seeking their feedback on the programme for the event is a good way of increasing their buy-in for the event. Establishing good relations with their staff before the event will help to ensure that the participation of the minister and other key policy makers is managed smoothly. You should also offer to provide the minister and the local MP with speaking notes. This will increase the likelihood that their inputs will be of maximum value to your organisation, and ensure that their speeches focus on the main issues which you wish to prioritise. The person in your organisation with lead responsibility for the media should also liaise with the minister's office, and with the local MP's office, about media coverage for the event. In this respect, a joint news release should be considered with quotes from your organisation's lead officer, from the minister and possibly also from the local MP.

Another important factor to bear in mind is that ministerial visits can provide useful opportunities to strengthen your organisation's relationships with its partners, and with other stakeholders such as business partners, investors, customers and service users. For organisations which rely on working closely with local government, for example, it is strongly advised that you assess which local politicians need to be involved in the event, and whether or not they must be given a formal role. It is recommended that there should not be too many formal inputs at the event, and you need to take a strategic view about which policy makers, apart from the Government minister, should provide a formal input. Important factors in this area will be the purpose of the event, your existing relations with the different policy makers and what type of inputs would be of most strategic benefit to your organisation.

These events will be important occasions for your organisation, and will provide your organisation with an opportunity to demonstrate to its partners and to other major stakeholders that it is a dynamic, highly effective and well connected organisation, which has made the right strategic connections with the main policy makers relevant to its work. The advantages are potentially considerable. Such events can help to strengthen your organisation's relationships with leading policy makers, and to raise its profile through good levels of media coverage. This, in turn, can present opportunities to help shape and influence policy development and legislation. Other benefits arising from these events could include securing increased levels of support from your partners and other stakeholders, whether in the form of increased investment, securing a grant, obtaining new contracts or being invited to participate in a Government task force or working group in a specific policy area. It is, therefore, important that, when you plan the event, you consider the outcomes you are hoping it will achieve in your relations not only with the key policy makers, but also with your partners and other stakeholders.

Summary of key points

The key points from this chapter can be summarised as follows:

- Organisations should prioritise influencing key policy makers in their public affairs strategies, as this will strengthen their capacity to shape policy development and legislation at Government level, and in Parliament.
- Identifying clear aims and objectives to underpin your organisation's engagement with leading policy makers will increase the effectiveness of its public affairs strategy.
- Correspondence will often be a limited way of engaging with policy makers. Seeking meetings with them, or inviting them to attend your events, will potentially offer more effective and productive means of engagement.
- Engaging with the different political parties on a cross-party basis is the approach most likely to influence national policy development and legislation.
- Securing the agreement of key policy makers to visit your organisation, or to participate in your events, can offer significant opportunities to influence policy and legislation, and to raise the profile of your organisation.

6

Engaging with MPs and Peers

Another major component of your organisation's public affairs strategy should be promoting engagement with MPs and Peers. Building up its connections with these policy makers will support your organisation to make an important contribution to policy development and legislation at Government level, and in Parliament. Working closely with MPs and Peers will, for example, help to ensure that your organisation participates effectively in key policy debates, and that its policy positions, best practice and evidence are able to influence those debates. It will also raise the profile of your organisation with Government and in Parliament, and strengthen the capacity of your organisation's public affairs strategy to deliver successful outcomes.

Approaching MPs

An important factor that your organisation should bear in mind, when assessing which MPs to engage with, is the different categories of MP that will be relevant to your public affairs strategy. These are:

- Local MPs;
- MPs who share your organisation's policy interests; and
- MPs who chair and/or are members of parliamentary committees.

One of the main categories for your organisation will be the local MPs who represent constituencies where your organisation is based, or in which it has business interests or operates projects or services. Local MPs have the potential to become major supporters of your organisation in Parliament, and to raise issues on your behalf with Government Ministers and with other leading policy makers. Most local MPs will have a deep-rooted interest in their constituency, particularly in relation to issues and developments which could have a positive or negative bearing upon their chances of re-election. Organisations should, therefore, seek to cultivate close links, and to have regular contact, with this group of MPs.

We have seen previously how links with local MPs can be developed through visits to your organisation, and through invites to attend showcase events hosted by your organisation. Such initiatives will help your organisation to build up strong connections with its local MP. To maximise the impact of these visits you should work with the office of your local MP to ensure that their visits attract good levels of media coverage, as this will be an important consideration both for your organisation and for the MP in terms of profile raising. Careful thought should also be given to ways in which social media can be used to promote and highlight the MP's visit. An additional benefit of such visits is that, when these visits go well, the MP may use appropriate opportunities in Parliament, such as during the course of a debate or at Question Time, to refer to your organisation and the work it is undertaking within their constituency. Positive references to your organisation and to its best practice and evidence will be invaluable in raising its profile with key policy makers, and in ensuring that it makes a contribution to policy development and legislation in areas relevant to your organisation and to its work.

Apart from inviting the MP to visit your organisation, and/or to participate in your events, there are other important ways of keeping the local MP updated about your organisation and its work or role within their constituency. In this respect, if there are policy issues arising for your organisation, either within or outside the parliamentary constituency in which it is based or has interests, you should seek meetings with your local MP to brief them about the issues and any concerns you may have, and to find out if they would able and willing to progress these issues on behalf of your organisation. The MP's ability to help your organisation in these circumstances will depend upon a number of factors, including whether or not the MP is a Government backbencher, and can use ministerial connections to deliver your organisation's 'policy asks'. Other factors will be how realistic these 'policy asks' are, and the steps which would be required to achieve them. The synergy between your organisation's 'policy asks' and the policies of the MP's own party will be another factor.

This will not prevent the MP raising the issues on your behalf, but it could naturally limit the outcomes they can achieve if what you are asking for is completely at odds with the policies of the MP's own party.

MPs receive a lot of information in circulars and briefings from numerous organisations and individuals. Receiving information about issues and developments arising within their constituency will be of particular interest to most MPs. It is, therefore, recommended that if your organisation provides regular briefings, or circulars or newsletters it should ensure that copies are sent to your local MP's office. This will help to keep the MP and their staff up to date about your organisation and its work within the constituency. Another option would be to develop links with the local MP, and to keep them updated, through social media. Your organisation's initial meetings with its local MP should help to clarify the MP's preferences about how they wish to be kept updated.

Careful consideration should be given by your organisation to how it engages with its local MP, if they are also a Government minister. The key thing with this category of MP is to be clear from the outset about the capacity in which you are seeking to engage with the MP. If you are seeking to engage with them as your local MP then you should route any contact through the MP's constituency office or their Westminster office if requested to do so by the MP's staff or website. If, on the other hand, you are seeking to engage with the MP in their ministerial capacity, any approaches should be directed through their department or by using the ministerial e-mail and postal addresses. Significantly, if you are inviting the minister as your local MP to attend one of your events or to visit your organisation, the fact that they are also a Government minister will potentially raise the level of media interest in the visit, and the levels of media coverage which the visit attracts.

Your organisation should also seek to engage with MPs who have an interest in the policy issues and areas on which your organisation and its work focus. Some within this category of MPs will be well known to your organisation, but it is recommended that you undertake research to establish the full range of potential supporters for your organisation, and its work amongst MPs. In this respect, you should look at *Hansard* and check to see which MPs have previously referred to your organisation or to the policy issues and areas on which your organisation focuses and/or campaigns. *Dod's Parliamentary Companion,*[1] *the House Magazine*[2] and *Vacher's Quarterly*[3] are other useful sources for researching MPs' policy interests, and areas of special interest. Identifying the MPs who are closest to your organisation in policy terms will strengthen the effectiveness of your organisation's public affairs strategy. It will, for example, ensure that your organisation will be able to quickly target the MPs who are most likely to be willing to progress, or to support, particular public affairs initiatives or activities in Parliament. This, in turn, will increase the chances that your organisation's public affairs activities or campaign will deliver tangible outcomes.

Another group of MPs which your organisation should seek to actively engage with are the chairs and other members of the various parliamentary committees relevant to your organisation and to its work in the House of Commons. The work of these committees is a key element of the Parliament, and of the legislative processes in both Houses. Influencing the work of committees should be a priority area for organisations, and is considered in more detail in Chapter 9. The committees in both House are responsible for dealing with significant amounts of parliamentary business. Engaging with the chairs of these committees, and with the other members, will offer your organisation significant benefits. Such engagement will, for example, raise your organisation's profile with these committees, and increase the likelihood that your organisation will be invited to give oral evidence for a particular parliamentary inquiry, or for its consideration of specific legislation. Developing relations with the chairs and members of committees relevant to your organisation's work will also place your organisation in a better position to receive early notification of the committee business likely to impact upon your organisation and its work. These relations will also ensure that your organisation is best placed to find out more about how the committee will approach, and deal with, business including legislation relevant to your organisation and its work. Organisations will be able to use this type of intelligence to inform their public affairs strategy, and to develop the response they make to specific committee work streams.

---

1   *Dod's Parliamentary Companion 2017*, (London, 2016).
2   *House Magazine*, (London, 2017).
3   *Vacher's Quarterly*, (London, 2017).

Engaging with Peers

Major opportunities exist in the House of Lords to influence key policy debates and legislation, and it is recommended that your organisation's public affairs strategy should include a strong focus on engaging with Peers. It is important, however, that your organisation, in launching an influencing strategy in the House of Lords, recognises from the beginning that the political landscape and dynamics in the Upper House are, in many respects, very different from those in the House of Commons. Peers, for example, will often be more willing to consider issues on their merits. Indeed, for some Peers belonging to one of the political parties represented in the House of Lords, this will sometimes translate into a greater willingness, than MPs, to vote against their own party's whip on Divisions on certain issues.

Another key dimension of the dynamics within the House of Lords is that there are significant numbers of Peers who belong to no political party. Apart from the sizeable group of Crossbench Peers, there are Bishops and other Peers who are not members of the Crossbench group or of any of the political parties represented in the House of Lords. The presence of these groups reinforces the House of Lords' willingness to often consider many issues on their merits, and on a cross-party basis. Significantly, the occasions on which MPs will, either individually or collectively, consider issues on a cross-party basis are much rarer in the House of Commons. These factors present many opportunities for organisations to engage with Peers, and to undertake public affairs activities in the House of Lords that deliver tangible outcomes.

Which Peers your organisation engages with will depend upon the context of such engagement, and the aims you are hoping it will achieve. Is your organisation, for example, seeking to raise issues in a particular debate in the House of Lords, or to influence a Government Bill or other legislation? Alternatively, is your organisation seeking to enlist the support of sympathetic Peers to help secure a meeting with a Government minister in the House of Lords, or to persuade a Peer to table a Starred Question for Question Time? These are all likely to have a bearing upon which Peers you engage with on a regular basis. Another major factor will be the policy areas and issues on which your organisation is seeking to engage with Peers. A further consideration will be if these policy areas or issues relate to a particular part of the UK or to a foreign country. Against this background, it is recommended that your organisation should undertake research to determine which Peers may have an interest in the relevant policy areas and issues. A useful starting point would be to check *Hansard*, which is available on Parliament's website, to see which Peers have previously participated in debates on these issues, or have asked Parliamentary Questions relating to the particular parts of the UK or to the specific countries. You should also check the membership of the committees in the House of Lords to identify Peers who might have an interest in the issues your organisation is seeking to raise. Another useful source will be the membership of relevant APPGs. The House of Lords section of the Parliament's website contains biographical sketches of Peers including a 'Member's Focus' section which outlines their policy interests. *Dod's Parliamentary Companion*, a guide to Parliament published annually, also provides some useful background information about the policy interests of individual Peers.

Different types of engagement

There are a wide range of ways in which your organisation's engagement with MPs and Peers can help to progress the aims and objectives of its public affairs strategy. This engagement can help your organisation to raise its profile, and make an important contribution to its capacity to influence policy development and legislation at Government level, and in Parliament. We have already seen in Chapter 5 the advantages of engaging with Government ministers, and this is just one area in which an MP or Peer can support your organisation to secure significant outcomes. Government ministers receive large numbers of approaches from organisations on a daily basis, including meeting requests and invites to attend events. Engaging with Government backbench MPs and Peers, and developing close relations with these groups, can be beneficial in this area. If, as part of your regular contact with, for example, a backbench MP, you confirm your approach or intended approach to the minister, the backbench MP will be able to update the minister and their special advisers on the merits of your organisation and its work, and of the strategic advantages to the Government of a positive response to your request.

MPs and Peers can also support your organisation by raising issues on its behalf during a parliamentary debate on a policy issue or area relevant to your organisation and its work. Debates can be a useful way of highlighting the best practice of your organisation, and of drawing upon the evidence of its business, or projects or services. These can be major opportunities to raise your organisation's profile, and to influence policy development at Government level, and the policy direction of the opposition parties. To maximise your organisation's impact you should engage early with MPs and Peers to update them on the policy areas and campaigns which your organisation is prioritising. You also want to put the MPs and Peers on notice that you will be seeking a chance to brief MPs and Peers in relevant debates as they arise. In this context, part of your engagement with the MP or Peer should be to investigate their willingness to lobby the Government, or the opposition party to which they belong, to table a Motion for debate on the policy issues that your organisation is seeking to prioritise. Alternatively, you should find out if they would be prepared to table a Motion for a Member's debate on these issues. Securing a debate through either of these routes would represent an excellent result for your organisation. It would, for example, increase the profile of your organisation, and provide an opportunity to secure support from the Government, the opposition parties and groupings, as well as individual MPs and Peers for the policy issues and 'policy asks' your organisation is seeking to raise.

Consideration should also be given to how MPs and Peers can support your organisation's response to legislation which affects your organisation and its work. In this respect, your organisation's parliamentary monitoring should alert you to the introduction of any relevant legislation. It is important that you assess the likely impact of the legislation on your organisation, including identifying any areas in which you consider that changes need to be made to improve the legislation. You should next approach MPs and Peers, depending upon which House the Bill commences and the stage it has reached in the legislative process, to outline the issues for your organisation presented by the Bill. You should then liaise with the MP and/or Peer to develop appropriate amendments to the legislation. This is an area in which the role of the MP and/or Peer will be critical. How to respond to legislation is considered in more detail in Chapters 10, 11 and 12. Another aspect of your organisation's engagement with MPs and Peers on legislation could potentially be liaising with an MP and/or Peer to consider taking forward a Private Member's Bill focusing on policy issues that your organisation believes require legislative change.

Parliamentary Questions can also make an important contribution to your organisation's public affairs strategy. You should, therefore, give consideration to policy issues which your organisation wishes to prioritise in this area. This could, for example, be linked to a long-term campaign that your organisation has been running. Approaching an MP, for example, to table a question for oral answer will provide a high profile opportunity to raise key issues for your organisation, to increase awareness of these issues and to try and generate a positive response from the Government. Oral questions will provide good media opportunities to enhance the profile of these issues and of your organisation, and you should work with the MP or Peer to maximise such opportunities, including through social media. The same considerations would apply for written questions, which will also potentially deliver significant outcomes especially if supported by media activities. How to use Parliamentary Questions to the best effect is addressed in Chapter 14.

Another useful way in which MPs can support your organisation to achieve the aims and objectives of its public affairs strategy is to lodge an Early Day Motion (EDM) on behalf of your organisation. EDMs are formal Motions for debate, although it is rare for EDMs to lead to a debate. The focus of the EDM could be on your organisation, its work and achievements. Alternatively, the EDM could highlight a specific campaign your organisation is running, or particular policy issues on which it is seeking to secure policy or legislative changes. EDMs can help to raise the profile of your organisation, and of policy issues it is seeking to prioritise. The most effective EDMs are those which are supported with media activity. EDMs are only tabled in the House of Commons. It is recommended that your organisation bears in mind the profile-raising opportunities presented by EDMs, and gives consideration to whether or not this is an initiative that you would like to progress with an MP. Issues around EDMs are considered in more detail in Chapter 16.

Summary of key points

The key points from this chapter can be summarised as follows:

- Building up your organisation's connections with MPs and Peers can support it to make an important contribution to policy development and legislation at Government level, and in Parliament.
- Engaging with local MPs can assist your organisation to progress key activities within its public affairs strategy, and steps should be taken to keep these MPs fully updated about your organisation, and its work within their constituencies.
- Undertaking research to identify those MPs and Peers who are most likely to support your organisation and its work will strengthen the effectiveness of its public affairs strategy.
- Major opportunities exist in the House of Lords to influence key policy debates and legislation, and it is recommended that your organisation's public affairs strategy should include a strong focus on engaging with Peers.

7

Influencing the Political Parties

The success of your organisation's public affairs strategy will depend
upon its capacity to build good relationships with the Government,
and with all of the opposition parties in Parliament. Establishing
close working relationships with the leaderships of all of the parties
and political groupings represented in the House of Commons and in
the House of Lords, as well as with individual MPs and Peers within
these parties and groupings, should be at the very centre of your
organisation's public affairs strategy. Ideally, you want to develop
relationships in these areas which will ensure that, if your organisation
does wish to raise an issue in either or both Houses of Parliament,
it will be able to rely on such relationships to engage with all of the
parties and political groupings at a senior level. By doing so, your
organisation can put itself in the best possible position to consistently
influence policy development and legislation at Government level, and
in Parliament. This will increase the chances that your organisation's
public affairs strategy, including specific public affairs activities and
campaigns, will deliver its aims and objectives.

Engaging with the Government

The overwhelming majority of the main policy development processes
undertaken at a UK level, and of the legislation introduced in
Parliament, will be initiated and progressed by the Government. It
is, therefore, vital that your organisation considers how best it can
engage with the Government in these areas, and develop a public
affairs strategy to maximise its influence with the Government. The
most successful public affairs strategies targeting the Government
will often take a multi-layered approach, and feature activities and

initiatives focusing on the different parts of Government. In this respect, an organisation seeking political support for its policy position in relation to a Government policy initiative, or for its response to a piece of legislation or for a particular service model it has developed, should progress activities targeting the Prime Minister and relevant Government ministers. It should also develop activities focusing on the Government's backbench MPs and/or Peers, while undertaking other activities aimed at senior Government civil servants and at the Government's special advisers. Successfully influencing policy development and legislation at a UK level will rely on securing the backing of the Prime Minister and/or the relevant ministers. Organisations will often, however, before achieving this support, have to invest time and effort in obtaining the backing of the Government's backbench MPs and Peers, of senior civil servants and of the special advisers, for a specific policy issue.

A major priority for your organisation should be manoeuvring itself into the policy thinking of the Prime Minister, and/or of the ministers most relevant to its work and with ministerial responsibility in the policy areas or issues being prioritised by your organisation. You can do so by keeping the Prime Minister and/or relevant Government ministers up to date about your organisation, its work and achievements and campaigns. We have already seen how visits to organisations and their businesses and services can help in this regard, along with meetings on key policy issues.

Your organisation can also try to develop, or maintain, a high profile with the Government by ensuring it regularly intervenes to raise issues in response to parliamentary business relevant to its work or to campaigns it is running. Briefing ministers on these issues, and engaging with the Government's backbench MPs and/or Peers on such business, will help to raise your organisation's profile with leading policy makers, and to strengthen its ability to influence the direction of Government policy development and legislation. Building your organisation's influence in this area can potentially deliver major success for its public affairs strategy. The key is to try and secure a meeting with the minister and with their senior civil servants as soon as your parliamentary monitoring and political intelligence gathering have identified Government and/or parliamentary business on policy issues or areas that your organisation is seeking to prioritise, or which are likely to impact upon your organisation.

Organisations seeking a ministerial meeting should ensure that their request highlights the interface between the governmental and/ or parliamentary business, and the strength of the evidence and best practice upon which the organisation's policy position is based in relation to this business. The organisation should emphasise the strategic importance to the Government of ensuring that the issues it is raising are heard, and listened to, within the policy debates around the Government business and/or parliamentary business in question. Ministers receive large numbers of meeting requests. Your organisation, therefore, needs to ensure that you make your request as persuasive as possible. If the issues are relevant to Government or parliamentary business, you could combine the meeting request with an invite to visit your organisation or its projects or services, especially where the evidence and best practice they offer are relevant to the Government or to parliamentary business.

By contrast, where the timescales of the Government and/or parliamentary business would not permit a ministerial meeting, e.g. the business is a Government debate in either House of Parliament, your organisation should prepare a briefing which can be sent to the relevant minister or ministers. The response to the briefing will depend upon a number of factors, including the Government's own policy position, and its strategic priorities. Your organisation can try and maximise the chances that the briefing will receive a positive response from the Government, and from its backbench MPs and/or Peers, by ensuring that it is based on strong evidence and on successful best practice. Responding to Government or parliamentary business on a regular basis will help to raise the profile of your organisation with the Government. Even if the Government does not agree with your arguments, it is more likely to engage with your organisation if your briefings are well presented, and are based on robust evidence and best practice, and your organisation has developed a proven track record in the policy area under consideration. The risk the Government may run is that simply ignoring your briefings on ideological grounds, without addressing the issues you are seeking to raise, could leave it open to criticism by the opposition parties and/or by the media if the briefing is supported by strong evidence, and the issues it presents are taken up by the latter.

Your organisation can also strengthen its relations with the Government by cultivating its ties with the Government's backbench

MPs and Peers. Indeed, developing your ties with the latter, and approaching them to raise issues on your behalf is often a highly effective way of influencing Government policy. In this respect, the minister will generally feel much less threatened by an approach from one of the Government's backbench MPs or Peers, and might accordingly be more willing to consider the issues on their merit. Approaching your constituency MP and those MPs with a particularly close association with your organisation or the sector it operates in, and who are Government backbench MPs, would be good starting points. The warmth or otherwise of a specific MP's relations with the Government and/or with a specific minister, will be another important factor in weighing up which MP to approach. Other relevant factors would include the depth of the MP's involvement in, and contribution to, the policy issues on which you are seeking to engage with leading policy makers.

Engagement with Government ministers in the House of Lords

In the House of Lords, the type of factors to be considered in weighing up an approach to the Government would be slightly different from those in the House of Commons. One of the main considerations is that it is generally junior ministers who are based in the Lords. In this respect, your organisation would need to identify specific reasons and advantages for approaching the Government's Ministers in the Lords, rather than its ministers in the Commons, on a particular issue. Engaging with the Government's ministers in the Lords would, for example, usually make most sense tactically when your organisation is seeking to influence business in the House of Lords, and the minister is leading on this business for the Government. In this context, it is important to remember that many Government Bills will start in the House of Lords. Where your organisation has an interest in a particular Bill, and the legislation is starting in the Lords rather than in the House of Commons, it is essential that you engage with the relevant minister in the House of Lords as early as possible in the legislative process.

Such approaches can also provide significant advantages where your organisation has strong ties with a particular junior minister in the House of Lords, and makes the initial approach to the latter in order to ensure that its issues or concerns are raised with the Government through the 'good offices' of the junior minister. This type of engagement has been known to get policy issues onto the Government's policy agenda. Part of that route to influencing the Government could also involve engaging with backbench Government Peers who are sympathetic to your organisation, and to the policy issues it is seeking to raise. The backbench Peers then, in turn, raise the issues with the Government's minister in the Lords. Engaging with the Government backbench Peers can be particularly productive where your organisation is seeking to respond to key business in the House of Lords. Persuading a Government backbench Peer to table amendments to a Bill, on your organisation's behalf, for example, is one of the major areas in which your organisation can engage with the Government in the House of Lords. This area is considered in more detail in Chapter 12.

Engaging with senior Government civil servants

An important aspect of an organisation's multi-layered approach to engaging with the Government should be ensuring that it develops good working relations with the Government's senior civil servants. Some organisations will have formal relations with these officials because they receive funding or grants from the Government, and are accountable primarily to civil servants in the sponsoring Government department. These organisations will generally have developed relations with the officials over a period of time. It will be in the interests of these organisations, for continuity of funding and to influence Government policy development and legislation, to try and ensure that such relations are as positive as possible. For those organisations which are not in receipt of Government funding or grants, there are also major advantages in developing good working relations with the Government, both at ministerial and at senior civil servant levels. Establishing such relations can increase the likelihood that your organisation will be able to secure meetings with the ministers and their officials, as the latter will brief the minister on the advantages of meeting your organisation, and on the risks of failing to do so.

Building good relations with senior officials can also pay significant dividends where the Government is seeking to establish working groups to develop policy proposals, including draft primary legislation, secondary legislation and statutory guidance. Being on the policy radar of the senior civil servants, and having good working relations with the latter, will help to improve the chances that your organisation will be invited to join the membership of a specific working group focusing on developing policies or pieces of legislation. Securing membership on one of these groups will be a major outcome for your organisation. It will provide your organisation with significant opportunities to contribute to policy development at Government level.

Developing good working relations with the senior officials will also be helpful in situations where your organisation is attempting to influence legislation in Parliament and, as part of its public affairs strategy, is seeking meetings with the Bill team, i.e. with the civil servants dealing with the legislation, and with other key officials. Establishing close working relations with the senior officials will often make it more likely that the Bill team and other officials will agree to meet your organisation to discuss possible lines of amendment to the legislation. Such meetings can provide invaluable opportunities to outline your organisation's concerns about aspects of the legislation, and to set out its proposals for amendments. These meetings can, at their best, help your organisation to secure significant concessions from the Government. The role of these meetings is considered in more detail in Chapter 12.

Special advisers

Other policy makers who should not be overlooked in developing your organisation's relations with the Government are the special advisers. These are appointed by the Government, and are responsible for providing ministers with political input and advice on areas such as political and parliamentary strategy, policy development and legislation. Their advice will focus on how specific Government policy positions will play out across the governing party, and with its backbench MPs and Peers, as well as with external stakeholders. The special advisers advise the Government on where it can press ahead with the full support of its party, or where it might be advisable to adapt or change policies, including postponing the progression or implementation of a policy initiative or legislation, due to concerns across the party or within particular constituent parts such as its backbench MPs.

Special advisers also advise on how specific policy initiatives or legislation will play out in the House of Commons and in the House of Lords, and on how the legislative processes could be managed in both Houses. In addition, special advisers provide the Government with insights into the likely strategic impact of particular policies on the Government's electoral fortunes at General Elections, or in relation to forthcoming by-elections or at the local government elections. They play an important role within Government, and individual special advisers will have varying levels of power and influence. It is recommended that your organisation's public affairs strategy should include activities to cultivate relations with the special advisers, as it will help to increase your organisation's access to ministers and to other key policy makers.

The special advisers, like senior civil servants, will play an important role in facilitating or restricting access to Government ministers, and the closeness of an organisation's relations with the special advisers will often have a direct bearing on the success of the organisation's requests for meetings with a specific minister. Horizon scanning and intelligence gathering are important functions of special advisers, and their 'political antenna' will focus on political opportunities and risks. The special advisers' advice and decision making will normally be based on political considerations and on the political environment, especially on their ongoing assessments of how particular decisions by the Government will impact upon their party's parliamentary, and electoral, fortunes. By contrast, the senior civil servants are generally responsible for developing and delivering Government policy and, unlike the special advisers, are not supposed to have a political role.

To put the role of the special advisers in context, there will be occasions on which organisations will find it difficult to persuade the civil servants that the issues they are raising have merit, or have a strong synergy with the Government's, and their minister's, strategic priorities. In many cases the civil service will not, largely as a result of the political restrictions on their role, have considered the political impact of a course of action to the same extent as the special advisers would. Civil servants, unlike special advisers, will generally not have the same political sensitivities, relations and acumen regarding how particular policy decisions or initiatives will play outside the governing party and its supporters, with both Houses of Parliament and with the electorate.

It is situations like these where your organisation will have scope to seek engagement with the minister's special advisers, and to outline the issues you are seeking to raise with the Government. This can provide your organisation with important opportunities to explain your organisation's policy position, and its 'policy asks'. Such opportunities are vital as they can provide your organisation with chances to talk through, and to overcome, any objections the Government has raised in response to your policy position and policy demands. As part of this process, your organisation will be able to discuss with the special adviser the political consequences for the Government of taking, or of failing to take, a particular course of action in response to your organisation's concerns and/or the policy issues or campaigns it is prioritising. Engaging with the special adviser, in these circumstances, will provide your organisation with an opportunity to outline its key issues and any concerns, and to highlight the political ramifications for the Government. The aim of this engagement is to ensure that, once the special advisers have considered all of the political options and consequences of how to respond to the issues you have brought to their attention, your organisation has succeeded in getting these issues firmly onto the Government's policy agenda. Furthermore, if the Government has raised concerns about your organisation's policy position or 'policy asks', your aim should be to reassure the Government, to overcome these concerns and to get it to support your organisation's policy position and 'policy asks'.

Taking a cross-party approach

Your organisation should take a cross-party approach to its public affairs strategy. This will help to maximise the impact of its strategy, and to increase the chances that it will deliver tangible outcomes by influencing policy development at Government level, and legislation in Parliament. Some organisations will, by their history, policy positions and aims and objectives, have close ties with a particular political party and will, in consequence, be under less pressure to adopt a cross-party approach. By contrast, most organisations' public affairs strategies will rely on, and draw strength from, building and maintaining good relations with all of the political parties. For these organisations, demonstrating that they are taking a cross-party approach, and engaging with all of the political parties, will highlight the transparency of their public affairs strategies, as well as the objective, non-partisan nature of their relations with the different parties. This approach will support your organisation to develop a public affairs strategy which will make it more likely that it will attract cross-party support for its 'policy asks', and campaigns.

Pursuing a cross-party approach will have particular benefits in the context of your organisation's response to legislation. Seeking changes to legislation will usually only be possible if an organisation can persuade the Government to make changes to its own legislation, or if the organisation can put the Government under pressure by building up a cross-party alliance in favour of its amendments to the legislation. Demonstrating that your organisation has support from other organisations, ideally across different sectors, and has, or is likely to attract the support of opposition parties, will improve your organisation's chances of securing concessions on the legislation from the Government in the House of Commons.

The scope for taking a cross-party approach is even greater in the House of Lords, where the Government does not have a built-in majority. Indeed, the Government will not always be able to rely on all of its own backbench Peers to support its stance on particular issues, or on specific provisions within a Bill. Peers are often more willing to consider policy issues, and amendments to legislation, on an objective, non-partisan basis to a far greater extent than MPs would do in the House of Commons. Furthermore, there are significant numbers of Crossbench Peers, as well as Bishops and non-affiliated Peers, which further highlights the opportunities for developing cross-party alliances behind different amendments to legislation. These are important areas, and are considered separately and in more detail in Chapter 12.

Working with the opposition parties

An important part of your organisation's public affairs strategy should be to seek, and secure, meetings with the leaders of all of the opposition parties. Such meetings can help to raise the profile of your organisation, its work, policy positions and campaigns, and to develop its relations with these key policy makers. Another way in which your organisation can build up its relations with the opposition parties is to arrange meetings with the parties' spokespersons for the policy areas most relevant to your organisation's work, policy priorities and campaigns. It is strongly advised that your organisation invests sufficient levels of time and resource to prepare for such meetings, because these meetings can potentially afford significant opportunities to influence the opposition parties' policy positions, and their internal debates on policy development. One of the first issues to consider is to identify the most appropriate opportunity or context for such meetings. Possible options might include meetings to discuss a Government policy initiative or legislation, with the aim of trying to secure support for your organisation's response to these developments. Other options could involve meetings to update the spokespersons on your organisation's launch of a campaign with specific policy demands, or of a policy initiative, which you wish to gain support for across the different political parties represented at Westminster.

Consideration should also be given to who will represent your organisation at any meetings it arranges with opposition parties' leaders, and with their main spokespersons. Ideally, any meetings with the opposition parties' leaders should be led by a senior member of your organisation's management team, or by a trustee or by a high-profile supporter. Meetings with party spokespersons should also be led by your chief executive or by another senior member of your organisation. It is advised that you choose someone who can engage confidently and knowledgeably about your organisation, both on the policy issues you are seeking to raise with the spokesperson, and on practice or service issues. It is also vital that you set clear aims and objectives for these meetings. This includes ensuring that any 'policy asks' your organisation makes at the meeting are realistic, focused and well presented, and are backed by robust evidence and best practice. These demands will be particularly important if you wish the meeting to deliver tangible outcomes. Examples would include securing the agreement of the opposition party to intervene on your behalf in relation to policy development and influencing legislation, as well as building or reinforcing your relations with specific opposition parties.

Engaging with other parliamentary contacts

An important aspect of your organisation's public affairs strategy will be engaging with the chairs of key committees in both Houses of Parliament relevant to your organisation and its work. This will potentially offer major opportunities to influence policy development and legislation, and is considered in more detail in Chapter 9.

The Government and opposition parties will have chief whips and junior whips who are responsible for maintaining their party's internal discipline in the House of Commons and in the House of Lords, and for organising their party's response to parliamentary business. Developing good relations with the offices of the respective parties' whips in the House of Commons and in the House of Lords is strongly advised. The whips' offices can be an invaluable source of information about parliamentary business, and may provide your organisation with significant political intelligence. Building close ties with these offices could, for example, help your organisation to gain early warning of forthcoming parliamentary business relevant to your organisation and its interests, including which Member will be leading on this business for the party in question. Developing good relations with the whips' offices could support your organisation to develop useful insights into how a particular party will respond to specific items of parliamentary business, and its likely policy positions in response to this business. The whips' offices might also be able to provide advice on which of their party's MPs or Peers would welcome a briefing on certain policy issues or Bills. Obtaining this information can be a major advantage because it will enable your organisation to start briefing the key policy makers who will intervene in response to the parliamentary business in question.

Other useful contacts would include the staff in the resource centres and/or research offices run by the opposition parties in both Houses. As with the whips' offices, there will be important advantages in developing strong relationships with these offices. The resource centres and/or research offices based in both Houses of Parliament are designed to support the respective political parties, principally by ensuring that their front bench spokespersons and backbench MPs and Peers have briefing material for key parliamentary business, including debates, questions and legislation. These offices will usually be very happy to receive copies of briefings from external organisations, and to distribute the briefings as background information to their party's spokespersons, and backbench MPs and Peers. Cultivating your relations with these offices in both Houses will improve the chances that MPs and Peers will use your organisation's briefing material in responding to key parliamentary business. Your organisation would first need to weigh up, however, the advantages and disadvantages of taking a targeted approach to briefing the ministers, party spokespersons, MPs and Peers as appropriate, against a more general approach in which generic briefing is widely circulated to these groups.

Influencing the political parties' manifestos

Organisations can also achieve the main aims and objectives of their public affairs strategies by influencing the manifestos of the different political parties. Helping to shape and influence aspects of the parties' manifestos will potentially deliver major outcomes for your organisation's public affairs strategy. To highlight the cross-party nature of your organisation's public affairs strategy, it is recommended that you engage with all of the political parties and groupings represented at Westminster to try and influence their manifestos. One way in which your organisation can try and influence the parties' manifestos is by drafting your own manifesto. You can then use this as a focus of your engagement with the political parties in the run up to the General Election or to the local government elections, and in influencing the policy debates in Parliament. You can also use your organisation's manifesto to try and ensure that at least some of your organisation's 'policy asks' are included in the programme of government introduced by the political party which wins the General Election.

Some of the political parties will be more willing than others to involve external organisations in the development of their manifestos. Certain political parties will have formal consultations, and will seek the views of a wide range of organisations on the type of policies which should be in their manifestos. For others, it will be a much more closed affair, with the overwhelming focus being on canvassing, and drawing upon, the views of internal party stakeholders.

To ensure that your organisation increases its chances of influencing the policy development processes which lead to the drafting of the political parties' manifestos, it is important that your organisation uses its political contacts and parliamentary monitoring to keep an eye on the timelines for these processes, and on the opportunities for external organisations to influence the parties' manifestos. The political parties will work to different timelines, so it is strongly advised that you use these sources to ensure that your organisation is in as strong a position as possible, from the outset, to influence at an early stage the policy development processes to shape the manifestos.

While it is recognised that your organisation might be closer historically, and by its policy positions, to a specific party or parties, this should not deter you from approaching all of the political parties. Many of them will be prepared to consider suggestions for policy initiatives or for models of best practice or service delivery on their merits, and on the basis of the supporting evidence. That said, the outcome of such approaches will often depend upon the extent to which an organisation's suggestions or recommendations strike a chord with the party's own policies and its strategic policy themes, and the extent to which your proposal is underpinned by robust evidence. This is where you need to demonstrate, using evidence and any objective, external evaluations that exist, the merits of what you are proposing, and the benefits which it would offer if adopted by the party in government.

Regardless of how open and accessible this process will be for individual political parties, it is recommended that, in addition to participating in any formal consultation events or processes hosted by particular political parties, you also engage with all of the party leaders, and with the spokespersons most relevant to your organisation's work and with your individual MP and Peer contacts, to try and ensure that your organisation's policy positions are reflected in the different parties' manifestos. In this respect, it is worth remembering that the parties are not just looking for policy input, they are also looking for examples of evidence and best practice which could inform the party's strategy in government. This could include supporting the roll out, by the party in government, of models of best practice or service delivery. Securing the Government's backing for your organisation's policy initiative or policy proposals, or of its service/practice models or innovations, would be a significant result for your organisation.

Summary of key points

The key points from this chapter can be summarised as follows:

- Developing good working relationships with political parties at a senior level will increase the chances that your organisation's public affairs strategy will deliver its aims and objectives.
- The most successful public affairs strategies targeting the Government will often require a multi-layered approach, and feature activities and initiatives focusing on the different parts of the Government.
- Organisations seeking to influence the Government should highlight the interface between their policy positions and campaigns, and the Government's strategic aims and objectives.
- Organisations can maximise the impact of their overall public affairs activities and campaigns by taking a non-partisan, cross-party approach to influencing the political parties.

8

Making the Most of Consultation Responses

The Government launches hundreds of public consultations each year, seeking views on policy issues covering a wide range of policy areas and themes. Consultations often help to shape and inform the Government's approach to specific policies and proposed pieces of legislation, and play a major role in the development of policies and legislation. Government departments use consultations to seek the views of stakeholders including, for example, organisations, agencies, specific sectors and the general public on various policy areas and on individual issues. The general aim of consultations is to enable the Government, and Government departments or other agencies, to obtain the views of stakeholders on policy matters, where they are proposing changes, and in some cases legislation, that could have a significant impact on, or consequences for, the economy, or the environment, or for services in particular policy areas such as, for example, health or education, or for the UK as a whole.

Responding to consultations will be a key aspect of many organisations' public affairs strategies, and it is recommended that your organisation should seek to submit responses to policy consultations relevant to its work and interests. Ensuring that your organisation submits responses to such consultations can offer a number of important advantages. It could, for example, provide important opportunities to influence policy development and legislation on policy issues and areas critical to your organisation, its work and interests. In addition, responding to a consultation could form the basis of further policy work by your organisation. Another strategic benefit is that responding to consultations can support your organisation to raise its profile with the Government, and with specific ministers, as well as with senior civil servants, and with the opposition parties. This, in turn, may improve your organisation's prospects of influencing the policy changes under consideration by the Government. Other potential spin-off benefits could include getting invited to join a Government working group focusing on a particular policy area. In addition, your organisation might be invited to give oral evidence to a parliamentary committee for a specific inquiry as a result of submitting a response to a consultation, and raising key issues and concerns which subsequently strike a chord with the members of the parliamentary committee.

Consultation updates

With so many consultations being launched each year by Government departments, it is important that your organisation keeps itself up to date about the launch of new consultations, and about the progress of existing consultations. One way of doing so is through developing, and maintaining, good relations with civil servants in the Government departments most relevant to your organisation, its work and interests. Some organisations will receive funding from Government departments, and will already have existing relationships which they can build on with the civil servants. If your organisation does not receive such funding, and has not developed working relationships with the civil servants, it should start to cultivate such relationships. In this way, you are likely to increase the chances that your organisation will receive early warning that a particular government consultation is due to be launched. Subject to the depth of your relations with specific Government departments, the civil servants may even seek your views on the scope of the consultation, its subject matter and the issues it will address prior to the formal launch of the consultation.

Similar considerations would apply to your organisation's relationships with the members of parliamentary committees in both Houses of Parliament, and with the parliamentary clerks supporting the work of these committees. Developing close ties with these groups will help to ensure that you receive sufficient notice that the committee is going to be taking evidence on a particular topic, or is due to launch a full inquiry in a specific policy area. This will potentially help to maximise the time available to submit evidence to the inquiry, and could improve the likelihood that your organisation will be invited to appear before the committee to give oral evidence for the inquiry.

Parliamentary monitoring is another important way of finding out about which Government consultations and parliamentary inquiries have been launched. As we have seen in Chapter 4, this can be done by organisations themselves undertaking their own parliamentary monitoring, or by taking out a subscription with a public affairs company to provide regular updates about parliamentary and governmental business including new consultations potentially impacting upon their organisation and its interests. If your organisation is undertaking its own parliamentary monitoring, it is important that it keeps a close eye on the web pages of the Government, and of those Government departments whose remit and responsibilities are most relevant to the work and interests of your organisation. These will feature details of new consultations and how to respond to them, as well as information about existing consultations including deadlines for responding, and key contacts for further information.

Parliamentary committees will also launch consultations, which take the form of calls for evidence on inquiries they are undertaking on specific policy themes or issues. As with government consultations, it is important that your parliamentary monitoring focuses on the parliamentary committees most relevant to your organisation's work and interests. In this respect, it is important to monitor the committees in the House of Commons and in the House of Lords, given that parliamentary inquiries and evidence sessions are launched by committees in both Houses. Equally, if your organisation has opted to take out a subscription for parliamentary monitoring with a public affairs company, it is important that the monitoring picks up both Government consultations, and parliamentary inquiries in the House of Commons and in the House of Lords.

Another way of keeping abreast of new consultations launched by the Government, and by specific Government departments, is to sign up for e-mail alerts which will let you know when a new consultation has been launched. You can sign up for such alerts on the main Government website,[1] and also by signing up to the alerts available through the websites of individual Government departments. Similar e-mail updates are available through the websites of the House of Commons and the House of Lords.

Organisations can also find out about new consultations, and about

---

1   UK Government website, www.gov.uk.

the progress of existing consultations, by following the Government and/or its individual departments on social media, as Government Facebook pages and Twitter accounts will often include details of relevant consultations. Details of consultations can also be found through the Facebook pages and Twitter accounts for the House of Commons, and for the House of Lords. This will include details of the policy issues being addressed by the consultation, of specific questions raised in the consultation, as well as the contact details for those requiring further information and the deadline for submitting responses.

If your organisation is a member of a trade association, a membership body or an umbrella organisation these agencies should also provide their members with full details and information about new Government consultations, and about new parliamentary inquiries initiated by the House of Commons', and House of Lords', committees. Such agencies will generally provide regular updates to their members, and your organisation should ensure it receives such updates if it is not already doing so. In addition, your organisation should confirm to the membership body that it is particularly interested in receiving notification of any new government consultations or parliamentary inquiries.

Processes and procedures

The normal process for consultations is that a Government department will launch a consultation document seeking views from a range of stakeholders on a series of questions relating to a specific policy area. The consultation document can be completed in paper form or online, and you should utilise the format most convenient for your organisation. Some consultations launched by the Government focus entirely on broad policy issues and themes, and your organisation will be invited to give its views on the same. Other consultations will feature a mixture of broad policy questions, and questions relating to specific areas of practice and service delivery. The fact that the Government is consulting on a subject confirms that it is of strategic importance, and that the Government is keen to canvass opinion on its proposed changes and direction of policy travel on particular issues. Alternatively, the consultation may relate to technical issues and the

Government is keen to receive the views of stakeholders with technical knowledge and expertise in the area under consideration. The processes and procedures for parliamentary inquiries are dealt with in Chapter 9.

With high profile consultations the Government, or the relevant Government department, may organise a consultation event. This will invite representatives from key stakeholders to attend, and the event will feature inputs from the Government and from other key stakeholders, highlighting the main issues raised by the consultation. The important thing is that your organisation keeps an eye out for details of such events, and tries to ensure it receives an invite to attend because attending will have a number of advantages. It will, for example, enable your organisation to raise issues with the Government and with other stakeholders which could help to shape the policy or legislation on which the consultation is focusing. Attending the event could also provide your organisation with an opportunity to hear more from the Government about the issues raised in the consultation. In addition, it would give your organisation a chance to learn more about the perspectives of other organisations on the consultation, which could be invaluable in helping your organisation to finalise its own response.

Developing your consultation response

Once your organisation has received notice of, or identified, a relevant consultation or parliamentary inquiry, it should start planning its response. Deadlines for submitting responses to consultations and parliamentary inquiries are often tight, and your organisation will need to develop internal processes and procedures to ensure that it is able to submit a response within the prescribed deadline for individual consultations or parliamentary inquiries. The nature of your organisation's response will depend upon the significance of the issues raised by the consultation. In this respect, it is vital that your organisation undertakes an initial assessment of the consultation, its importance to your organisation, the issues it raises and the type of response your organisation should make to the consultation.

Some consultations will not raise any substantial issues for your organisation, and in such instances your response may be fairly brief or not require significant capacity to develop a response. By contrast, other consultations will present issues of major importance which will require a high level, strategic response from your organisation. Where a consultation does present such issues, it is recommended that you take an integrated approach to developing a strategic response. In this respect, it is important that you capture your organisation's views and experience from a policy perspective, but also from the practice or business side of things.

One approach would be to establish a short-life, internal working group which would meet to consider the policy and practice or business issues highlighted by the consultation, and develop a draft response. Using such an internal group to consider the different questions outlined in the consultation will have a number of advantages. It will, for example, ensure that your organisation takes an integrated approach, and that its response is informed by policy and practice or business expertise and experience from across the organisation. This will potentially strengthen the impact of your consultation response, and underline the relevance and credibility of its answers to the questions contained in the consultation. Where capacity or geographical issues would prevent such a group meeting physically, alternative approaches would be to get colleagues with the appropriate skills sets and experience to contribute to your organisation's development of its draft response to a consultation by e-mail, or by social media. The key thing is that your organisation draws on perspectives from policy and from the practice or business side of the organisation, regardless of whether the staff with expertise and experience in these areas physically meet, or if their views are provided by e-mail or through social media.

Organisations which belong to a membership organisation will need to decide if they will rely on the representative organisation to submit a collective response on behalf of all of the members, or if they will also seek to submit a separate response to highlight specific issues relating to their organisation. This could be because the organisation either does not completely support the representative body's stance on particular issues raised in the consultation, or because it supports the latter's policy position but has additional, specific issues it wants to raise. For emphasis, and to increase support, on particular issues, membership organisations will sometimes submit a collective response on behalf of their members, but also encourage individual members to submit their own responses. To assist this process the membership organisation will circulate the headline points and messages which it is recommended that the members should highlight in their own responses. Such initiatives can be particularly beneficial to organisations which have an interest in a particular consultation or parliamentary inquiry, but lack the capacity to submit their own response. Receiving this type of information from the membership organisation can support such organisations to develop responses, and to cover the key areas they wish to raise.

Joint responses

If your organisation is not a member of a membership organisation, another way to maximise the impact of your consultation response is to work with other organisations to submit a joint response. If this is a realistic option for your organisation, you should consider which organisations will be affected in similar ways to your organisation by the issues raised in the consultation. Your organisation could be under significant time pressures to submit a consultation response, so the starting point would normally be those organisations operating in the same sector. You should also consider approaching organisations in other sectors where the consultation raises issues of mutual interest or concern. Joint responses can potentially be highly effective, and will demonstrate to the Government that there is strong support on particular policy issues in the consultation. If such responses are to be effective, however, early agreement must be secured between the different organisations on which one will lead the drafting process, and on the issues that will be raised collectively. Agreement should also be reached about who will manage and lead any media engagement around the consultation. Participating organisations also need to retain the freedom to submit their own response, in addition to any collective response, where they want to highlight issues that are specific to their organisation or where there is no consensus with their partner organisations on particular issues.

Maximising the impact of consultation responses

The Government will often receive hundreds, and sometimes thousands, of responses to its consultations from a wide range of organisations and agencies, as well as from individual members of the public. Against this background, if you want your organisation's consultation response to help influence the Government's policy development and legislation, it is vital that the response stands out from other responses for the right reasons. As previously indicated, your organisation can do so by taking an integrated approach to the drafting of its consultation responses, and by ensuring that its response captures both your organisation's policy, and practice or business, perspectives on the issues raised by the consultation. This will significantly strengthen the credibility of your answers to the questions set by the consultation document.

Another factor which can assist in this regard is where your organisation has undertaken research. Your organisation can then use the findings of the research to illustrate and emphasise key points you are making in your response. In many instances the fact that your response is reinforced by research will increase the likelihood that your response will be given serious consideration. The same factors would apply where an organisation uses references to other organisation's research to support particular issues it is raising in its consultation. This will strengthen the credibility of your response, and make it more likely to be taken into account by the Government in its policy development and legislation.

You should also try and maximise the impact of your consultation response by drawing on your organisation's best practice to illustrate the main points and issues in your response. The Government will be interested in examples of good practice, and you should develop case studies from your organisation's services or business, or from other organisations' services and businesses of which you are aware, that emphasise the key issues you are raising in your response. This will enhance the credibility of your organisation's response, especially if the examples presented of your organisation's best practice have been externally evaluated or have been deemed to be best practice by reference to other objective criteria. Being able to draw upon such evaluations will highlight to the Government that the best practice presented could be utilised as part of any practical solution to the issues outlined in the consultation, particularly where the consultation is seeking views on practical solutions to specific problems.

With high profile consultations it is strongly recommended that, when you submit your organisation's consultation response to the relevant Government departments, you should also send a copy of the response to the minister with the policy lead for the issues covered by the consultation. Where your organisation has referred to its best practice in the consultation response, you should give consideration to inviting the minister and their officials to visit the services or business in question. This will underline the connection between your organisation and its work, and the issues on which the Government is consulting, and in some cases could generate a positive response from the Government. In any event it will highlight to the Government that your organisation has a very strong locus for responding to the consultation, and that its response is based on the direct experience and evidence of its services or business.

It is also recommended that, with high profile consultations, as well as sending a copy of your response to the relevant minister, you also send copies of your organisation's consultation response to other senior policy makers, including the appropriate spokespersons for the Official Opposition party, and for the other opposition parties. Subject to the nature of the consultation, and the importance of the issues raised in the consultation, consideration should be given to sending a copy of your response to the chairs of any parliamentary committees and All-Party Parliamentary Groups with an interest in the issues addressed in the consultation, as well as to other organisations and agencies with such an interest. This will help to raise awareness of the issues you are raising, and also increase support for these issues. By building up support for your policy positions this will increase the chances that your organisation will be able to influence the policy debates on the policies and legislation on which the government is consulting. This, in turn, will make it more likely that your organisation will be able to have a direct influence on the government's policies and legislation arising from the consultation.

Summary of key points

The key points from this chapter can be summarised as follows:

- Responding to Government consultations can help to raise the profile of your organisation, and provide important opportunities to influence policy development and legislation critical to your organisation, its work and interests.
- Organisations should use different approaches, including parliamentary monitoring, to keep themselves up to date about the launch of new consultations.
- Taking an integrated approach, and drawing upon your organisation's views and experience from a strategic policy perspective, but also from the practice or business side of your organisation, will help to maximise the impact of its consultation response.
- Drawing upon your organisation's best practice, and research, will help to strengthen the impact of your organisation's response.
- Consideration should be given, where appropriate, to working with other organisations to submit a joint response to consultations.

9

Engaging with Parliamentary Committees

Committees play a major role in both the House of Commons and the House of Lords. They deal with a significant amount of business in both Houses on a daily basis. It is, therefore, important that your organisation engages with those committees in the House of Commons and the House of Lords which focus on the policy subject areas and issues most relevant to your organisation and its work. The main responsibilities of the committees include playing a key role in the scrutiny of legislation, undertaking committee inquiries and evidence gathering sessions on a wide range of issues, and holding the Government, Government departments and other public bodies to account. A more detailed look at the role of committees in both the House of Commons and in the House of Lords in the scrutiny of legislation can be found in Chapters 11 and 12. Further details about the roles, remits and procedures for committees in the House of Commons and in the House of Lords can also be found in the Standing Orders of the House of Commons[1] and of the House of Lords.[2] In addition, a full list of all of the committees in both Houses is available on the websites of the House of Commons, and of the House of Lords, respectively.[3]

---

1   UK Parliament, Standing Orders of the House of Commons – Public Business 2017, (April 2017 Edition), UK Parliament website, www.parliament.uk.
2   UK Parliament, The Standing Orders of the House of Lords Relating to Public Business, (18 May 2016 (HL3)), House of Lords section of the Parliament's website, www.parliament.uk.
3   UK Parliament, UK Parliament website, www.parliament.uk.

Select Committees

One of the main types of committees in Parliament are the Select Committees in the House of Commons and in the House of Lords. The principal role of the Select Committees in the House of Commons is to scrutinise, and to report on, the work of specific Government departments, and on the policy areas covered within the remit of these departments. There is a specific Select Committee in the House of Commons for every Government department. Each Select Committee's work, including its inquiries, focus on the spending, policies and administration of the corresponding Government department. Examples include the Education Committee which scrutinises the administration, expenditure and policies of the Department of Education and other relevant public bodies, and the Health Committee which undertakes a similar role in relation to the Department of Health, and the Exiting the EU Committee appointed to "examine the expenditure, administration and policy of the Department for Exiting the European Union and matters falling within the responsibilities of associated public bodies".[4]

The Public Accounts Committee and the Environmental Audit Committee, on the other hand, can take a cross-departmental focus as appropriate.[5] Other key Select Committees in the House of Commons include the Backbench Committee, which makes decisions about the backbench business to be taken in the main Chamber, and in Westminster Hall; and the Public Petitions Committee which considers petitions presented to the House and e-petitions.

When House of Commons Select Committees launch inquiries, they will take oral and written evidence, and report their findings to the House of Commons, which are then printed and uploaded on the Parliament's website. Upon receipt, the Government will usually have 60 days to consider these findings, and to respond to the committee's findings and recommendations. The Government's response to the committee's inquiry will be either to publish the committee's report as a Command Paper, or to send a memorandum to the committee.

---

4   UK Parliament, 'House of Commons' select committees', UK Parliament website, www.parliament.uk.
5   UK Parliament, 'About Parliament, Committees – Select Committees', UK Parliament website, www.parliament.uk.

The committee can then publish the Government's response along with any further comments from the committee, or take more evidence.[6]

By contrast, Select Committees in the House of Lords focus on six key subject areas. The main Select Committees in the House of Lords are currently the European Union Committee, the Science and Technology Committee, the Economic Affairs Committee, the Communications Committee, the International Relations Committee and the Constitution Committee. Other select Committees in the House of Lords are set up on an ad hoc basis.[7] Sub-committees will be established for the different Select Committees, where there is a recognised need to consider specific topics or themes within the remit of the Select Committee in more detail. Examples include the House of Lords' Economic Affairs Finance Bill Sub-Committee, the House of Lords' EU External Affairs Sub-Committee and the House of Lords' Science and Technology Sub-Committee.

Joint Committees

Some business in Parliament is dealt with by joint committees consisting of MPs and Peers. The powers of joint committees are similar to Select Committees, and joint committees can conduct inquiries into specific policy issues or deal with particular areas including draft legislation. Some joint committees will be permanent, and will meet regularly throughout the parliamentary session to examine specific policy areas. These include the Joint Committee on Human Rights, the Joint Committee on National Security Strategy and the Joint Committee on Statutory Instruments. In addition, temporary joint committees can be established to deal with short-life tasks such as considering proposals for draft legislation. Examples include the joint committees set up to consider the draft Investigatory Powers Bill, and the draft Protection of Charities Bill.[8] Consolidation Bills to update and consolidate legislation, and Bills to update and rewrite tax statutes, will also be

---

6   UK Parliament, 'About Parliament, Committees – Select Committees', UK Parliament website, www.parliament.uk.
7   UK Parliament, 'About Parliament, Committees – Select Committees', UK Parliament website, www.parliament.uk.
8   UK Parliament, 'About Parliament, Committees – Select Committees', UK Parliament website, www.parliament.uk.

referred to joint committees. Once a joint committee has published a report, it will normally then be debated in both Houses.

General committees

The general committees in the House of Commons include the Scottish Grand Committee, the Welsh Grand Committee, and the Northern Ireland Grand Committee. These committees sit on an ad hoc basis to deal with, for example, legislation, ministerial statements, questions, Motions and short debates relating to Wales, Northern Ireland and Scotland respectively.[9] The Legislative Grand Committee (England) has been appointed to consider Bills which have been amended, and the Speaker has certified the Bills relate to England and Wales, or to England only, and fall within devolved legislative competence. The committee must then pass a consent Motion to the Bill, or to the relevant parts of the Bill, before the legislation can proceed to its Third Reading.[10] The House of Commons also currently has general committees focusing on European documents, and on delegated legislation, i.e. legislative changes implemented through the powers existing in Acts of Parliament and usually made by statutory instrument.

The main task of general committees is the scrutiny of legislation in the House of Commons. General committees are used by the House of Commons to consider the Committee Stage of Public Bills and Private Members' Bills. A Public Bill committee or a Private Member's Bill Committee will usually be established to consider each Public Bill or Private Member's Bill introduced in the House of Commons, or to undertake the Committee Stage of legislation

---

9   Information provided by the House of Commons Enquiry Service confirms that the Scottish Grand Committee, the Welsh Grand Committee, and the Northern Ireland Grand Committee, meet infrequently. The Scottish Grand Committee has not met since 2003, the Welsh Grand Committee last met on 3 February 2016, and the Northern Ireland Grand Committee last met on 9 September 2013. Decisions about meetings of the Grand Committees are taken through the usual channels, i.e. the behind the scenes negotiations involving, and agreements made by, the leaders and Chief Whips of the respective parties about the management of parliamentary business; House of Commons Enquiry Service.

10   UK Parliament, 'English votes for English laws: House of Commons bill procedure', UK Parliament website, www.parliament.uk.

that has started in the House of Lords. In this respect, the appointed committee will examine the principles underpinning, and the specific provisions in, the legislation. The committee, as part of its line-by-line scrutiny of the legislation, will be able to take oral and written evidence. The committee can also seek to amend the Bill. Parliamentary procedure requires that the composition of each committee reflects the political make-up of the House of Commons and, in consequence, the Government will always have a majority in the committees.

The House of Lords, on the other hand, will invariably consider the Committee Stage of a Bill in the Chamber as a 'Committee of the Whole House' with the whole House sitting in Committee, unless the Bill has been allocated to a Grand Committee sitting outside the Chamber in a committee room known as the 'Moses Room'. The procedures in the Grand Committee are similar to those used where the legislation is dealt with by a Committee of the Whole House. The main difference is that there are no Divisions, i.e. votes, and an amendment to a Bill in the Grand Committee will require the support of all members of the committee if the amendment is to be passed.[11]

Monitoring key committee business

Given the potential importance of the parliamentary committees in both Houses to your organisation and its work, you should ensure that your parliamentary monitoring includes tracking committee business. In this respect, it is vital that your parliamentary monitoring, or the monitoring service you receive on subscription, tracks the main business in the committees most relevant to your organisation, and to its interests. This is a starting point, and it is recommended that your organisation should also monitor the work of other committees. There could, after all, potentially be cross-cutting issues that are of interest to your organisation, and which, in some instances, may be dealt with by other committees beyond those that normally deal with the parliamentary business and policy areas most relevant to your organisation. Closely monitoring committee business will help to maximise your organisation's opportunities to engage effectively with particular committees, and to try and influence their business.

11 UK Parliament, 'About Parliament, Committees – General Committees'. UK Parliament website, www.parliament.uk.

The home pages of each parliamentary committee contain a lot of significant information, which can help to inform your organisation's public affairs activities. These pages confirm the role and remit of the specific committee, its membership, when it will meet as well as details of the committee's work including its inquiries and its scrutiny of parliamentary legislation. Details of major new developments, and news releases, are usually available on a committee's home pages, along with links to formal documents such as reports and responses to reports, evidence to committee inquiries, minutes of meetings, correspondence and other relevant documents relating to the work of the committee.

Information about any sub-committees will also feature on the committee's home pages, such as, for example, the Sub-Committee on Education, Skills and the Economy formed from sub-committees of the Education Committee and of the previous Business, Innovation and Skills Committee. Committee home pages will also contain links to home pages for specific inquiries being undertaken by the committee. Examples include the Defence Committee's inquiry into Russian defence policy and its implications for UK defence and security, and the Home Affairs Committee's inquiry into hate crime and its violent consequences.

Your organisation can also keep itself up to date on key business being considered by the committees, and on major developments in relation to the committee's business, by subscribing to the e-mail updates which committees offer. These updates can be a very useful way of ensuring your organisation remains up to speed on work being undertaken by the committee that is relevant to your interests. Another way in which your organisation can keep itself up to date about the work of those committees is to follow the committee's Twitter accounts. These will provide you with details of key news and developments.

The benefits of monitoring committee business can potentially be highly rewarding. At the start of each new Parliament, the different committees will develop their work plans. Monitoring the committee's website will help your organisation to identify the best opportunities to try and influence the work plans of those committees. It will, for example, give your organisation early notice of the inquiries which the committees will undertake, and of the legislation which it will be responsible for scrutinising. Early identification of such opportunities will enable your organisation to undertake public affairs activities designed to influence the committee's work, and to ensure that the committee takes into account your organisation's views in delivering the various aspects of its work plan. The type of activities which will be most effective in this context are considered in more detail below.

Engaging with committees

Once the membership of committees has been agreed by Parliament, your organisation should seek early engagement with these committees as a major part of its public affairs strategy. It is recommended that you contact the chairs, deputy chairs and members of those committees most relevant to your organisation's work, and request meetings to discuss the potential interface between your organisation's work and the policy issues and areas it is interested in, and the committee's remit and work plan. By doing so, you will raise the committee's awareness of your organisation and its work, and improve the chances that the policy issues and themes you are seeking to raise will be taken into account by the committee in developing its work plan for the parliamentary session. This, in turn, will increase the likelihood that your organisation will be invited to give oral evidence to the committee's inquiries, and that its evidence and best practice will feature prominently in the committee's inquiry reports.

To secure such outcomes, it is recommended that you review the remits of the parliamentary committees, and identify those most relevant to your work. You should also look at the membership of the committees and review what current contacts, if any, you have with MPs and Peers who are members of these committees. Ideally your existing contacts will include some of the chairs, deputy chairs and individual members of the committees. This would provide your organisation with solid foundations on which to build its engagement with the committees in the new parliamentary session. If, however, your organisation does not have strong existing ties with the members of a committee, you should check to see if the members of the committee include your local MP, or Peers with specific geographical links to an area or areas with which your organisation has ties. Your organisation should also check to see if any of the MPs or Peers have previously supported your organisation through, for example, attending one of your events, referring to your organisation during a parliamentary debate or lodging an amendment on your behalf to a Bill. These connections should be used to strengthen your organisation's approach to the MP or Peer as appropriate, and to put this in context and to help promote your engagement with the MP or Peer. Building up such contacts through regular meetings to discuss issues of mutual interest will help to increase the impact of your organisation's written evidence submitted to committee inquiries, and make it more likely that your organisation will be invited to give oral evidence to the committee for an inquiry.

As well as cultivating your organisation's relations with the MPs and Peers who are members of the committees most relevant to your organisation's work and interests, it is important that you also engage with the clerks who support the work of these committees. The clerks play an important role in the administration and daily running of the committees. They work closely with the chair and deputy chairs to plan meetings of the committee, and to ensure that it delivers its work programme. Developing your organisation's ties with the clerking teams for the main committee's relevant to your organisation can deliver major benefits. Such links can potentially make an important contribution to your organisation's parliamentary monitoring and political intelligence gathering. In this respect, developing close ties with the clerks will increase the chances that your organisation will receive early notice from the clerks of committee business that will cover policy issues and areas relevant to your organisation. Building strong working relationships with the clerking teams can also contribute to increasing the committee's awareness of your organisation, and of the policy issues and themes in which it has an interest. This, in turn, will help to ensure that serious consideration is given to any written evidence submitted by your organisation, and to your organisation being invited to give oral evidence, to a parliamentary inquiry.

Another way in which your organisation can raise its profile with a committee, and to underline the persuasiveness of the policy issues it is raising, especially in the context of a parliamentary inquiry, is to invite the committee to visit your organisation. This would be worth considering if your organisation is running a business or delivering services which are relevant to the policy areas covered within the committee's remit, or to a parliamentary inquiry the committee is conducting. In this respect, it is recommended that your chief executive or lead officer contacts the chair of the committee to invite the committee's members to visit your organisation. It is further recommended that, even if your chief executive or lead officer has strong ties with the chair or other members of the committee, a formal invite letter should be sent as a follow-up to any informal contact. Such a visit would offer invaluable opportunities to raise the profile of your organisation, and to demonstrate how the evidence and best practice from its business or services interfaces with aspects of the committee's work, and with the policy issues being considered in its inquiry.

Influencing committee inquiries: written evidence

Committees in both Houses of Parliament will undertake inquiries on a wide range of policy issues and themes. These inquiries can offer significant opportunities for your organisation to raise its profile, and to promote its policy positions on different issues. By developing your organisation's contacts with members of the committees and with the clerking teams, and by keeping on top of your parliamentary monitoring, your organisation should be ready to respond to any new inquiries announced by relevant committees. When a new inquiry has been launched, the committee will normally issue a call for written evidence seeking views from interested parties, including organisations, agencies and individuals. The committee will also agree those witnesses it will invite to give oral evidence to the inquiry. Witnesses will be called to give evidence on behalf of, for example, organisations and agencies, while certain individuals will be invited to give evidence in a personal capacity. To maximise the influence of your organisation on the committee's inquiry, and on the committee's inquiry report, your organisation should seek to submit written evidence, and to also try and ensure it is invited to give oral evidence to the committee.

A wide range of organisations, agencies and individuals will often submit written evidence to committee inquiries. The level of interest in a specific parliamentary inquiry, and the volume of written evidence received by the relevant committee, will depend upon a number of factors. These will include the background policy context, and the political environment, against which the inquiry is being undertaken.

Is the inquiry, for example, focusing on issues which have generated political controversy and debate, and attracted wider public interest? Alternatively, is the inquiry looking at technical issues that will appeal to a much narrower audience? The relevance of the inquiry to high-profile Government business and strategic priorities, and in particular its synergy with current or forthcoming legislation or policy initiatives and strategies, could also heighten interest in the inquiry. This, in turn, is likely to increase the level of written evidence received by the committee for its inquiry.

Against this background, you should assume that your organisation's written evidence will have to compete with that of various other organisations, agencies and individuals if it wishes to influence the committee's thinking on the issues under investigation. It is, therefore, critical that your organisation takes steps to enhance the persuasiveness of its evidence. This would include, for example, ensuring that the written evidence submitted by your organisation is concise, measured and well argued. The impact of your organisation's evidence will be strengthened if it is underpinned by robust evidence. Commissioning research, or supporting key points in your evidence by reference to independent research, can make a useful contribution in this respect. You should also seek to support your organisation's evidence with examples of best practice. When your organisation does refer to its best practice, you should, where possible, include details of any independent evaluations which highlight the strengths of its practice.

When drafting your evidence, it is recommended that your organisation focuses both on influencing the committee's inquiry report, and also on influencing the Government's response to the report, and in particular on how the latter responds to the committee's findings and recommendations. Ideally, you want the committee to support the 'policy asks', evidence and best practice outlined in your evidence, and for the Government to also back your organisation in these areas when it responds to the committee's report. To achieve these outcomes you should, prior to submitting your evidence, seek meetings on a cross-party basis with members of the committee. This will give your organisation opportunities to raise its policy positions on the issues raised by the inquiry, and to highlight to the committee members the evidence and best practice on which your evidence is based. It will also give your organisation an opportunity to take on board any feedback received from the members of the committee about the issues you are seeking to raise in your evidence, and to update and adapt your evidence accordingly.

If you are unable to secure meetings with individual members of the committee, you should try and arrange a meeting, or discussion by phone, with a member of the committee's clerking team to find out more about the committee's likely approach to, and priorities for, the inquiry. Meetings with the members of the committee, and with the clerking team, can be particularly helpful in clarifying the areas of the inquiry on which the committee is likely to concentrate. These meetings can also give your organisation a chance to finesse its evidence in the light of this feedback. Using such meetings to develop your written evidence can help to strengthen the persuasiveness of this evidence and, in consequence, increase the likelihood of your organisation's evidence influencing the recommendations in the committee's report. It will also improve its prospects of being invited to give oral evidence to the inquiry.

The committee's call for evidence will confirm to whom in the clerking team you should submit your written evidence. To raise the profile of your organisation's written evidence it is recommended that, in addition to sending your written evidence to the clerking team or other lead person, you should also send a copy to the chair, deputy chair and to the individual MP members of the committee. You should include a request to give oral evidence to the inquiry, as well as an offer to meet the individual MPs on the committee to discuss your evidence if they require more information. In view of the fact that you want to influence both the committee and the Government minister who will be responding to the committee's report, it is strongly advised that you also send a copy of your organisation's evidence to the minister and his or her senior civil servants, as well as to their special advisers.

Subject to the nature of the inquiry, and to the level of political, media and public interest it attracts, you should also consider requesting a meeting with the minister and their officials to discuss the issues raised by your evidence. Alternatively, you might take the view that, at this stage in the inquiry process, it would be a more effective approach to try and secure a meeting with the minister's special adviser, and to ensure that they are aware of the issues you are seeking to raise. Such meetings can help to ensure that the issues presented in your organisation's evidence are given serious consideration by the Government, and that the Government focuses on the key issues raised by your evidence. Meeting the special adviser could also help to open up a dialogue with the Government, and potentially lead to important concessions being made if the special adviser provides positive feedback to the minister after your meeting.

Influencing committee inquiries: oral evidence

Committees in the House of Commons and in the House of Lords undertaking inquiries will take oral evidence from a range of organisations, agencies and individuals. Where a parliamentary inquiry is relevant to your organisation and to its interests, you should lobby the committee to secure an invitation to give oral evidence. Submitting persuasive written evidence, based on robust evidence and best practice, will put your organisation in strong contention to be called to give oral evidence. It is strongly recommended, however, that you flag up your interest in giving oral evidence to the committee as soon as details of the inquiry have been announced, and before you submit written evidence, to increase the likelihood that you will be invited to give oral evidence.

Your organisation can improve its chances of being called to give evidence by contacting the chair and other members of the committee, as well as the clerking team, and seeking meetings to discuss the inquiry. Your organisation can use these meetings to flag up the key issues it will be raising in its evidence to the inquiry. Organisations can also stimulate the committee's interest in their evidence, and improve their prospects of being invited to give oral evidence, by submitting evidence which draws upon new research, and best practice, to give perspectives on the issues being considered in the inquiry. In this respect, where committees are seeking to identify solutions to specific policy and/or practice problems through the inquiry, you can try and increase the probability of being invited to give oral evidence by ensuring that you get across to the committee, both in your organisation's meetings with individual members of the committee and/or with members of the clerking team, that your organisation is able to provide such solutions through its best practice and approaches.

If your organisation is invited to give oral evidence to a committee in the House of Commons or in the House of Lords, it is important that you are fully prepared. Appearing as a witness before a parliamentary committee is a major, high profile opportunity to showcase your organisation, and to get your organisation's policy positions across to, and to share your best practice with, key policy makers. If, however, you are to successfully use the opportunity to influence the policy issues and legislation under consideration by the committee, it is strongly recommended that your organisation gets its preparation right. Some organisations will have experience of giving oral evidence, and will have a clear understanding of the process and of what to expect. By contrast, many organisations will have limited knowledge of the formal inquiry process, and of what being called as a witness to give oral evidence will involve. If your organisation falls into the latter category, it is strongly recommended that one of the first steps your organisation should take is to look at the committee's webpage, and to look at evidence sessions held by the committee either for the current inquiry or for previous inquiries. This will give you an insight into the structure and format of the evidence sessions, and possibly also of the dynamics within the membership of specific committees and how they may approach an inquiry.

As part of your organisation's preparation, you should also take steps to identify the purpose of the committee's evidence session, and dig deeper than the initial invite letter received from the committee. Is the committee conducting a general inquiry into a policy area, or is the committee's inquiry focusing on specific issues such as the aims and purpose of legislation? The inquiry remit will normally be available on the committee's website, or in the relevant *Hansard* relating to the committee's previous proceedings. If not, it is recommended that you get in touch with the clerking team to clarify any queries you may have around these issues. In any event, it is recommended that you get in touch with the clerking team to get a sense of the policy issues that the evidence session will focus on, and of the type of questions which are likely to be raised by the members of the committee. This will not always be easy to anticipate, and the line of questioning that develops during an evidence session will depend upon a number of factors. These will include the subject matter of the inquiry, and whether or not the issues under consideration are of a technical nature or if the inquiry is likely to raise high profile, political issues. With the latter there is always the risk that members of the committee, particularly in the House of Commons, may use the evidence session to score political points, which could overshadow their questioning.

In preparing for a committee evidence session, your organisation should give consideration to ways in which the person giving evidence can avoid getting dragged into political point scoring between the committee members should this escalate, and threaten to dominate proceedings. Including an assessment of the issues likely to be controversial during the evidence session, and preparing your organisation's answers to potential questions in these areas, would be a wise precaution. Your representative might not be asked about these issues but, if they are, being able to rely on a clear organisational position based on your organisation's role and remit, with evidence of the best practice of its services or business, will help to keep your focus on the key points you wish to get across. In certain cases, outlining your organisation's position in these terms may be enough to move the committee's focus along onto other areas. A lot will depend, however, upon the nature of the inquiry, the level of controversy generated by the issues being considered, the way in which the committee is being chaired and the dynamics within the committee.

Against this background, it is important that organisations choose a representative who is able to speak knowledgeably about the organisation, and who can answer questions confidently in a high-profile setting. Your organisation should support its representative by trying to anticipate the type of questions which will arise during the evidence session, including any politically motivated questions that its representative is likely to face. It should then work with its representative to ensure that they are fully briefed, and prepared, for the evidence session. In this respect, it is worth considering if the representative would benefit from a 'mock' evidence session to rehearse their answers. Many witnesses would benefit from this before the evidence session, particularly in terms of supporting them to ensure they focus on getting your organisation's key messages across in their answers.

Another useful step to take in your organisation's preparation for the evidence session is to check *Hansard* to see what type of questions any previous witnesses were asked by the committee during the inquiry, and to analyse their written evidence to see what issues were taken up by the committee. This research is definitely worth undertaking where there have been previous evidence sessions. It will help your organisation to identify key themes, and areas of questions, which have emerged during the inquiry, and could feature in the evidence session. In addition, it will enable your organisation to identify any specific areas of policy and practice that individual members of the committee have a particular interest in, and which they may raise in questions to your organisation's representative. Your organisation should also undertake research to see if any members of the committee have made statements in Parliament or in articles or interviews about the subject and issues to which the inquiry relates. This will often help organisations to identify the specific areas of interest held by individual members of the committee, and give an indication of the type of issues they may ask you about during the evidence session. Analysing the previous evidence sessions will also allow your organisation to get a sense of where the committee has given a positive response to answers it has received, and where its response has been negative or sceptical. This information will enable you to work with your representative to adapt your key issues and messages as appropriate. You should also monitor which other organisations, agencies and individuals have given oral evidence, and you may wish to contact some of them to get a sense of how the evidence session went for them, and to see if they can offer any insights to support your preparation.

Above all else, your organisation needs to develop clear policy positions in relation to the policy issues being covered in the inquiry. Your organisation should also consider and agree the key issues and messages which its representative should convey in its oral evidence. Evidence sessions can present organisations with opportunities, but can also expose them to significant reputational risks. It is likely that your organisation will be asked to give evidence as part of a panel of witnesses. If that is the case, your representative will need to bear in mind that they will generally only have limited opportunities to get your organisation's headline issues and messages across to the committee. This is where ensuring that your organisation rehearses answers to anticipated questions with its representative can pay dividends. You want to ensure that your representative is fully prepared, and has the necessary background knowledge to answer all questions confidently, regardless of which direction the committee's questions take during the evidence session.

Debates on committee reports

Following the completion of committee inquiries in both Houses, the committee's final reports will be published, and will normally be debated at a convenient time in the parliamentary calendar. Such debates can offer important opportunities for organisations to engage with the Government and with MPs on a cross-party basis on the main issues presented by the report. The primary aims of such engagement will be to raise awareness of the key issues arising from the committee's inquiry and final report, and to secure support from the Government, the opposition parties and individual MPs or Peers for the specific 'policy asks' that your organisation has made in response to the inquiry. To ensure that such engagement delivers tangible outcomes, you should prepare a briefing for the debate. This should draw upon your organisation's evidence to the inquiry as appropriate. It is recommended, however, that if your organisation's briefing for the debate on the report is to have a positive impact that it does not simply repeat your original written evidence. If your briefing is to be persuasive it is important that its key issues and themes include references to, and take account of, the main developments emerging from the inquiry. The debate will be an opportunity to progress the debates around the inquiry, and it is, therefore, important that your briefing is relevant, and as current as possible. In particular your organisation should focus on key statements made by the Government during the inquiry, and in its response, and welcome or challenge these statements as appropriate. It is also important that your briefing includes specific recommendations about where further action is required by the Government and by other agencies in relation to addressing the issues raised by the inquiry.

Apart from drafting and circulating a briefing for MPs or Peers for the debate on the committee's report, you should also consider trying to arrange meetings with the Government, with the opposition parties' relevant spokespersons and with individual MPs or Peers to brief them prior to the debate. The appropriateness of seeking such meetings will depend upon a number of factors, such as how high profile the debate will be, and the significance of the debate for your organisation. If the debate does present major issues for your organisation you should try and arrange these meetings to ensure that the Government, the opposition parties and individual MPs and Peers are aware of your organisation's policy positions on the issues raised by the inquiry. In this respect, you are seeking support for your 'policy asks', and a commitment from the Government that it will take action to address any concerns your organisation has raised in its evidence.

Developing media interest

Engaging with parliamentary committees will potentially present your organisation with different opportunities to develop media interest, including through social media, in your organisation, and in its contribution to the committee's work. Generally there will be greater media interest in committee business in the House of Commons, where the focus is more likely to be on high profile policy and political issues that will attract greater levels of media and public interest, than in the House of Lords. Media interest in committee business in the House of Lords will depend upon a number of factors, including how much political profile the issues under consideration have, and the extent to which the committee's business is feeding into national policy and political debates. Legislation being considered by the House of Lords sitting as a Committee of the Whole House, or by a Grand Committee in the House of Lords, could also generate media interest, subject to the issues presented by the legislation and the political debate it has promoted. In this respect, the possibility of Government defeats on Divisions on key amendments could further increase media interest.

Regardless of whether or not you are engaging with committees in the House of Commons or in the House of Lords or with joint committees involving members from both Houses, it is important that you consider the opportunities to secure media interest in your contribution to the committee's work. A starting point would, for example, be to issue a news release confirming that your organisation is submitting written evidence to a parliamentary inquiry, and outlining the key issues outlined in your evidence. This would work well using social media, as would providing details of a committee's evidence gathering session at which your organisation is scheduled to give oral evidence. You should also brief the media where your organisation is seeking to influence legislation, and an MP or Peer has agreed to lodge amendments to the legislation on your behalf. Ensuring that the media understands the aims and effects of your amendments will help to increase the chances that you will secure media interest in the key issues you are seeking to raise. Legislation does not always attract high levels of media interest, and legislation which has provoked significant political debate and public interest is generally more likely to generate such interest.

Summary of key points

The key points from this chapter can be summarised as follows:

- Committees play a major role in Parliament, and organisations should engage with those committees most relevant to their work and policy interests.
- Organisations can strengthen their engagement with committees by ensuring that their parliamentary monitoring includes tracking key committee business in both Houses.
- Cultivating relations with the members of committees in both Houses, and with the clerking teams supporting these committees, will help to improve organisations' chances of being invited to give oral evidence for inquiries, and of influencing committee reports.
- Flagging up your organisation's interest in giving oral evidence to a committee as soon as details of an inquiry have been announced, and before you submit written evidence, will increase the likelihood that your organisation will be invited to give oral evidence.

10

Legislation: Influencing the Pre-legislative Stage

Legislation is used by the Government, and by Parliament, to introduce new laws, and to repeal, change or update existing laws, in a wide range of policy areas. Under the current legislative process in Parliament, the Government can present Public Bills for debate in either the House of Commons or in the House of Lords. Individual members of both Houses can also introduce Private Members' Bills to propose new laws, or to repeal or facilitate changes to existing laws. A Public Bill or Private Member's Bill outlines the new law and the provisions which will give it effect, or the proposals to repeal, change or update an existing law. Once the Bill has been introduced in either House, it must then go through different stages in both Houses before it can then be approved. After both Houses have agreed the content of a Bill, it can then be presented to the Monarch for final approval known as Royal Assent.[1] After the Bill receives Royal Assent it becomes an Act of Parliament, and part of UK law.

A major aspect of Parliament's role is its scrutiny and passing of legislation, with both Houses making an important contribution in this area. The House of Commons and the House of Lords will seek to improve legislation through amendments, i.e. changes, to Bills where this is considered necessary, and where the House of Commons and the House of Lords, as appropriate, agree to these amendments.

Legislation, once it has been agreed by both Houses of Parliament and has received Royal Assent, can have a major impact upon different areas of policy and practice. It can, for example, facilitate major changes in the economy, in education, in health, in the environment

---

1   UK Parliament, 'Glossary', UK Parliament website, www.parliament.uk.

and in various other aspects of our society. How Parliament scrutinises legislation can, in effect, have a significant bearing, both directly and/ or indirectly, on many parts of our everyday lives. Laws passed by Parliament, once they have received Royal Assent, can impact upon the whole population of the UK, or upon specific groups within the general population. By influencing legislation, therefore, your organisation will potentially be able to help make important changes to the law in relation to policy and practice issues relevant to its interests. This will be a major outcome for your organisation's public affairs strategy, and could provide wide-ranging benefits for your organisation.

Assessing the scope for legislative change

To ensure that your organisation is able to secure such outcomes from its engagement with the Government, with the opposition parties and with individual MPs and Peers, on issues around legislation, it is strongly recommended that your organisation begins this engagement as early as possible. In this respect, it is vital that your organisation gives careful consideration to engaging, if necessary, from the pre-legislative stage when the proposals for legislation are still being developed, right through to all of the different stages of the legislation in both the House of Commons and in the House of Lords. Your organisation should also develop a public affairs strategy that will enable it to participate in the main debates around the legislation during key stages of the legislative process, and until such times as it is able to secure the legislative changes it requires.

An important part of this process is the pre-legislative stage of a Parliamentary Bill. This is the stage prior to the formal introduction of a Bill, whether a Public Bill introduced by the Government or a Private Member's Bill introduced by an MP or Peer. The pre-legislative stage can afford important opportunities to influence the policy direction of travel of the proposals for legislation, as these are developed prior to the introduction of a Bill in Parliament. This will often have a direct effect on the nature and character of the Bill introduced by the Government, or by individual MPs and Peers.

For any organisation seeking to progress major changes in policy development and in practice through legislation, it is important to have a clear view of which legislative changes it wishes to make.

Furthermore, if its advocacy in support of these changes is to be successful, it is important that the organisation has developed strong policy positions underpinned by robust evidence and best practice in relation to the proposed changes. This will help to strengthen the persuasiveness of the organisation's calls for legislative change, and improve the chances that the Government, the opposition parties and other political groupings and individual MPs and Peers will respond positively to its calls for legislative change. In addition, taking this approach will increase the likelihood that the organisation will be able to secure backing for its proposed legislative changes from other organisations and from the general public. This, in turn, could help to increase support for the organisation's policy positions within the Government, and amongst the opposition parties and other key policy makers.

Moreover, organisations seeking legislative change must give careful consideration to what they want to achieve, and about how these changes can be secured. In this context, it is important to clarify at an early stage in your public affairs strategy if your organisation has identified issues and concerns with existing legislation, or is aware of policy and practice gaps requiring new laws, as well as the type of legislative change that will be required to address these issues. A fundamental aspect of this will be determining if the proposed changes can be facilitated through amending an existing piece of parliamentary legislation or by introducing secondary legislation, or if a new public Bill will have to be introduced by the Government. Alternatively, if the Government is unwilling to amend existing legislation or to introduce new legislation, your organisation may wish to give consideration to working with an individual MP or Peer to progress a Private Member's Bill. In certain cases, Private Members' Bills can be progressed by the MP or Peer in the knowledge that the Government is sympathetic to the aims of the Bill, and will not vote against it or to try and block its progress. Private Members' Bills are considered in more detail in Chapter 13.

Opportunities for influencing during the pre-legislative stage

Once your organisation has decided what type of legislative changes are required, and how these can be achieved, it should take action to influence the Government, the opposition parties and other political groupings, as well as individual MPs and Peers during the pre-legislative stage before the introduction of a Bill. Key actions during this stage would include seeking meetings with the relevant Government minister. Securing such a meeting would provide an invaluable opportunity to outline to the Government the case for or against legislative change, and to present the evidence upon which your arguments are based. To increase the chances that the minister will respond positively to a meeting request, it is recommended that your organisation sets out its case as clearly as possible, including how you believe the changes could be achieved and the benefits or disadvantages that will arise from the proposed changes. This will have a direct bearing on the minister's decision on whether or not to meet your organisation to discuss its proposals for legislative change. It will also enable the minister to consider the practicalities of the changes you are proposing, and to weigh these up with their senior civil servants and special advisers before providing your organisation with a formal response to its request for legislative change. A key aspect of this process will be for the Government to determine that your organisation's proposals will not incur prohibitive costs. The Government will also want to be satisfied that your organisation's proposals will not have any unintended consequences in the relevant policy and practice areas or in other areas, or for specific groups of people or for the population as a whole.

As well as seeking a meeting with the relevant minister or ministers to discuss your organisation's proposals for legislative change, steps should also be taken to engage senior civil servants in discussions about these proposals. Such discussions should be used by your organisation to outline the background for its demand for legislative change, highlighting why the changes are necessary and the consequences if positive action is not taken in response to your demands for such change. The senior civil servants will update the minister on the issues you have raised, and their reports of your meetings and discussions will feed into the Government's internal deliberations on whether or not to accept your organisation's arguments for legislative change in a particular policy and practice area. It is, therefore, vital that you make the most of your discussions and meetings with the senior civil servants, and present your arguments for legislative change in a clear and persuasive manner. Being able to demonstrate your organisation's expert knowledge of the legislative context, and of the legislative changes you believe are necessary to accomplish the required changes, will strengthen your case.

Another element in your organisation's efforts to persuade the Government of the need for legislative change in a particular area of policy should be engaging with the Government's special advisers. Such engagement will be particularly important in enabling your organisation to build up support within Government for the case for legislative change. In this respect, any meetings your organisation can arrange with the relevant special advisers will be critical. The special advisers will consider your organisation's arguments in support of the case for legislative change in the context of the Government's policy priorities, and of the overarching policy and legislative framework. They will also weigh up the political advantages and disadvantages of the proposed changes, and of the risks of progressing or declining to progress the required legislative changes. A key part of their assessment will be an analysis of the strategic interface, if any, with the Government's policy and legislative priorities, and with the wider political landscape.

Bearing these factors in mind, it is important that your organisation gives careful thought to how it plans for such meetings. Apart from focusing on the evidence and best practice on which you will draw upon in support of the case for legislative change, you should also consider any arguments that are likely to be made in objection to your proposed legislative changes. Once you have done so, it is recommended that those attending the meeting with the special adviser, on behalf of your organisation, are well versed in the arguments your organisation will raise in rebuttal of any such objections. The meeting with the special adviser will give you an important opportunity to persuade a key member of the minister's staff about the merits of your case for legislative change. Getting the special adviser on board would be a major step towards persuading the minister to accept your organisation's demand for legislative change in a specific policy area. This underlines the importance of ensuring that your organisation is fully prepared for any meeting with the special advisers to discuss proposals for legislative change. Part of this process could be further exploring with the special adviser any objections to these proposals raised by the civil servants at a previous meeting, and emphasising to the special adviser the ways in which the proposals closely align with the Government's own policy priorities.

Your organisation should take a cross-party approach to building up support for any demands it may have for legislative change. Apart from approaching the Government, you should also, therefore, get in touch with all of the opposition parties and other political groupings, including the crossbench Peers in the House of Lords, to discuss your organisation's proposals for legislative change. Ideally, you want to build up a cross-party alliance in support of the proposed legislative changes, and to get all of the political parties, and groupings, represented at Westminster on board. Securing support from the opposition parties could be particularly useful if the Government has still to decide whether or not to agree to your organisation's proposals, and is waiting to assess what levels of support these proposals are likely to attract within Parliament. In this context, demonstrating that your proposals have cross-party support could help to make it more likely that the Government will accept the case for legislative change. This would, however, depend upon the nature of the legislative changes proposed, on the political landscape and on how your organisation's suggested legislative changes would fit with the Government's own policy and legislative priorities. Furthermore, the timing of the proposals would be critical, given that the Government would also need to consider if there would be sufficient time available in the legislative timetable to develop your organisation's proposals into a Bill, to introduce it, and to take it though all of its stages in both Houses of Parliament.

Influencing the political parties' manifestos

Another major opportunity to try and influence the political parties during the pre-legislative stage is to engage with the different political parties when they are developing their manifestos, an area already touched upon in Chapter 7. The political parties will all have different approaches and timelines for developing their manifestos. You should, therefore, use your contacts with the different political parties to clarify what opportunities there are likely to be for your organisation to contribute to this process. Once you have been able to determine when, and how, you can engage with the different political parties in this area, your organisation should raise the issue of legislative change in the specific aspects of policy and practice it has identified. Against this background, your organisation should seek to persuade the respective political parties to include a commitment in their manifestos to introduce the required legislative change your organisation is seeking if their party is elected to government. Securing such commitments would be a major step towards achieving legislative change. In this context, where a party is elected to government, and has included a commitment to progress legislative change in an area demanded by your organisation, you should then work with the governing party to help shape and influence the Bill prior to its formal introduction in the House of Commons or in the House of Lords.

Petitions

The petitions system in the House of Commons also offers opportunities to progress proposals for legislative change. Your organisation could potentially use a petition to campaign for legislative change in a particular policy area. In this respect, you could use the petition to secure support for your policy position from key policy makers, from other organisations and from members of the public. The petition could become the focus for your organisation's campaign. It would, for example, offer good opportunities to publicise your organisation's campaign for legislative change, and to raise the profile of the case for legislative change. This would include raising awareness of the campaign through social media. Building up support for the petition could also secure a parliamentary debate on the case for legislative change, and this would be a significant outcome. Such a debate would put your organisation in a strong position to work with the Government, the opposition parties and with individual MPs and Peers to develop its proposals for legislative change into a Bill. Further information about how organisations can use public petitions in their public affairs strategies can be found in Chapter 17.

Responding to Green Papers

Government Green Papers are discussion papers which outline draft proposals for policy changes, as well as potential options for progressing these changes. Examples include the 2010 Defence Green Paper, *Adaptability and Partnership: Issues for the Strategic Defence Review* which was the first stage of a process that led to a Strategic Defence Review[2] the 2010 *Modernising Commissioning Green Paper* which focused on how Government could support charities, voluntary groups and social enterprises to bid for public services contracts;[3] and the 2012 *Green Paper on Parliamentary Privilege.*[4] Green Papers will often include proposals for legislative change, or will identify areas of policy change that will require legislation. This can provide organisations with opportunities to influence Government proposals for legislation prior to the introduction of a Bill. Examples include the 2015 *Green Paper on Higher Education Reform,*[5] and the 2015 *Green Paper on the Review of the BBC's Royal Charter.*[6]

Responding to Government Green Papers will give your organisation opportunities to comment on the Government's legislative proposals, and to try and influence the direction of legislative travel. Your parliamentary monitoring will give you notice of any new Government Green Papers relevant to your organisation, and to its interests. Another useful source for such information will be signing up for e-mail alerts from the Government departments whose remit and work are most relevant to your organisation. This will enable you to track any announcements by these departments that they have published Green Papers likely to be of interest to your organisation.

Where a Green Paper has been published that covers policy areas in which your organisation has an interest, you should review the document and identify the issues most relevant to your organisation. Your organisation's response should draw as much as possible upon robust evidence and best practice, including, where relevant, case

2   Ministry of Defence, 'Adaptability and Partnership: Issues for the Strategic Defence Review', (February 2010), UK Government website, www.gov.uk.

3   Cabinet Office, 'Modernising commissioning Green Paper', (December 2010), UK Government website, www.gov.uk.

4   Cabinet Office and Leader of the House of Commons, Parliamentary Privilege Green Paper, (April 2012), Cabinet Office website and Office of the Leader of the House of Commons, UK Government website, www.gov.uk.

5   Department for Business Innovation & Skills, 'Fulfilling our potential: Teaching Excellence, Social Mobility and Student Choice', (November 2015), UK Government website, www.gov.uk.

6   Department for Culture, Media & Sport, BBC Charter Review: Public Consultation, (July 2015), UK Government website, www.gov.uk.

studies. The main points to get across are whether or not you think there is a case for the legislative changes proposed by the Government, and if you think the Government's approach is appropriate. You should also highlight any ways in which your organisation believes the Government's proposals, or its approach, can be improved. In this context, suggesting specific amendments to the proposals, particularly where the Green Paper includes a draft Bill, will help to strengthen your organisation's response, and improve the chances that the Government will respond positively to the issues you are raising, and take them on board before it introduces a Bill in Parliament.

Responding to White Papers

White Papers are policy statements issued by the Government for consideration by a wide range of policy makers including the opposition parties, and individual MPs and Peers as well as by other stakeholders including organisations with an interest in the subject matter and issues raised in the White Paper. These publications often build upon proposals initially set out in Government Green Papers, and confirm how these proposals will be progressed, including through legislation. Examples include the White Paper on *Educational Excellence Everywhere* which outlined the Government's plans for schools in England;[7] and the Government's White Paper setting out its proposals for the future of the BBC, *A BBC for the Future: a Broadcaster of Distinction.*[8]

Many White Papers include proposals for legislative change, and some will seek comment through consultations prior to the formal introduction of a Bill. An example of this was HM Treasury's consultation on the *White Paper: A New Approach to Financial Regulation: the Blueprint for Reform.* This White Paper, which included a draft Bill,[9] was published as a consultation document, and views were sought from a wide range of stakeholders. The Financial

---

7   Department for Education, White Paper: Educational excellence everywhere, (March 2016), UK Government website, www.gov.uk.
8   Department for Culture, Media and Sport, *A BBC for the Future: a Broadcaster of Distinction*, (May 2016), UK Government website, www.gov.uk.
9   HM Treasury, White Paper: *A new approach to Financial Regulation: the Blueprint for Reform*, (June 2011), UK Government website, www.gov.uk.

Services legislation, subsequently introduced in Parliament by the Government[10] drew upon the White Paper, and upon the responses received to the consultation on the White Paper, including the provisions in the draft Bill.

Where your organisation has an interest in the policy issues addressed in a White Paper, and the Government is consulting on the document, you should take the opportunity to submit a response to the consultation. This will provide your organisation with a chance to help shape and inform the legislative changes introduced by the Government following the publication of the White Paper. The extent to which your organisation will be able to do so, however, will depend upon the persuasiveness of your consultation response. Another major factor will be your organisation's engagement with the Government, the opposition parties and with individual MPs and Peers in support of your policy positions in response to the issues presented in the White Paper. Where the White Paper presents significant issues for your organisation, it is recommended that you try and secure meetings with the relevant minister, their senior civil servants and special advisers to outline any concerns and issues that you may have concerning the White Paper.

Draft Bills

Another way in which your organisation can influence the pre-legislative stage of legislation is by responding to Draft Bills introduced by the Government in either House of Parliament. The introduction of Draft Bills enables the Government to consult various stakeholders about its proposed legislation, and to improve the Draft Bill through the pre-legislative scrutiny of the legislation. Recent examples include the introduction of the Draft Investigatory Powers Bill focussing on the powers used by the police and the intelligence and security forces; and the Draft Wales Bill designed to increase the powers devolved to the National Assembly for Wales, both of which were introduced as Draft Bills for consultation prior to their formal introduction in Parliament.

Once a Draft Bill has been introduced, it is referred to a Select Committee in the House of Commons or in the House of Lords, or to

10 The legislation was passed as the Financial Services Act 2012, www.legislation. gov.uk Delivered by The National Archives.

a Joint Committee of both Houses. The Committee will then determine how to progress scrutiny of the Draft Bill, and its approach may involve taking oral and/or written evidence.[11] Once the committee has completed its scrutiny of the Draft Bill it will publish a report. The Government will then consider and respond to the committee's report. This will include confirming if it wishes to proceed with its legislative proposals. If the Government decides to press ahead with its proposals, it may take into account recommendations made by the committee in its report when preparing the final version of the Bill. This will then be formally introduced in the House of Commons, or in the House of Lords.

The pre-legislative scrutiny of Draft Bills could offer your organisation important opportunities to influence legislation relevant to its interests. In this context, it is important to bear in mind that the Government, by having decided to publish, and to consult on, a Draft Bill is seeking improvements to the legislation, and will often be willing to consider different issues and arguments raised by organisations in relation to the legislation. This underlines the scope available for helping to influence Government thinking on the direction of legislative travel. It is, therefore, important to ensure that your parliamentary monitoring tracks Draft Bills on policy areas relevant to your organisation, and that your organisation is aware of the publication of new Draft Bills that are relevant to its work. You then need to undertake a review of the legislation to determine what are the key issues, if any, it presents for your organisation. You should also identify any amendments to the Draft Bill which you believe would be necessary to improve the legislation. Your organisation's policy positions in these areas will be greatly strengthened if you can demonstrate that your proposed amendments are underpinned by robust evidence and best practice. This information should then be set out clearly in your written evidence to the committee. You should also contact the chair of the committee and offer to give oral evidence to the committee to help inform its consideration of the Draft Bill. Identifying your organisation's main issues, and any specific amendments to the legislation, could help to increase the chances that your organisation will receive a positive response to its request to give oral evidence to

---

11 House of Commons Library, 'pre-legislative scrutiny', Standard Note, (9 April 2010), SN/PC/2822, UK Parliament website, www.parliament.uk.

the committee. By taking these steps your organisation is more likely to be able to influence the legislation at this critical, pre-legislative stage.

Working in partnership

If your organisation is committed to securing legislative change, and is seeking to progress such change or to influence the pre-legislative stage of the Government's proposals for legislative change, it should give serious consideration to enlisting support from other organisations with similar interests. Some organisations will be large enough, or possess a significant track record in the policy area under consideration, to have a major impact at the pre-legislative stage without the need to secure the backing of other organisations. For those organisations not in this position, however, getting other partners on board to support their organisation's campaign for legislative change, or their response to the pre-legislative scrutiny of the Government's legislative proposals, could help to increase the levels of support their organisation receives for its policy positions from the Government, the opposition parties and from individual MPs and Peers. This, in turn, will make it more likely that their organisation will be able to secure the introduction of the legislative changes it is seeking, or to ensure that the Government's response to the pre-legislative scrutiny of its Draft Bill takes into account the issues raised by their organisation.

In terms of securing such support, an initial starting point could be those organisations which have made similar calls for legislative changes. The membership of any relevant APPGs, and membership organisations or associations that have raised similar issues might also be productive sources in terms of identifying potential partners and supporters. Consideration should also be given to approaching those organisations with which you already work in partnership, or have mutual interests in the policy areas that you are seeking legislative change. Approaching other organisations in these different areas will help to build up support for your organisation's efforts to secure legislative changes. Demonstrating to the Government that your organisation has wider support for its policy positions could help to ensure that you receive a positive response to the issues you are raising and that, as a result, the Government introduces legislation to address the issues you have raised, or alternatively reflects these issues in the Bill that is formally introduced following its consultation on the Draft Bill.

Summary of key points

The key points from this chapter can be summarised as follows:

> - Influencing legislation can help to make important changes to the law in policy and practice areas relevant to your organisation's interests.
> - The pre-legislative stage can afford important opportunities for organisations to influence parliamentary legislation prior to its introduction in Parliament.
> - Organisations can strengthen their calls for legislative change if these are underpinned by robust evidence.
> - Organisations should take a cross-party, and cross-organisational, approach to building up support for their calls for legislative change to improve their chances of receiving a positive response from the Government and other key policy makers.

11

Legislation: Overview of the Parliamentary Process

The previous chapter highlighted the important role which legislation plays in our political system, and within society as a whole. It also signposted the significant focus it can have in organisations' public affairs strategies, and the major outcomes responding to legislation can deliver for these strategies. This chapter provides guidance on how your organisation can engage effectively in the legislative process in both the House of Commons and in the House of Lords, and on how to ensure your organisation can help to shape and influence legislation relevant to its interests. It provides an overview of the key stages of Public Bills in both Houses. These Bills introduced by the Government are the main types of Bill considered in Parliament. In addition, this chapter provides useful background for Chapter 12 which looks at how your organisation should respond at each stage of the legislation. It also emphasises key differences in the legislative processes in the House of Commons and in the House of Lords that your organisation should be aware of, as it plans its engagement for each stage of a Bill. This guide does not seek to provide a detailed study of parliamentary procedure, but instead concentrates on how organisations can develop public affairs strategies that can ensure they place themselves in the best possible position to influence parliamentary legislation relevant to their work and interests.

Taking stock

When a Bill is introduced to Parliament in which your organisation has an interest it is important that you review the legislation to determine what major issues it raises, if any, for your organisation.

One of the first issues is to consider which House the legislation has been introduced in, as this will have a direct bearing on how your organisation develops its public affairs strategy in response to the legislation. Another important factor to take into account will be the question of whether or not the Bill has been developed from a consultation launched by the Government or by another body or agency, or from the pre-legislative scrutiny of a Draft Bill on which your organisation has already provided comments. Alternatively, has the Bill been introduced in response to calls for legislative change made by your organisation and by other organisations with similar interests? Or has the legislation been introduced by the UK Government as a 'Flagship' Bill, i.e. one of the key high profile Bills, announced in the Queen's Speech at the beginning of each parliamentary session? Putting a Bill in this context will be a critical factor in supporting your organisation to develop the most effective response, and strategy in relation, to the Bill as it goes through the legislative processes in both Houses of Parliament.

Having put the Bill in context, your organisation should then develop its analysis of the main issues presented by the legislation, and its response to these issues. Does your organisation, for example, fundamentally oppose the legislation? Conversely, does it broadly welcome the legislation, but believe the Bill needs to be improved in certain key areas? This is critical as your organisation's response to these questions will have a direct bearing on how it responds to the legislation as it goes through its different stages in both Houses of Parliament. In this respect, if your organisation is fundamentally opposed to the legislation then you should work with MPs to mobilise their support to speak against the Bill receiving a Second Reading in the House of Commons.[1] Second Reading is the stage of a Bill where MPs or Peers – depending upon in which House the Bill commences – debate the general principles of the legislation, and its provisions.

If your organisation can galvanise enough support amongst MPs to win a Division, i.e. a vote, on a Reasoned Amendment against the Motion that a parliamentary Bill be read a second time, then the legislation will not proceed any further in that parliamentary session. It is important, however, to take a realistic view of the likelihood that

---

1   Under the Salisbury Convention Peers generally do not vote against the Second Reading of Public Bills which have been included in the Election Manifesto of the Party of Government.

a Bill will be defeated at Second Reading, as this happens only rarely, and usually where the Government lacks a majority in the House of Commons. Indeed, the last time this happened was in 1986 when the Shops Bill designed to liberalise Sunday trading was defeated in the House of Commons.[2]

Where an organisation does not fundamentally oppose a Bill, but believes it requires significant improvement in certain key areas it should give consideration to doing so through progressing amendments to the legislation. Where you wish to change the legislation you will generally need amendments which can be considered by the House of Commons and/or by the House of Lords as appropriate. Amendments can add text to a Bill, or delete text from the legislation. Drafting amendments is a specialised area, and guidance on drafting amendments is beyond the scope of this guide. In general terms, however, it is recommended that, as background information and to put amendments in context, you look at a Marshalled List for any Bill. The Marshalled List features all of the amendments tabled for the Committee or Report stages of a Bill in the House of Commons, or for the Committee or Report or Third Reading stages of a Bill in the House of Lords. Consulting a Marshalled List will give you an insight into the style and structure of amendments. If your organisation lacks the capacity to draft amendments to a Bill, but wishes to secure changes to a Bill, its options will include engaging with the Government to persuade it to accept your requests for specific amendments to be made to the legislation. If this proves unsuccessful you should consider approaching the relevant spokesperson of the Opposition or one of the other opposition parties, or an individual MP or Peer, and to work with them and their staff to develop some basic text for amendments. If the relevant spokesperson of the Opposition or of one of the other opposition parties, or an MP or Peer agrees to table the amendments they can work with the Public Bill Office in the House of Commons or in the House of Lords as appropriate to finalise the text of the amendments. Once this has been done, the amendments will appear in the Marshalled List, and the Groupings document will confirm which amendments, if any, your amendments have been 'grouped' with for the purpose of the order of debate.

2   Parliament's Information Sheet, Parliamentary Stages of a Government Bill, Factsheet L1 Legislation series, (revised August 2010), House of Commons website www.parliament.uk.

Key stages of a parliamentary Bill

One preliminary issue to emphasise is that Parliament will only be able to legislate on a matter normally devolved to the Scottish Parliament, or to the Northern Ireland Assembly or to the National Assembly for Wales if the devolved body in question passes a Legislative Consent Motion to allow the UK Parliament to do so.

The key stages of a Public Bill in the House of Commons and in the House of Lords are outlined in the table below. This also highlights, where appropriate, the main procedural differences between the approaches taken in both Houses to these stages.

Stage of a Parliamentary Bill	House of Commons	House of Lords
First Reading	This is the formal introduction of a Bill. The introduction of a Bill will be confirmed in the House of Commons' Order Paper. The introduction of the Bill will be noted by the House of Commons with the announcement of the Bill's Short Title and an order for it to be printed. First Reading will not involve or require any formal action at this stage in terms of debate and scrutiny. There is no opportunity for engagement at First Reading.	This is the formal introduction of a Bill. The introduction of a Bill will be confirmed in the House of Lords' Order Paper. The introduction of the Bill will be noted by the House of Lords with the member in charge of the Bill announcing its Long Title. First Reading will not involve or require any formal action at this stage in terms of debate and scrutiny. There is no opportunity for engagement at First Reading.
Second Reading	Second Reading normally takes place no earlier than two weekends after the First Reading of a Bill.[3] At Second Reading MPs will consider and debate the	Second Reading normally takes place a minimum of two weekends after the First Reading of a Bill.[4] At Second Reading Peers will consider and debate the

3   UK Parliament, 'Second Reading (Commons)', UK Parliament website, www. parliament.uk.

4   UK Parliament, Companion to the Standing Orders and Guide to the Proceedings of the House of Lords, (2015), UK Parliament website, www.parliament.uk.

Stage of a Parliamentary Bill	House of Commons	House of Lords
	general principles of, and provisions in, the Bill. MPs will vote on the Bill receiving its Second Reading at the end of the debate. If the House votes in favour of the formal Motion "That the Bill be now read a second time" the legislation will proceed to its Committee Stage.	general principles of, and provisions in, the Bill, and discuss potential areas for amendment and improvement. Under the Salisbury Convention the House of Lords does not oppose Public Bills included previously in the Party of Government's election manifesto. There is generally no vote at the end of a Public Bill's Second Reading.[5]

Committee Stage	The Committee Stage of a Bill normally takes place a few weeks after its Second Reading.[6] A Public Bill Committee will generally be appointed to deal with the Committee Stage.
	    The Committee Stage of a Bill will see the legislation subject to line-by-line scrutiny by the Public Bill committee appointed for this purpose. This scrutiny will be undertaken through the committee's consideration of amendments to the Bill.
	    All amendments will be published on a Marshalled List of amendments. A list of 'Groupings' will also be published. The Groupings
		The Committee Stage of a Public Bill generally takes place approximately two weeks after the Second Reading debate.[7]
		    The House of Lords considers the Committee Stage of a Bill in the Chamber ('On the floor of the House') with the whole House sitting in Committee unless the Bill has been allocated to a Grand Committee sitting outside the Chamber ('Off the floor of the House'). As with the Committee Stage in the House of Commons, the Committee Stage in the House of Lords will focus on the line-by-line scrutiny of the legislation.

5   UK Parliament, 'Second Reading (Commons)', UK Parliament website, www.parliament.uk.
6   UK Parliament, 'Second Reading (Lords)', UK Parliament website, www.parliament.uk.
7   UK Parliament, 'Committee Stage (Commons)', UK Parliament website, www.parliament.uk.

Stage of a Parliamentary Bill	House of Commons	House of Lords
	outline the order in which amendments will be considered by the committee, as well as how the amendments will be grouped for debate, i.e. amendments dealing with the same issues and themes will usually be debated in a group together. Amendments for debate will be selected by the chair of the committee. Amendments will be considered and debated by the committee, and the amendments, unless the amendments receive unanimous support or are withdrawn without being pressed to a Division, i.e. a vote, will either be agreed to or rejected by the committee on a Division.	All amendments will be published on a Marshalled List of amendments, which are updated and printed before each Committee day. A list of 'Groupings' will also be published. The Groupings outline the order in which amendments will be considered by the committee, as well as how the amendments will be grouped for debate, i.e. amendments dealing with the same issues and themes will usually be debated in a group together. The procedures in the Grand Committee are similar to those used where the legislation is dealt with by a Committee of the Whole House. The main difference is that an amendment to a Bill in the Grand Committee will require the support of all members of the committee if the amendment is to be passed.
Report Stage	After the Committee Stage of a Public Bill has been completed, the Report Stage of the Bill in the House of Commons will be considered by the whole House. There is no prescribed timescale between the end of the Committee Stage and start of the Report Stage of a Public Bill.[8]	The Report Stage of a Public Bill normally takes place 14 days after Committee Stage has been completed. The Report Stage of a Bill in the House of Lords will be considered by the whole House. At Report Stage the House will have a further opportunity to consider amendments to the Bill.

---

8   UK Parliament, 'Report Stage (Commons)', UK Parliament website, www.parliament.uk.

Stage of a Parliamentary Bill	House of Commons	House of Lords
	At Report Stage, MPs will have a further opportunity to consider amendments to the Bill. As with the Committee Stage of a Bill, all amendments tabled for the Report Stage will be published in a Marshalled List of Amendments. The order in which the amendments will be debated will also be set out in the Groupings. Amendments relating to the same issues, or linked by the same issues, will be grouped together. Amendments tabled for the Report Stage of a Bill will tend to be those amendments considered to be the most important. Significantly, not all amendments will be debated at Report Stage, and it will be up to the Speaker to decide which amendments will be selected for debate. Where an amendment has been voted on, and defeated at Committee Stage it is unlikely that the Speaker would call the same amendment, or one with the same effect, at the Report Stage.	As with the Committee Stage of a Bill, all amendments tabled for the Report Stage will be published in a Marshalled List. The order in which the amendments will be debated will also be set out in the Groupings. Amendments relating to the same issues, or linked by the same issues, will be grouped together. The amendments lodged for the Report Stage of a Bill in the House of Lords by the Official Opposition party, and by the other opposition parties and groupings, will tend to be those amendments considered to be the most significant. Where an amendment has been voted on, and defeated at Committee Stage the same amendment, or one with the same effect, cannot be tabled at the Report Stage.[9]

9   There is no identical rule in the House of Commons, but it is considered unlikely that the Speaker would call an amendment for debate at Report Stage in the House of Commons if it had already been defeated on a Division during the Committee Stage in the House of Commons; *Erskine May: Parliamentary Practice*, 24th Edition, (23 June 2011); UK Parliament, 'Taking part in Public Bills in the House of Lords: A Guide for Members', UK Parliament website, www.parliament.uk.

Stage of a Parliamentary Bill	House of Commons	House of Lords
English Votes for English Laws (EVEL) process	The Speaker will consider if a Public Bill, or parts of the Bill or proposed changes to the Bill relate to England and/or Wales only. Where that is the case the Speaker will issue a certificate confirming that the EVEL process will apply. Where the Bill relates to England and/or England and Wales only, there are three new stages which could apply between Report Stage and Third Reading, depending upon decisions made by MPs. These stages are the Legislative Grand Committee (LGC), Reconsideration and Consequential Consideration. If the Speaker issues a certificate confirming that the EVEL process applies, and that the Bill falls within the devolved legislative competence, a consent Motion must be passed by the LGC. Where this relates to England and Wales it will be considered by the LGC, and if it concerns England only it will be dealt with by the LGC on the floor of the House of Commons. If the LGC gives its consent, the Bill will then proceed to its Third Reading. If the LGC does not give its consent to the Bill or to parts of the Bill, it will be subject to reconsideration by the whole House to try and resolve the dispute between the LGC and	The EVEL process is not applied to legislation in the House of Lords. Any issues arising from the EVEL process are addressed in the House of Commons.

Stage of a Parliamentary Bill	House of Commons	House of Lords
	the House. If the LGC still refuses to give its consent, after reconsideration, the Bill will not proceed to its Third Reading. Where consent is withheld in relation to certain parts of a Bill, those clauses and schedules will be removed and the Bill will then progress to its Third Reading. The Bill will be subject to the Consequential Consideration stage if certain minor technical changes are required following the removal of certain provisions in the Bill at the Reconsideration stage. Under the EVEL process, if the Speaker issues a certificate in relation to a Lords' amendment, a majority of all MPs and a majority of all MPs representing English and Welsh constituencies must approve the amendment. Where the MPs decline to do so, the amendment will be sent back to the House of Lords as disagreed.[10] After the Bill has completed these stages, it will proceed to its Third Reading.[11]	
Third Reading	The Third Reading of a Public Bill normally takes place	Third Reading will normally take place a minimum of three

---

10 UK Parliament, 'English votes for English laws: House of Commons bill procedure', UK Parliament website, www.parliament.uk.

11 The section on the 'English Votes for English Laws' (EVEL) process draws upon information provided in the UK Parliament's, 'English votes for English laws: House of Commons bill procedure', UK Parliament website, www.parliament.uk.

Stage of a Parliamentary Bill	House of Commons	House of Lords
	immediately after the Report Stage. The Third Reading will feature a short debate on a Motion "That the Bill do now pass" which formally ends the proceedings. The debate will focus on the contents of the Bill, and no amendments will be debated. After the debate, the House of Commons will vote on whether or not to give the Bill its Third Reading.	sitting days after the Report Stage of the Bill.[12] This is seen as the House's last chance to address any outstanding issues, including the 'tidying up' of any drafting errors or outstanding policy issues. Amendments can be tabled at Third Reading, provided they have not been previously considered and voted on at the Committee Stage or at the Report Stage. These are, however, largely amendments which have been brought forward by the Government or by the Official Opposition party or by other opposition parties or groupings in response to ministerial commitments to make concessions on the legislation, or technical amendments to address drafting errors. The Third Reading will feature a short debate on a Motion "That the Bill do now pass" which formally ends the proceedings. Under the Salisbury Convention the House of Lords will generally not vote against the Third Reading of a Public Bill.
Consideration of Lords' amendments	If the Bill was introduced and commenced in the House of Commons, upon completion of its Third Reading, the Bill	

---

12 UK Parliament, Companion to the Standing Orders and Guide to the Proceedings of the House of Lords, (2015), UK Parliament website, www.parliament.uk.

Stage of a Parliamentary Bill	House of Commons	House of Lords
	will then be considered by the House of Lords. All amendments made to the Bill by the House of Lords will then, after the Third Reading in the House of Lords, be considered by the House of Commons. There is no prescribed timescale between Third Reading in the House of Lords and the consideration of any Lords' amendments by the House of Commons. The Lords' amendments will either be accepted or rejected by the House of Commons, or the latter will suggest alternatives. If the House of Lords made no amendments to the Bill, after Third Reading in the House of Lords it will go to the Monarch to receive Royal Assent. If, on the other hand, the House of Commons rejects the Lords' amendments made to the Bill or suggests alternative proposals, it will be sent back to the Lords. The Bill may then go back and forward between the two Houses in a stage known as 'ping-pong', until agreement can be secured to accept or reject the Lords' amendments. If no agreement can be reached, the Bill could fall or the Parliament Act 1911 might be applied in certain circumstances. In this context, the House of Commons could pass the Bill in the next	

Stage of a Parliamentary Bill	House of Commons	House of Lords
	parliamentary session without the Lords' agreement.[13] The use of the Parliament Act is, however, very rare. Only seven Bills have become Acts using this procedure, with a further three Bills introduced in a second parliamentary session with the intention of following this procedure only for the three Bills to be agreed by the Lords without the need for this procedure to be applied.[14]	
Consideration of Commons' Amendments		If the Bill was introduced and commenced in the House of Lords, upon completion of its Third Reading it will then be considered by the House of Commons. All amendments made to the Bill by the House of Commons will then, after its Third Reading in the House of Commons, be considered by the House of Lords. The Commons' amendments will either be accepted or rejected by the House of Lords, or the latter will make alternative proposals. If the House of Commons made no amendments to the Bill, after Third Reading in the House of Commons it will go to the

---

13 UK Parliament, 'Consideration of Amendments', UK Parliament website, www. parliament.uk.

14 UK Parliament, 'The Parliament Acts', UK Parliament website, www.parliament. uk.

Stage of a Parliamentary Bill	House of Commons	House of Lords
		Monarch to receive Royal Assent.
		If, on the other hand, the House of Lords rejects the House of Commons' amendments made to the Bill or suggests alternative proposals, it will be sent back to the House of Commons. The Bill will then go back and forward between the two Houses, in a stage known as 'ping-pong', until agreement can be secured to accept or reject the Commons' amendments.
		If no agreement can be reached, the Bill could fall or the Parliament Act 1911 might be applied in certain circumstances. In this context, the House of Commons could pass the Bill in the next parliamentary session without the Lords' agreement.[15]
		As previously mentioned, the use of the Parliament Act is very rare. Only seven Bills have become Acts using this procedure, with a further three Bills introduced in a second parliamentary session with the intention of following this procedure only for the three Bills to be agreed by the Lords without the need for this procedure to be applied.

---

15 UK Parliament, 'Consideration of Amendments', UK Parliament website, www. parliament.uk.

Stage of a Parliamentary Bill	House of Commons	House of Lords
Royal Assent	Once a Bill has completed all its stages in the House of Commons and in the House of Lords, it will then receive Royal Assent from the Monarch, and become an Act of the UK Parliament, and part of UK law. There is no prescribed timescale between the completion of all of the Bill's stages in both Houses of Parliament and it receiving Royal Assent.	Once a Bill has completed all its stages in the House of Commons and in the House of Lords, it will then receive Royal Assent from the Monarch, and become an Act of the UK Parliament, and part of UK law. There is no prescribed timescale between the completion of all of the Bill's stages in both Houses of Parliament and it receiving Royal Assent.
Delegated or secondary legislation	Once a Bill has received Royal Assent, delegated legislation (also known as secondary legislation) will often be introduced in Parliament relating to the implementation of different aspects of the primary legislation (also known as the 'Parent Act'). This secondary legislation (usually in the form of Statutory Instruments) will be introduced through the order making provisions in the primary legislation. As previously noted, Parliament can accept or reject a piece of secondary legislation, but cannot, subject to certain rare exceptions, amend the legislation.[16]	Once a Bill has received Royal Assent, delegated legislation (also known as secondary legislation) will often be introduced in Parliament relating to the implementation of different aspects of the primary legislation (also known as the 'Parent Act'). This secondary legislation (usually in the form of Statutory Instruments) will be introduced through the order making provisions in the primary legislation. As previously noted, Parliament can accept or reject a piece of secondary legislation, but cannot, subject to certain rare exceptions, amend the legislation.[17]

16. Information provided by the House of Commons Enquiry Services confirms that it is only on rare occasions that secondary legislation can be amended, such as where the primary Act permits the secondary legislation to be amended as in the case of the Census Act 1920. The Government can also amend Statutory Instruments, and introduce revised drafts, in response to representations received under the super affirmative procedure.

17. Information provided by the House of Commons Enquiry Service.

Stage of a Parliamentary Bill	House of Commons	House of Lords
	The aim of the secondary legislation is to add greater detail to the legislation, and to often add provisions which were considered too complex to be included in the primary legislation. Statutory Instruments relating to a specific piece of legislation can assume different forms, including orders, regulations, rules, guidance and codes of practice.[18] The primary legislation will determine what, if any, parliamentary scrutiny will apply to a specific statutory instrument. These will normally be considered by the whole House of Commons, or by a Delegated Legislation Committee.[19]	The aim of the secondary legislation is to add greater detail to the primary legislation, and often to add provisions which were considered too complex to be included in the primary legislation. Statutory Instruments relating to a specific piece of legislation can assume different forms, including orders, regulations, rules, guidance and codes of practice.[20] Secondary legislation will be subject to scrutiny by the Secondary Legislation Scrutiny Committee. This draws the House of Lords' attention to any pieces of secondary legislation that raise issues of special interest, or which are flawed or require further clarification by the Government.[21]

18 UK Parliament, 'Delegated Legislation', UK Parliament website, www.parliament. uk.; R. Kelly, House of Commons Background Paper: Statutory Instruments, (18 December 2012), SN/PC/6509, UK Parliament website, www.parliament.uk.

19 UK Parliament, 'Delegated Legislation', UK Parliament website, www.parliament. uk.; R. Kelly, House of Commons Background Paper: Statutory Instruments, (18 December 2012), SN/PC/6509, UK Parliament website, www.parliament.uk.

20 UK Parliament, 'Delegated Legislation', UK Parliament website, www.parliament. uk.; R. Kelly, House of Commons Background Paper: Statutory Instruments, (18 December 2012), SN/PC/6509, UK Parliament website, www.parliament.uk.

21 UK Parliament, 'Delegated Legislation', UK Parliament website, www.parliament. uk.; R. Kelly, House of Commons Background Paper: Statutory Instruments, (18 December 2012), SN/PC/6509, UK Parliament website, www.parliament.uk.

Summary of key points

The key points from this chapter can be summarised as follows:

- When a Bill is introduced in which your organisation has an interest, review the legislation to determine what major issues it raises, if any, for your organisation.
- Your organisation must decide if it is fundamentally opposed to a Bill, or if it is seeking to improve it, and develop its public affairs strategy accordingly.
- Organisations wishing to halt a Bill must focus on persuading enough MPs to vote against the legislation's Second Reading, but this is rarely successful.
- Organisations wishing to improve legislation will generally have to progress amendments to the legislation, either by persuading the Government to table amendments to meet their concerns, or by persuading the opposition parties or groupings, or individual MPs or Peers, to table amendments.

12

Legislation: Influencing the Parliamentary Process

When your organisation is seeking to influence the Government, the opposition parties and other political groupings, and individual MPs and Peers on issues raised by the introduction of a Parliamentary Bill, it is vital that your organisation is ready and able to engage with these policy makers at all key stages in the legislative process. The sections below provide guidance on how your organisation should approach each stage of a Public Bill in the House of Commons, and in the House of Lords. Following this advice will help to maximise the impact of your organisation's public affairs strategy in relation to a specific Bill, and strengthen your organisation's capacity to ensure this strategy delivers tangible outcomes.

Making the most of Second Reading debates in the House of Commons

Once a Public Bill has been formally introduced in either House through its First Reading, a date will be set for its Second Reading. This will normally take place no sooner than two weekends after its First Reading in the House of Commons, and a minimum of two weekends after its First Reading in the House of Lords. The Second Reading debates of major Government Bills are generally high profile, politically charged events in which Government ministers and opposition parties' spokespersons will deliver set-piece speeches outlining their respective parties' policy positions on the legislation. The debate will normally feature a mixture of detailed analysis of the provisions in the legislation, and political point scoring. Second

Reading debates in the House of Commons can nevertheless offer organisations important opportunities to raise key issues in response to Government legislation, and to try and influence the Government's, and the opposition parties', thoughts on the direction of legislative travel that the Bill should take as it progresses through both Houses by flagging up potential areas for amendment and improvement.

If a Bill presents issues or concerns for your organisation, and it is keen to help shape the legislation, your organisation should closely monitor the introduction of the Bill and the scheduling of a date for the Second Reading debate. You will be able to obtain this information through the parliamentary monitoring service your organisation receives, or by ensuring a staff member follows the timetabling of the Bill on Parliament's website or by telephoning the House of Commons' Public Information Office to find out if a date has been set for Second Reading. It is advised that, as soon as your organisation is aware of the issues presented by the Bill, it should start preparing a briefing paper for the Second Reading debate. Ideally, this should be a short briefing paper of two to four pages (ideally two pages), depending upon the type of legislation introduced, the issues raised for your organisation and the complexity of the changes proposed by the legislation. This briefing paper should highlight the main issues raised in the legislation for your organisation. Is your organisation, for example, against the legislation in principle? Or does your organisation generally support the legislation, but consider that it requires significant amending in certain areas? If so, your organisation's briefing should outline the lines of amendments it is seeking the House of Commons to make to the Bill.

Once your organisation has prepared its Second Reading briefing, you should send a copy of the briefing to the relevant Government minister or ministers, with responsibility for the legislation, prior to the debate. In this respect, it is important to bear in mind that some legislation raises issues across different policy areas, Government departments, and ministerial remits. Against this background, it is important to brief those ministers who will lead on the Bill, but also to ensure that you send a copy of the briefing to other ministers who may have a policy interest in the legislation. With regard to the lead Government minister, you should try and secure a meeting with the latter as soon as the Government has announced its intention to introduce a Bill that will impact upon your organisation and its work.

You should also engage with the Government's special advisers and senior civil servants to highlight the key issues presented by the Bill for your organisation, and to discuss any amendments you are seeking to the legislation. Early contact in this area can play a vital part in kick-starting discussions with Government about possible concessions it may be prepared to make, during the parliamentary progress of the legislation, in response to the issues your organisation wishes to raise concerning the legislation.

As well as engaging with the Government, you should send copies of your organisation's briefing to the relevant spokespersons of the different opposition parties. Ideally, you should also try and arrange meetings with these spokespersons to discuss the main issues raised by the legislation for your organisation. If this does not prove possible (and it is important to recognise that spaces in their diaries will often be at a premium), you should at least try and meet their researchers or other members of their staff to ensure your organisation's policy position and 'policy asks' are taken into account when the respective parties' spokesperson's Second Reading speeches are being drafted. Briefing the opposition parties for the Second Reading debates will give your organisation important opportunities to influence the opposition parties' thinking on the legislation, and to potentially secure their support for specific amendments to the legislation. This could be a critical element in determining whether or not the Government will be willing, or if enough pressure can be brought to bear on the Government, to make concessions in response to amendments tabled by one of the opposition parties on your behalf.

To try and maximise the chances that your organisation's policy issues will be highlighted during the Second Reading debate your organisation should circulate its briefing paper to individual MPs. It is often the case that large numbers of organisations will be briefing MPs for Second Reading debates. This will depend upon the type of legislation being considered, the differences in policy positions the legislation generates between the Government and the different opposition parties and the wider interest it attracts from those most affected by the legislation, including specific sectors, organisations and the public. It is recommended that, where the Second Reading debate will be a high profile debate, your organisation may wish to consider taking a more targeted approach to briefing MPs.

If your organisation decides to take a targeted approach, it should prepare personalised briefings for a limited number of MPs prior to the debate. This could be your organisation's local MP, and/or other MPs who have close associations with your organisation or with policy areas related to the legislation under consideration. Alternatively, you could simply circulate a general briefing to all MPs for the Second Reading debate. The risks inherent in such an approach, however, are that there could already be a significant amount of general briefings in circulation from other organisations with an interest in the legislation, and with which your briefing will then be in competition, particularly if it is a high profile debate. Following this approach could, therefore, see your briefing vanish without trace. A lot will depend upon the existing profile of your organisation, and on its relations with Government and other policy makers. The type of legislation on which your organisation is lobbying, the strength of your organisation's key messages and their resonance with the Government, with the opposition parties and with individual MPs and the extent to which these messages are underpinned by robust evidence will also be major factors.

Against this background, regardless of whether or not your organisation decides to opt for a targeted or general approach to briefing MPs for specific Second Reading debates, it needs to try and ensure that its briefing paper stands out from those of any competing briefings. Drafting concise, well written briefing papers with clear messages, based on persuasive evidence and best practice, can all help to increase interest in your briefing. Including factual case studies to illustrate how the legislation is likely to impact upon your organisation or on the sector in which it operates or on the wider economy or upon specific groups of people or society as a whole, will also help to strengthen your organisation's briefing paper. Taking these factors into account when preparing briefings can increase the likelihood that your briefings will secure a receptive audience from different MPs. This, in turn, could encourage cross-party support for amendments to specific parts of the legislation subsequently tabled on behalf of your organisation.

Apart from sending MPs a copy of your organisation's Second Reading briefing you should also try and secure a meeting with MPs to discuss the key issues presented by the legislation. This could take the form of a briefing meeting at which your organisation features different speakers to brief MPs about the legislation, and invites MPs to attend, on a cross-party basis. In addition, or alternatively, your organisation could try and arrange meetings with individual MPs. Your organisation could use these meetings to provide the MPs with information and questions for the minister, on an exclusive basis, which they could then use in the Second Reading debate. Briefing meetings with groups of MPs, and meetings with individual MPs, can be a useful way of engaging with MPs on legislation, and of bringing them up to speed on the key issues relevant to your organisation. By doing so, you are more likely to secure commitments from MPs that they will take up issues on your organisation's behalf at the Committee Stage, and during the subsequent stages of the legislation. Such commitments will strengthen your organisation's engagement on the legislation, and increase the likelihood that an opposition party or individual MP raising issues on your behalf will be able to secure concessions from the Government.

Making the most of Second Reading debates in the House of Lords

Second Reading debates in the House of Lords can also provide your organisation with significant opportunities to help shape and influence legislation. If the legislation has started in the House of Commons, and is now being considered in the House of Lords, it is important that your organisation drafts a Second Reading briefing for the House of Lords. The themes and issues highlighted in your briefing will depend upon whether or not the Bill was amended during its passage in the House of Commons to address your organisation's concerns. Your briefing will focus on any issues and concerns that remain outstanding for your organisation following the completion of its stages in the House of Commons. In this respect, when drafting your Second Reading briefing for the House of Lords it is important that your briefing has taken into account, and reflected key arguments and developments from the House of Commons' stages. You should also include, and address, any major points made by the minister. In particular, if the Government has rejected your arguments for specific amendments to be made to the Bill, you should tackle these arguments in your Lords' Second Reading briefing. This should outline why the amendments are still necessary, notwithstanding the Government's objections expressed during the legislative process in the House of Commons.

If a Bill starts in the House of Lords, and it has attracted significant political discussion in Parliament and in the media, this will increase the legislation's profile, and create chances for your organisation to engage in key debates on its provisions. The approach your organisation should take to preparing for a Second Reading debate in the House of Lords will be similar in many areas to that which it should take for Second Reading debates in the House of Commons. It is equally important in both Houses, for example, that you ensure the Government minister leading on the Bill receives a copy of your organisation's briefing. In addition, just as with your organisation's approach to Second Reading in the House of Commons, you should ensure that all of the spokespersons for the different opposition parties and groupings represented in the House of Lords receive a copy of this briefing.

Your organisation should also keep an eye on the Speakers' List on the Government whips website in the House of Lords[1] to see which Peers have put their names down to speak in the debate. This will assist your organisation to ensure that it is able to send a copy of its briefing to those Peers with an interest in the legislation. It is recommended that you should also undertake research to identify which Peers have an interest in the policy areas covered by the legislation. A good source for this information will be the House of Lords' *Hansard*. This will provide details of which Peers intervened in previous legislation dealing with similar policy areas, or in relevant debates or who have tabled Parliamentary Questions on these issues. Another useful source will be the House of Lords section of the Parliament's website which contains biographical details for many of the Peers, including a 'Member's Focus' section.[2] This includes the policy areas in which individual Peers have an interest. Building up this background detail about Peers will support your organisation to decide which Peers to target in its Second Reading briefings. Furthermore, it will help your organisation to decide which Peers it should try to secure briefing meetings with prior to the Second Reading debate.

To maximise support for your organisation's policy positions on the legislation you should consider approaching a Peer to sponsor a briefing meeting in the House of Lords on behalf of your organisation.

---

1   UK Parliament, Government Whips' Office House of Lords website, www. lordswhips.org.uk.
2   UK Parliament, UK Parliament website, www.parliament.uk.

This will enable your organisation to update Peers about key issues presented by the legislation, and to promote debate on the policy issues you are raising in response to the Bill. Such meetings will also provide good opportunities to identify Peers who might be prepared to table amendments on your behalf at the Committee Stage, and/or at the subsequent stages, of the Bill. The added advantage of briefing meetings is that, if they attract attendance from Peers of all parties and groupings, this will help your organisation to secure cross-party support for any amendments that are tabled on its behalf. This will increase the chances that the Government will make a concession in response to the amendment or agree to the amendment, or that the amendment will be won on a Division of the House.

A major difference between the two Houses, and one which your organisation should bear in mind when developing its public affairs strategy and progressing public affairs activities, is the political composition in the House of Commons and in the House of Lords. This has contributed to the development of very different dynamics in the House of Commons, and in the House of Lords. By way of further background, in the House of Commons, MPs will generally approach Bills on a party political basis, and will vote in compliance with their Party's Whip. There will, however, be some occasions in which some MPs may decide to vote against the Party Whip on specific debates or Bills, or at least on certain issues related to the debates or legislation on which they find themselves at odds with their party's policy on the grounds of principle. An example would be where an MP fundamentally disagrees with their party's policy on the topic for debate, or on a Bill, or where the legislation could have an adverse impact upon their constituency and their constituents. In most cases, however, MPs will approach Bills on a party political basis, will view legislation through the prism of their party allegiance and will vote in accordance with their Party's Whip.

By contrast, the situation in the House of Lords can sometimes be more fluid. In this respect, all of the political parties in the House of Lords will provide a Party Whip to their members, with instructions on how to vote in particular divisions should they arise, but there is less capacity for the party to compel its Peers to vote on, for example, amendments to Bills, and Peers can feel less constrained by the Party Whip. This means that amendments to Bills in the House of Lords will often attract cross-party support, and that Government backbenchers will occasionally vote with the opposition parties and with other groupings to vote against the Government, which can lead to Government defeats on specific amendments. Another important element of the dynamic in the House of Lords is that, in addition to the various political parties represented in the House of Lords, there are other significant groupings of Peers. These include the Crossbench Peers, the Bishops and Peers sitting as 'Independents' or with 'No affiliation'. How organisations can use the dynamics of party representation in the House of Lords is considered in more detail below.

Maximising impact at Committee Stage in the House of Commons

If your organisation wants to influence the Committee Stage, and subsequent stages, of a Bill, it will need to draft amendments to the legislation. If, on the other hand, it lacks the capacity to do so, your organisation should identify possible lines of amendments to the Bill, which it can then suggest to the Government, to the opposition parties and to individual MPs. Against this background, it is advised that, even before the Second Reading debate on a Bill has taken place, your organisation should give consideration to the type of amendments it believes are necessary to improve the legislation. To help inform this process your organisation should spend time analysing the Bill along with the explanatory notes accompanying the Bill, copies of which will be available on Parliament's website.[3] You should also analyse other relevant documents including, for example, any overarching impact assessments providing an analysis of the overall impact of the legislation. Undertaking this exercise will enable your organisation to develop its thinking around which aspects of the Bill require amendment. It will also allow your organisation to identify which amendments are necessary to facilitate these improvements, the aims of the amendments and why it thinks the latter are necessary.

Once your organisation has completed this exercise, it should highlight the amendments it is seeking to the legislation in its Second Reading briefing for MPs, and engage with key policy makers on a

---

3   UK Parliament, UK Parliament website, www.parliament.uk.

cross-party basis. Furthermore, prior to the Second Reading debate, your organisation should ensure it raises the potential amendments to the Bill with the relevant minister, their special advisers and with the Bill Team (the civil servants responsible for managing the legislation). In addition, your organisation should highlight these amendments to the spokespersons of the various opposition parties, as well as to individual MPs. If, however, this engagement fails to secure a commitment from the Government that it will bring forward its own amendments at the Committee Stage of the Bill to meet the issues raised by your organisation, you should give consideration to working with the opposition parties and with individual MPs to amend the Bill during its Committee Stage, or during its subsequent stages.

Influencing the legislation will require amendments to be drafted to the Bill, which can then be debated at Committee Stage. Your organisation can either draft these amendments itself, or contract with someone who has specialist expertise in this area to draft the amendments, and to then approach an MP to table the amendments on behalf of your organisation. Alternatively, you could work with an individual MP and their staff to develop your organisation's suggested lines of amendment into amendments which the MP can table on your organisation's behalf. Another option would be to use your organisation's engagement with the minister to call on them to bring forward Government amendments to the legislation based on the issues raised by your organisation. If the Government is persuaded by the merits of such amendments, it may confirm that it will bring forward amendments to address the issue raised by your organisation either at the Committee Stage, or at the Report Stage, of the legislation. Such positive responses will often be accompanied by confirmation from the Government that the Bill Team will work with the organisation raising the policy issues to draft appropriate amendments to address these issues.

To maximise the likelihood of the Government doing so, it is recommended that your organisation should build up as wide an alliance of organisations as possible in support of your organisation's proposal for a specific amendment or amendments. You should also work with the opposition parties and with MPs from all parties, including the Government's own backbenchers, to try and secure their support for your proposed lines of amendments. Securing the backing of other organisations for your suggested lines of amendments, and the support of the opposition parties and individual MPs, will demonstrate to the Government the depth of support for your proposal, and make it more likely to bring forward Government amendments to address the issues you have raised.

Another key aspect of your organisation's public affairs strategy, prior to the Committee Stage of a Bill, should be engaging with the minister's special advisers. Securing a meeting with the special advisers would give your organisation an opportunity to persuade them of the merits of your proposed amendments, and of the benefits which would accrue from these amendments for the Government, for your organisation and for other stakeholders. Persuading the special advisers of these merits will increase the likelihood of the Government responding positively to your proposed amendments. As well as engaging with the Government's special advisers, your organisation should also engage with the Bill Team to outline the significant advantages of your proposed lines of amendments, and how these amendments could improve the legislation. A productive meeting with the Bill Team would also help to improve the prospects that the Government will respond positively to your organisation's proposed amendments.

If your organisation has persuaded an MP to table amendments on its behalf, it should provide background briefing papers for each amendment tabled. Ideally, you should provide the MP with speaking notes which can be used in support of the amendments. Providing background briefing papers and/or speaking notes will enable your organisation to set out the reasons why the amendments are necessary, and how they will improve the legislation. The briefing papers and/or speaking notes should take on board any key issues raised during the Second Reading debate. It is particularly important that this material directly addresses any objections raised by the Government in response to your proposals for amendments. Building a rebuttal of any such objections into your briefing paper/speaking notes for Committee Stage amendments will help to develop the debate in relation to your amendments. It will also strengthen the case for these amendments by demonstrating that the Government's objections were groundless, or can be overcome by following specific steps or actions suggested by your organisation in its briefing paper/speaking notes.

A copy of the briefing paper should be sent to the minister, to their special advisers and to the Bill Team. By taking these steps, you will help to ensure that the minister is more likely to provide an informed and detailed response to each amendment at Committee Stage. Giving the Government the background to the amendments will also increase the chances that the Government will make a concession in response to each amendment. The Government might, for example, accept the amendments or confirm that it will bring forward its own amendments to address the issues you have raised. Other concessions could include the Government giving a commitment that the issues or concerns you have raised will be addressed in secondary legislation, or in the statutory guidance accompanying the legislation. Alternatively, the minister might offer your organisation an opportunity to meet, and discuss the issues further. All of these concessions would be excellent outcomes for your organisation. Achieving a positive outcome will be more likely if you have been able to demonstrate the merits of your amendments to the Government, and that your proposed amendments have significant levels of support from MPs and from other organisations. Furthermore, you need to persuade the Government that accepting your amendments, or making some other concession, will not have unintended consequences for the Government or cut across its policies and strategic objectives.

To increase support for your organisation's amendments at Committee Stage you should also provide briefing material to the individual members of the Public Bill committee with responsibility for the Bill. This briefing material should be provided on a cross-party basis to maximise support in the committee for the amendments tabled on behalf of your organisation. You should also try and arrange meetings with the opposition parties, and with individual MPs, to update them on the amendments, and to outline the objectives of the amendments and the reasons why they are necessary. In doing so, you should co-ordinate with the MP sponsoring the amendments, and agree with them what actions your organisation can most usefully take to increase support for the amendments.

As a reality check it is important to approach Bill proceedings in the House of Commons in the full knowledge that the Government, and the opposition parties represented in the Public Bill Committee dealing with the legislation, will generally vote on party lines. Against this background, it is important that your organisation tries to secure Government support for your amendments, or for the principles which the Government can then address in Government amendments.

If your organisation's approaches to the Government in support of its amendments fail to draw a positive response, you should try and maximise cross-party support for your amendments with a view to putting pressure on the Government to either accept your amendments or to make concessions in response to your amendments during the Committee Stage in the House of Lords.

As indicated above, some amendments will be tabled by MPs with a view to seeking a Division in the committee, or to secure concessions from the Government. By contrast, other amendments called 'probing amendments' will be tabled by MPs seeking clarification of the Government's intentions and policy thinking behind the Bill, or to clarify how specific provisions in the legislation should be interpreted. Getting the Government's statement reported in *Hansard*, i.e. on the record, in response to a probing amendment can play a significant role in the implementation stage of the legislation after it has received Royal Assent. The case of *Pepper v Hart* established the principle that such statements can sometimes be used to help settle disputes over how parliamentary legislation should be interpreted. Against this background, organisations, agencies and individuals can use such statements to aid their interpretation of a government's aims with regard to the legislation, its meaning, objectives and effects.[4] This can make an important contribution to how the legislation is implemented, particularly in relation to, for example, how any duties and responsibilities placed on organisations or agencies or individuals should be interpreted, or how they should exercise any powers given to them under the legislation.

Maximising impact at Committee Stage in the House of Lords

Many of the above approaches and methods for the Committee Stage of a Bill in the House of Commons can, with careful adaptation, be utilised for the Committee Stage of the Bill in the House of Lords. There are, however, certain significant differences between the Committee Stages in the House of Commons and in the House of Lords, which can often

4   UK Parliament, House of Commons Library, (22 June 2005), Standard Note: SN/PC/392, 'Pepper v Hart', UK Parliament website, www.parliament.uk.

be attributed to the different dynamics within each of the two Houses. These are considered in more detail below.

If your organisation has had amendments tabled on its behalf during the Committee Stage, it is important that, upon completion of the proceedings in the House of Commons and before the commencement of the Bill in the House of Lords, you consider your strategy for the Bill's stages in the House of Lords. It is strongly recommended that your organisation analyses the Committee Stage proceedings, and the subsequent stages of the Bill in the House of Commons to assess the main points made by the Government, and by the opposition parties, in response to the amendments tabled on your behalf. This will give you a clear idea of the strengths of the amendments, as well as any weaknesses highlighted by the minister or by the opposition parties or by individual MPs. The key things are to evaluate the debates around your amendments, and any other policy issues in the legislation in which your organisation has an interest, and to take a view on whether or not you wish to revisit the amendments, and related policy issues, in the House of Lords.

Another key reference point for your organisation should be the Second Reading debate on the Bill in the House of Lords. In this respect, it is important that your organisation reviews and evaluates the debate to see what statements the Government made about the specific provisions in the Bill, and on the related policy issues, in which your organisation is potentially seeking to progress amendments. The Second Reading debate in the House of Lords will also give you a chance to identify which Peers are most interested in the policy areas and issues that would potentially be addressed by your organisation's amendments. Undertaking this type of analysis will enable your organisation to determine which Peers are most likely to table amendments to the Bill on your behalf. You can then approach these Peers to find out if they would be prepared to table the amendments, and work with them to draft the amendments. In some cases the Peer may seek assistance from the Public Bill Office in the House of Lords to finalise the amendments, and to ensure that they are in a form which can be accepted for tabling.

Your organisation may have various reasons for progressing amendments in the House of Lords that have previously been debated in the House of Commons. Some amendments may raise issues of such fundamental importance and principle to your organisation that raising these issues in the House of Lords will help to keep the issues in the political spotlight. In this respect, ensuring the amendments are tabled in the House of Lords would help to further raise the profile of the issues with Government, with the opposition parties and other groupings represented in the House of Lords, with individual Peers, with the media and with the public. Another major reason for ensuring the amendments are tabled in the House of Lords would be to tune into, and to utilise, the dynamics in the House of Lords where Bills are often approached by Peers on a cross-party basis. This often results in amendments to Parliamentary Bills being judged on their merits, and the Government being defeated on Divisions by cross-party alliances of opposition Peers, crossbench Peers, independents, and Bishops. It is also part of the House of Lords' dynamic that Government backbench Peers will sometimes be prepared to vote against the Government, even if it risks defeat for the latter. This can occur where the Government backbencher supports an amendment on the basis of their personal views and principles, which on the specific issues presented by the amendment are at odds with the Government's policy position.

If your organisation decides that it wishes to have amendments tabled on its behalf at Committee Stage in the House of Lords, either on legislation that is starting in the House of Lords or which has previously been through its different stages in the House of Commons, there may be opportunities to use the unique composition of the House of Lords to secure concessions on amendments. The Government and the opposition parties will issue a Whip on Bills, and confirm to their members how they are expected to vote on different amendments should they be pushed to a Division. There is, however, a greater tendency for Peers to ignore the Party Whip on a specific amendment, or throughout a Bill, if their personal views are at odds with their party's policy position, than in the House of Commons where such behaviour would be more likely to result in political consequences for 'rebelling' MPs. Apart from this willingness of Peers to vote against their own Whip, in certain situations, there is also the role of other groups of Peers in the House of Lords to be considered. In this respect, the Crossbench Peers, the independents and the Bishops can all have an influence on Divisions and, if mobilised, along with the opposition parties can help to defeat the Government on specific amendments to Parliamentary Bills.

The dynamics in the House of Lords, created in part by such factors, can present your organisation with important opportunities to influence legislation when it is considered in the House of Lords. The secret is to try and build up a cross-party alliance in support of any amendments lodged on your organisation's behalf. Developing such alliances will increase the likelihood that the Government will make concessions in response to your amendments, or that the Government will be defeated if the amendment is pushed to a Division. To construct such an alliance you should try and get a respected Government backbencher to table the amendment on your behalf, and then approach Peers from the other parties and groupings represented in the House of Lords, to try and secure cross-party support. Alternatively, you could approach a member of one of the opposition parties or from the Crossbench Peers with a particular interest or proven track record in the policy issues underpinning the amendments you are seeking to the legislation. The key to successfully developing such an alliance is to have a good issue which is likely to attract cross-party support, and to get the amendments lodged by a Peer who is widely respected in the House. This will help your organisation to secure cross-party support for the amendment, and to ensure that representatives from other parties and groupings add their names to the amendment.

With high profile issues it would be worth asking a Peer to host a briefing meeting in the House of Lords. This would give you an opportunity to brief Peers on a cross-party basis, and to identify Peers who would be prepared to support a particular amendment. Once you have secured the agreement of a Peer to table the amendments, and you have been able to identify Peers who would be willing to support the amendment, you should circulate briefings to these Peers, and to any others who have an interest in the policy issues you are seeking to raise through the amendment. Apart from sending copies of the briefing to individual Peers, copies of the briefing should also be sent to the Government Whips' office, to the Opposition Whips' office (of the Opposition party in the Lords), to the whips office of any other political parties in the House of Lords, as well as to the resource office for the Crossbench Peers. The staff in these offices should be able to circulate the briefing to Peers belonging to their respective parties, or groupings. Maximising the circulation of your briefing will raise awareness of the related policy issues amongst Peers, and potentially increase support for your amendments. Furthermore, the Peer sponsoring the amendment will be able to make a significant contribution to securing support for the amendment through their own networks within the House of Lords.

Influencing the Report and Third Reading Stages in the House of Commons

After the Committee Stage, the Bill will be reprinted with all of the amendments made at Committee Stage incorporated into the new version of the Bill. If your organisation is seeking to have amendments tabled at Report Stage it is essential that you use the correct version of the Bill as amended in committee. If the Government failed to accept your amendments at Committee Stage, or to make suitable concessions, your organisation should liaise with the MP who sponsored your amendments, and other MPs who supported the amendments, to consider your next steps, and how best to take forward the policy issues raised by your amendments. The main options would be:

- not to take forward the amendments; or
- to seek to have the amendments tabled again at the Report Stage in the House of Commons; or
- to revisit them in the House of Lords.

If you decide to approach an MP to table the amendments again at Report Stage, you should liaise with the sponsoring MP about approaching the Government prior to the Report Stage, to request that it accepts the amendments at Report Stage or brings forward its own versions of the amendment to address the policy issues your organisation is raising.

If such an approach fails to secure a positive reaction from the Government, you should proceed with the option of persuading an MP to table the amendments at Report Stage. If the amendments were debated previously at the Committee Stage, you will in principle be able to have the amendments re-tabled at Report Stage, provided the amendments were not pushed to a Division at the Committee Stage as these are unlikely to be called for debate by the Speaker. Whether or not the amendment is debated will, however, depend upon a number of factors. Significantly, you should bear in mind that, at the Report Stage of a Bill in the House of Commons, the parties tend to focus on key issues, and on their main amendments. This means that you will have to persuade an MP of the importance of revisiting the amendment, and to agree to table the amendment. The MP (if not the party's lead spokesperson on the Bill), in turn, is likely to have to persuade their Party's lead spokesperson and the Chief Whip that the amendment should be tabled again, and should be supported by their party. The party in question will then take a decision about this in the light of its priorities for Report Stage, and as part of its overall assessment of the issues it wishes to progress at Report Stage. Your organisation will, therefore, need to argue persuasively in favour of the amendment, and to highlight its synergy with the political party's own priorities, if it is to be tabled at Report Stage. Another significant factor is that, even if an MP wishes to table your amendments and secures support from their own party to do so, it will be up to the Speaker to decide if the amendment should actually be debated. It is important to recognise that the Speaker will be unable to call all amendments for debate. The Speaker will generally tend to select only those amendments that they consider to be the most important and which, in the Speaker's view, are likely to benefit from further debate.[5]

Amendments tabled at Report Stage, and called for debate, will be considered by the whole House of Commons. MPs will generally vote for amendments along party lines. Indeed, it is less likely that an MP will vote against their party's Whip compared to the House of Lords. Peers are generally more likely than MPs to defy their Party Whip on an amendment where their personal views are at odds with their party's policy position on a Bill, or on particular parts of the Bill. Against this background, the consideration of the Report Stage by the whole House of Commons will nevertheless potentially give your organisation significant opportunities to influence MPs on a cross-party basis. You should liaise with the MP who has agreed to table the amendment on how best you can help to build cross-party support for the amendment. The extent to which this can be achieved will, however, largely be the result of negotiations between the respective opposition parties. Ensuring that MPs all have a copy of briefing material in support of your amendments prior to the Report Stage will, at least, increase awareness of the issues you are seeking to raise. This, in turn, could make it more likely that MPs will consider the issues presented by your

---

5   *Erskine May: Parliamentary Practice*, 24th Edition, (23 June 2011).

amendments more sympathetically. The chances of this translating into support for your amendments will depend upon the extent to which these amendments strike a chord with a particular party's priorities for Report Stage, or raise issues for individual MPs that mean they are willing to consider supporting your amendment and, if necessary, voting against their own party's Whip.

Report Stage and Third Reading are generally taken at the same time in the House of Commons, and amendments are not debated at Third Reading. Prior to Third Reading, therefore, if your organisation has been unable to secure concessions at Committee Stage, it will have to try and obtain concessions at Report Stage or wait until the Bill goes to the House of Lords if it has started in the House of Commons. If your organisation has had amendments lodged on its behalf at Report Stage in the House of Commons, but the amendments were not accepted by the Government or were defeated on a Division, this will, in essence, have been the last chance to amend the legislation prior to it going to the House of Lords.

The Report Stage in the House of Commons will conclude with a Third Reading debate on the Motion that 'The Bill do now Pass'. This will give the Government and the opposition parties a final chance to reflect on the legislation, and to highlight any key issues remaining from its consideration by the House of Commons. If your organisation has raised high profile issues, and these have not been resolved during the Bill's stages in the House of Commons, you should try and persuade the party or parties which have supported your amendments to refer during the Third Reading debate to the policy issues raised by the amendments. This will help to flag up to the Government that these are issues of substance which you will be seeking to revisit when the Bill commences in the House of Lords.

Influencing the Report and Third Reading Stages in the House of Lords

If your organisation's amendments are debated at Committee Stage in the House of Lords, but are not agreed to or fail to secure concessions from the Government, you need to take stock, and to review how to take forward your amendments (if at all). Part of this process should be analysing the key debates during the Committee Stage in *Hansard*.

Particular attention should be paid to assessing debates on parts of the legislation where the Government has confirmed it is willing to make concessions, or that it is not prepared to make any concessions. This analysis should include an assessment of the level of support for the policy issues raised by your amendments from the Government, from the opposition parties and groupings represented in the House of Lords and from Peers. You should also look very carefully at the statements made by the Government in response to your organisation's amendments.

Did the Government, for example, reject your amendments outright? Did the amendments fail to galvanize significant levels of support amongst the opposition parties, and other groupings represented in the House of Lords, and from individual Peers? Alternatively, did the Government oppose the principles behind your amendment, but the amendments themselves secured significant levels of support from Peers on all sides of the Chamber? In this context, it would definitely be worth pursuing the amendments at the Report Stage. Another situation in which your organisation should give serious consideration to progressing amendments at Report Stage is if, at the Committee Stage, the Government stated it would not agree to your amendments, but confirmed it might do so if the sponsoring Peer was prepared to make certain changes to them. Making these changes could be the difference between your organisation securing, or failing to secure, an important change to the Bill. This could potentially represent a significant outcome for your organisation's public affairs strategy. Undertaking an analysis of the Committee Stage proceedings will, therefore, enable your organisation to take a view on how best to proceed at Report Stage.

The Report Stage of a Bill in the House of Lords will tend to focus on substantial issues, and your organisation should decide which key issues it wishes to progress. Once your organisation has made this decision, it should work with the Peer or Peers who sponsored your amendments at Committee Stage to progress the amendments. Prior to Report Stage you should liaise with the Peer/Peers and with other partner organisations to write to the Government, seeking a commitment that it will either agree to your amendments at the Report Stage, or bring forward Government amendments at the Report Stage or Third Reading to address the policy issues raised by your amendments. You should also engage with the opposition parties and with the other groupings represented in the House of Lords, and in particular with the Crossbench peers and the Bishops, to raise awareness about your amendments and to try and enlist their support should these amendments be pushed to Divisions at the Report Stage. Building up a cross-party alliance, including Government backbenchers, will increase the chances that you will be able to defeat the Government on a Division on an amendment at Report Stage or to secure a concession from the Government wishing to avoid the embarrassment of a defeat.

By comparison with the House of Commons, the Third Reading Stage in the House of Lords will generally not take place on the same day as the Report Stage. In the House of Lords the Third Reading will normally take place a few days after the Report Stage. The Third Reading will be an opportunity for the Government to bring forward any amendments it promised as concessions during the Committee or Report stages. In this respect, if the Government did make a concession in response to amendments tabled by a Peer on your behalf, it is important that you keep an eye on the amendment/amendments introduced by the Government at Third Reading to make sure this meets your expectations. It is recommended that you liaise with the Peer who sponsored the original amendments about the Government amendments. The sponsoring Peer will be able to engage with the minister to ensure that the Government's amendments give full effect to the concessions promised at Committee or Report stages.

Consideration of Lords' and Commons' Amendments

Another stage of a Bill that your organisation should monitor (where it has been active in the previous stages of the legislation), is Consideration of Commons' Amendments Stage, and the Consideration of Lords' Amendments Stage. Where a Bill started in the House of Lords, and then goes through all of its stages in the House of Commons, all the amendments made by the House of Commons will then be considered in the House of Lords as the 'Consideration of Commons' Amendments' stage. The same process will apply where the Bill has started in the House of Commons, and then goes through its different stages in the House of Lords. In this respect, all the amendments agreed by the House of Lords will then be considered in the House of Commons as 'Consideration of Lords' Amendments'.

In certain cases there will be situations in which either the House of Commons or the House of Lords objects to amendments made by the other. This can lead to a process known as 'ping-pong' where the amendments will go back and forward between the two Houses until agreement is reached to accept or reject the Commons' or Lords' amendments as appropriate. If no agreement can be reached, the Bill could fall or the Parliament Act 1911 may be applied. Where the Parliament Act 1911 is invoked, the House of Commons can pass the Bill in the next parliamentary session without the Lords' agreement.[6] This sanction, however, has rarely been used, as the 'Usual Channels', i.e. negotiations involving the Government ministers and whips and their counterparts in the opposition parties, have tended to resolve matters before this expedient has become necessary.

This stage of legislation can have an impact upon organisations where the legislative 'ping-pong' relates to amendments tabled on their behalf. To take the example of a Bill starting in the House of Commons, and undergoing significant amendment in the House of Lords, if the changes made in the Upper House include amendments secured on your behalf, your organisation needs to be mindful that the amendments could be lost when the Bill returns to the House of Commons. This is likely if the amendments you have secured are significant and cut across the Government's own policy positions, and the Government can rely on a majority of MPs to vote against your amendment should it be pushed to a Division. In these circumstances your organisation will face a major challenge to ensure that its amendments are not defeated on a Division when the House of Commons deals with the 'Consideration of Lords' Amendments'. To try and avoid such an outcome your organisation should engage with the Government to highlight the merits of your amendment or amendments, and how they have strengthened the legislation. In this respect, if it is not possible to arrange a meeting with the minister you should try and meet with the Government's special advisers to outline the case for your amendments, and the advantages the amendments will bring. The major aim of such meetings would be to try and persuade the Government not to vote

---

6   UK Parliament, 'Consideration of Amendments', UK Parliament website, www. parliament.uk.

against your amendments when they are considered by the House of Commons.

As part of this process, you should also ensure that your organisation's chief executive or other senior officer writes to the minister to outline the case for retaining your amendment or amendments in the legislation. Getting the chief executives or senior officers of partner organisations to support the letter would help in this regard, by demonstrating that your amendments have wider support. Building up cross-party support for the amendments, by engaging with the opposition parties and with individual MPs and Peers including the Government backbenchers, would also increase the pressure on the Government, and improve the chances that it will be willing to accept the amendment or amendments, particularly if they do not cut across fundamental policy positions held by the Government.

After Royal Assent: responding to secondary legislation

Once a Bill has been through all of its stages in the House of Commons and the House of Lords, and both Houses have agreed its content, the legislation will receive Royal Assent from the Monarch and become an Act of Parliament. The legislation will then enter its implementation stage. There are a couple of important areas which organisations, that have had an interest in a specific Bill, should keep an eye on and, where appropriate, seek to influence. One of these areas is the laying of Commencement Orders by statutory instrument confirming when the Act, or part of the Act, will come into force at a date later than when the Act was passed. This will let organisations know when the Act will have effect, and impact on their work and interests.

Another significant area is the introduction of delegated or secondary legislation through any regulation-making powers in the primary legislation. Most primary legislation will contain such powers, as the use of these powers to introduce secondary legislation will give Government a discretion and flexibility to put in place many of the detailed provisions necessary to give effect to the legislation. Secondary legislation will mainly be introduced by statutory instrument, and can take the form of orders or regulations or guidance. Both Houses of Parliament will then consider the secondary legislation. The primary legislation will confirm if the secondary legislation is to be subject to the Affirmative Procedure or to the Negative Procedure. Secondary legislation subject to the Affirmative Procedure will require the statutory instrument introducing the secondary legislation to be expressly approved by both Houses. By contrast, under the Negative Procedure, the secondary legislation will automatically become law unless there is an objection from either House, i.e. an MP or Peer lodges a Motion to Annul (known as a 'Prayer') within 40 days of the statutory instrument being laid objecting to the statutory instrument and requiring that it be annulled.[7] Secondary legislation can often include significant details which give effect to the Government's legislative intent, and will provide significant shape and structure to many of the provisions contained in the Act of Parliament. This type of legislation can have a major impact upon organisations and their work, and on those on whose behalf they work. Secondary legislation is, however, often obscure and is rarely prioritised by the politicians themselves, and often receives little, if any, interest from the media and from the general public. Given the importance of the legislative provisions sometimes introduced by secondary legislation this is perhaps surprising, but can be put in perspective by considering that any high profile debates and issues around the legislation will mainly have passed when the Bill completed its parliamentary stages and became an Act. If your organisation retains a major interest in the primary legislation it is recommended that it uses its parliamentary monitoring to follow the progress of the introduction of any secondary legislation through the regulation powers in the Parliamentary Act. It is also advised that you keep in touch with the Government officials responsible for the legislation, and with the MPs and/or Peers who tabled and/or supported your amendments to the Bill as it progressed through Parliament. This will help to keep your organisation posted on when to expect the introduction of the secondary legislation, and its likely content.

If your organisation becomes aware through its monitoring or through its contacts that a statutory instrument is being introduced and a date has been set for its consideration by either House of Parliament you should brief the Government, MPs and Peers on any issues presented

---

7   UK Parliament, 'Negative Procedure', UK Parliament website, www.parliament. uk.

for the organisation by the secondary legislation. Such legislation is often obscure but can contain significant provisions, and the MPs or Peers on the committees with the task of considering secondary legislation will welcome briefings from your organisation which flag up key issues. Without such briefing, it is likely that the statutory instrument will go through on 'the nod', i.e. with little formality and with hardly any detailed scrutiny. Where the secondary legislation does raise issues of substance for your organisation it is, therefore, important that, to ensure the scrutiny of the statutory instrument is well informed, you brief the Government, the opposition parties, MP and Peers about these issues. In this respect it is recommended that you seek meetings with the Government officials dealing with the legislation, and also with the individual members of the committees dealing with the statutory instrument in the House of Commons and in the House of Lords respectively. Taking these steps can help to improve the chances that the Government, the opposition parties and groupings and individual MPs and Peers will be able to consider the issues you are seeking to raise in their discussions about the secondary legislation. Either House will be able to approve or reject the statutory instrument, but cannot, subject to certain rare exceptions, amend the statutory instrument. If your organisation has concerns about a statutory instrument, getting partner organisations to support your organisation's briefing of the MPs and Peers considering the statutory instrument will increase the likelihood that either House will be willing to oppose the secondary legislation becoming law.

Influencing statutory guidance and directions

Where your organisation has been active on part of a Bill that has received Royal Assent, it will also have opportunities to influence the implementation of the legislation by contributing to the development of any statutory guidance that is to accompany the legislation. Many Acts will include powers for Government to develop and introduce such guidance. This 'statutory guidance' will outline ways in which the Government suggests different parts of the legislation can be implemented, including how different public bodies, agencies and persons should fulfil their duties and responsibilities under the legislation. Some legislation will place a duty on the Government to consult various bodies and persons about the development of the statutory guidance. If this duty relates to statutory guidance in which your organisation will have an interest you should ensure your parliamentary monitoring includes tracking the publication of the draft statutory guidance.

When the statutory guidance has been published, you should respond to the Government's consultation to try to help shape and influence the statutory guidance. Sometimes the Government will develop draft statutory guidance, which will be subsequently put out to consultation, through working groups, including various stakeholders with an interest in, or which are likely to be affected by, the guidance. In such cases, if the minister did not give a commitment during the passage of the legislation to involve your organisation in the working group, you should contact the minister to try to secure a place on the working group, citing your organisation's experience and expertise in the area under consideration. Helping to progress the statutory guidance could potentially provide your organisation with significant opportunities to influence the implementation of the legislation. It is, therefore, important that your organisation engages with the Government in the development of such guidance by contributing to the work of any working group established by the Government to develop the guidance, or responds to any consultation launched by the Government relating to the statutory guidance.

Another area in which there might be opportunities for your organisation to influence the implementation of an Act is in the provision of Directions. Some legislation will give the Government the power to introduce Directions, i.e. instructions to public bodies which operate outside the Government's direct control. These give various bodies and agencies, such as local authorities, instructions on how to comply with the legislation, and to fulfil and implement their duties and responsibilities under the legislation. Such legislation will sometimes place a requirement on the Government to consult various bodies, agencies and organisations about the Directions prior to their introduction. Where the Government does consult on Directions, and the Directions relate to an area of policy or practice which will impact upon your organisation and its work, you should ensure you respond to the Government's consultation. This will provide your organisation with an opportunity to influence the Directions which will be issued to various bodies, agencies and organisations to determine how they meet and exercise their duties and responsibilities under the legislation. This could impact upon your organisation, so it is important that you try and influence the framing of these Directions as much as possible.

Summary of key points

The key points from this chapter can be summarised as follows:

- Second Reading debates can offer important opportunities to raise substantial issues in response to Government legislation, including flagging up potential areas for amendments.
- You should seek meetings with the Government, with the opposition parties' spokespersons, and with individual MPs and Peers to discuss the main issues raised by legislation.
- Building up a cross-party alliance, as well as a cross-organisational alliance, in support of amendments lodged on your behalf offers the best chances of securing concessions on a Bill.
- Where a Bill raises major policy issues, you should engage with the national and local media to raise awareness of these issues, and to maximise support for your amendments from the Government, the opposition parties, as well as from individual MPs and Peers.

13

Private Members' Bills

Parliament prioritises legislation introduced by the Government of the day. There are, however, some opportunities for MPs and Peers to introduce Private Members' Bills. These are a type of Public Bill, which can be introduced by backbench MPs and Peers (who do not hold ministerial responsibilities). As with Public Bills introduced by the Government, Private Members' Bills seek to facilitate policy and legislative changes through law reform. Over the years there have been a number of high profile Private Members' Bills which have made significant changes to the law. These include the Murder (Abolition of the Death Penalty) Act 1965 which abolished capital punishment, and the Abortion Act 1967 legalising abortion. Recent examples include the Forced Marriage (Civil Protection) Act 2007, and the Autism Act 2009.

Due to the lack of time available, the success of Private Members' Bills introduced by MPs or Peers will usually depend upon the level of support they secure from the Government, and on the level of cross-party support they attract. As a result, very few Private Members' Bills become law. This, however, should not deter organisations from pursuing this option with sympathetic MPs and Peers. Private Members' Bills can often, after all, offer organisations major opportunities to raise the profile of key policy issues. They can also provide organisations with the means to undertake high profile, national campaigns which seek to change the law in significant areas of public policy. There are, therefore, potentially substantial benefits in progressing Private Members' Bills, even where a specific bill may have limited, if any, chance of success.

Private Members' Bills in the House of Commons

House of Commons' Standing Orders confirm that Private Members' Bills will take precedence over Government business on 13 Fridays in each session.[1] Private Members' Bills are introduced in the House in the following ways:

- through the 'ballot' for Private Members' Bills; or
- through the 'Ten Minute Rule'; or
- through Presentation.

Further information about Private Members' Bills can be found on Parliament's website.

The ballot for Private Members' Bills route offers MPs the best opportunity for their Bill to become law. Ballot Bills are given priority in the limited debating time available. The ballot of Members' names is held on the second sitting Thursday of the parliamentary session. Twenty names are picked out, and the MPs successful in the ballot are then entitled to put their bills down for a Second Reading on one of the Fridays allocated for Private Members' Bills. Once the ballot has been completed, other MPs can introduce Private Members' Bills by giving appropriate notice on a sitting day.[2]

Under the 'Ten Minute Rule' MPs have an opportunity to speak for no more than ten minutes in support of their proposal to introduce a Private Member's Bill on a specific policy issue or area of the law that they believe requires reform. Other MPs will be entitled to give speeches against the principle that the Bill should be presented. The House will then decide, sometimes on a Division, whether or not the MP should be allowed to present the Bill. MPs can use the 'Ten Minute Rule' to raise awareness of particular issues, and to gauge if their proposal for a Private Member's Bill is likely to secure sufficient support.

MPs can also introduce Private Members' Bills by presentation under Standing Order No. 57. An MP introducing a Private Member's Bill through presentation simply announces the title of the Bill, but

---

1   UK Parliament, Standing Orders of the House of Commons – Public Business 2017, (April 2017), UK Parliament website, www.parliament.uk.
2   UK Parliament, House of Commons Background Paper, 'Public Bills in Parliament', (17 December 2012), UK Parliament website, www.parliament.uk.

does not need to speak in support of the proposed Bill. These Bills do not often become law.

Private Members' Bills introduced through the ballot, the Ten Minute Rule or presentation are all subject to the same legislative process as Government Bills. They will all receive a formal First Reading. If the Bill is permitted to progress it will receive a Second Reading, and then it will be sent to a Public Bill Committee. A Bill reported from the Public Bill Committee will be considered at Report, followed by Third Reading. If the Bill completes all of these legislative stages in the House of Commons, it is then considered in the House of Lords, and vice versa, if the Bill was first introduced in the Lords. Private Members' Bills which successfully complete all of their legislative stages in both Houses will then receive Royal Assent, and become law.

Private Members' Bills in the House of Lords

There is no equivalent of the House of Commons' ballot for Private Members' Bills in the House of Lords, and any Peer can introduce a Private Member's Bill.[3] Private Members' Bills introduced in the House of Lords must generally follow the same legislative procedure as those in the House of Commons, and with the same qualification that the level of support secured by the Bill will determine how far the Bill will reach in the legislative process in the Lords, and if the legislation will progress to the House of Commons. If a Private Member's Bill successfully completes all of its stages in the House of Lords and, if it secures the support of a sponsoring MP, it will then be introduced in the House of Commons. It is important to note, however, that, although Lords' Private Members' Bills will generally be treated like any other Private Member's Bill in the House of Commons, those Private Members' Bills introduced in the House of Commons will take precedence over those introduced in the House of Lords. This will increase the odds against a Peer's Private Member's Bill being allocated enough time for scrutiny in the House of Commons.

---

3   UK Parliament, House of Commons Background Paper, 'Public Bills in Parliament', (17 December 2012), UK Parliament website, www.parliament.uk.

Advantages of a Private Member's Bill

It is recognised that there are many challenges for an MP or Peer to steer a Private Member's Bill through all stages of the legislative process, and to become law. Indeed, securing enough time on the parliamentary timetable in both Houses often proves an insurmountable hurdle for many of these Bills, regardless of how meritorious the issues raised in the Private Member's Bill. Steep as these challenges are, the advantages of Private Members' Bills far outweigh the disadvantages. A Private Member's Bill can provide your organisation with an opportunity to, for example, fix a problem for people including those on whose behalf your organisation works, or for the sector or industry in which your organisation operates. It can also raise awareness of specific policy issues, and initiate high profile public debates on these issues. In this respect, the Bill could offer your organisation the parliamentary focus for a national campaign on a key area of public policy. Such campaigns should be linked, and geared, to each stage of the legislative process to ensure that your organisation raises awareness within the Government, within the opposition parties, with individual MPs and Peers and with the public, of the issues being addressed in the Private Member's Bill. This will support your organisation to maximise the effectiveness of its engagement with the Government, with the opposition parties and with individual MPs and Peers on the issues raised in the proposed legislation.

Apart from strengthening your organisation's external engagement with key policy makers on vital issues, launching a national campaign with a focus on a Private Member's Bill can offer other advantages. Campaigning for a Private Member's Bill can assist some organisations to strengthen their public profile and association with certain issues and policy areas. Significantly, for organisations which rely on fundraising, the focus provided by a campaign around a Private Member's Bill will present potential donors with a clear picture of what the organisation does, its aims and objectives and which groups or individuals benefit from its work. Similarly, where the Bill is being progressed on behalf of a membership organisation such as a trade union, it will provide the organisation with an opportunity to demonstrate how the legislation will benefit the members, and the action being taken to improve outcomes for the members.

Key factors in progressing a Bill

You need to remember that the likelihood of sufficient time being available for most Private Members' Bills to complete all of their stages in both Houses is generally slim. Against this background, most Private Members' Bills will only become law if they secure backing from the Government, and if they obtain sufficient levels of cross-party support. These factors will be important considerations for organisations seeking to persuade an MP or Peer to introduce a Private Member's Bill on their behalf. One of the key factors for any organisation wishing to progress a Private Member's Bill will, therefore, be to choose the right issue. Against this background, your organisation should focus on an issue and policy area which has the potential to gain support from the Government, or at least not to incur the Government's active opposition. The issue must also be one that will gain cross-party support, ideally in both the House of Commons and in the House of Lords.

Having identified an issue which satisfies these criteria, your organisation must then decide whether or not to seek the introduction of the Bill in either the House of Commons or in the House of Lords. It must also decide which MP or Peer it will approach to sponsor the Bill. Some organisations will be able to draw upon their existing close ties with individual MPs and Peers, and it may be that they have already received offers of support from individual MPs and Peers willing to sponsor a Private Member's Bill. For those organisations which are unable to rely on such ties, however, and are having to approach MPs and/or Peers from 'scratch', there are a number of issues you should consider.

A good starting point would be to approach your local MP, which could be the MP in whose constituency your organisation is based. Alternatively, you could approach any MP or Peer you have previously been in touch with, possibly through, for example, attending the annual conferences of the political parties, and who has expressed an interest in your work. Another option is to undertake research and to identify those MPs and Peers with an interest in the public policy issues on which the proposed Private Member's Bill will focus. Important sources in this respect would be *Hansard* for relevant debates and questions in which they have intervened, as well as membership of relevant APPGs and checking to see which MPs and Peers have supported organisations with similar interests to your own. Parliament's website also includes biographical details of MPs and Peers, including the areas of their public policy and legislative interests, and this can be another useful source of information for potential sponsors for a Private Member's Bill.

Once your organisation has agreed on the policy issues and areas on which the Private Member's Bill will concentrate, and identified a supportive MP or Peer to take it forward, you need to also consider the logistics of drafting the Bill. Options include drafting the Bill yourself, or instructing counsel, or seeking support from the Public Bill Office in the House of Commons or in the House of Lords as appropriate, or even approaching the Government to see if they have any draft legislation which could be used (known as 'Hand Out Bills'). In the House of Commons the MP must publish the full text of the Bill before its Second Reading. Failure to do so will result in the Bill being removed from the Order of Business. By contrast, Private Members' Bills cannot be presented in the House of Lords until they have been published.[4]

Maximising support

This guide has outlined above the challenges for organisations seeking to progress Private Members' Bills with a sponsoring MP or Peer, as well as the advantages which this type of legislation can offer. The lack of parliamentary time available highlights the need for organisations, wishing to progress a Private Member's Bill, to work with the sponsoring MP or Peer to build up a broad alliance both outside and within Parliament in support of the proposed Bill. It is recommended that the sponsoring MP or Peer hosts a meeting with a range of stakeholders with an interest in taking forward the Bill. Apart from increasing support for the legislation, such meetings can also help to consolidate and clarify thinking around the policy issues to be progressed, and on the overall strategy for taking these issues forward.

With regard to maximising external support for a Private Member's Bill, social media can play an important role in this area. It can help to raise awareness of the policy issues your organisation is seeking to progress through the proposed legislation, and also to broaden

---

4   UK Parliament, House of Commons Background Paper, 'Public Bills in Parliament', (17 December 2012), UK Parliament website, www.parliament.uk.

the alliance in support of the legislation by obtaining the backing of other organisations and members of the public. Taking time to build up this external alliance will help to underline to the Government, to the opposition parties and to individual MPs and Peers that the sponsoring MP or Peer will be able to draw upon significant levels of external support. These factors can help to generate backing for the proposed Private Member's Bill within Parliament which, in turn, could strengthen the prospects of the legislation becoming law.

The strength of the alliance of political support for the Private Member's Bill which the sponsoring MP or Peer can rely on within Parliament will be critical to its success. Once your organisation has secured a sponsoring MP or Peer willing to lodge the Private Member's Bill you should seek an early meeting with the relevant Government minister and their advisers. The purpose of this meeting would be to discuss the policy issues that the proposed Bill will focus on, and to determine the Government's attitude to the legislation. Gaining the support of the Government at this stage will significantly increase the chances that the legislation will become law, while confirmation that the Government will oppose the legislation would highlight the scale of the challenge facing the sponsoring MP or Peer and their supporters.

Apart from meeting the minister and their officials, action should also be taken to secure early meetings with the relevant spokespersons of all of the opposition parties. These meetings should be used to discuss the main issues presented by the legislation, and to address any concerns these parties may have about the proposed legislation. Where concerns are raised you need to work with the sponsoring MP or Peer to determine if these concerns can be overcome in order to secure the support of the political party in question. Meetings should also be arranged to brief MPs and Peers about the Private Member's Bill, and about the issues it raises. A cross-party approach should be taken to these briefings to increase support amongst individual MPs and Peers. In the House of Lords your organisation should remember to ensure that it briefs Crossbench Peers and Bishops, as well as the main parties represented in the House of Lords, to ensure that the cross-party alliance within Parliament in support of the Bill is as wide as possible.

Developing a media strategy

If your organisation is seeking to work with an MP or Peer to progress a Private Member's Bill, it is important that careful consideration should be given to developing a media strategy to support the legislation. This will help to promote awareness of the Bill, and of the issues it is seeking to address. It will also support the process of building up the alliance of support, both within and outside Parliament, which will be vital if the Private Member's Bill is to successfully complete all of its legislative stages in both Houses of Parliament. As soon as your organisation has secured the support of a sponsoring MP or Peer for the proposed Bill, you should work with the latter to develop a media strategy to raise awareness of the legislation, and to make the most of the influencing opportunities presented at each stage of the legislative process. To maximise the effectiveness of this strategy, it is important that you reach agreement with the sponsoring MP or Peer about who will take the lead in undertaking media activity around the Private Member's Bill.

A media briefing, for example, should be prepared prior to the presentation of the Private Member's Bill. This should be circulated to all journalists with an interest in the policy issues and areas addressed in the Bill. Consideration should also be given to holding a news conference to launch the Bill. In addition, meetings with individual journalists should be organised to update them about the Bill, and to persuade them that the legislation is sufficiently newsworthy to merit their covering it during its different parliamentary stages. If the Bill receives a Second Reading, briefings should be provided to journalists at all of the remaining key stages of the Private Members' Bill. Your organisation's aim should be to create a media spotlight on the Bill, which will help to raise awareness of the legislation, and to maximise support for the Private Member's Bill during its parliamentary passage. Achieving this aim will significantly increase the Bill's chances of completing all of its parliamentary stages, and of becoming law. It should, therefore, not be neglected.

As part of this process, your organisation should use social media to support its campaign for the Private Member's Bill. Social media could be used to launch a consultation on the Bill, or on specific aspects of the legislation. This will enable your organisation to gather important feedback about the Bill, which can then be used to fine tune and strengthen the provisions in the Bill, and its campaign for the Private Member's Bill. The use of social media will also allow your organisation to kick-start an interactive public debate on the issues around the proposed legislation, and to raise awareness of the key issues with Government, with the opposition parties, with MPs, with Peers, with other organisations and with the general public.

You can then use the engagement through social media to encourage members of the public to contact their local MP or Peers to persuade them to give their backing to the Bill. In this respect, engaging with the politicians through social media, and/or encouraging members of the public to fill the minister's post bag and inbox, and those of MPs and Peers, with expressions of support for the proposed legislation, could help to increase support for the legislation both within and outside Parliament. Social media will also ensure that your organisation is able to provide regular updates about progress on the Bill, and on the campaign as a whole. The odds against a Private Member's Bill becoming law are great, but building up a cross-party alliance in support of the Bill, and backing it with a focused media strategy, can significantly reduce those odds in your favour.

Summary of key points

The key points from this chapter can be summarised as follows:

- The success of Private Members' Bills will usually depend upon the level of support they secure from the Government, and on the level of cross-party support they attract.
- Private Members' Bills can offer organisations a means to fix a problem, or to promote opportunities, relevant to their work.
- Private Members' Bills can also provide organisations with an opportunity to raise the profile of key policy issues, and to undertake prominent, national campaigns to change the law in significant areas of public policy.
- Developing a media strategy will help to promote awareness of the Bill, and to build up the alliance of support, both within and outside Parliament, which will be vital if the Private Member's Bill is to become law.

14

Parliamentary Questions

This chapter provides an overview of the procedure for Parliamentary Questions in the House of Commons and in the House of Lords. Outlined below you will find advice on how organisations can use Parliamentary Questions to best effect within their public affairs strategies. Following the advice in this chapter will enable your organisation to maximise the opportunities presented by Parliamentary Questions in both Houses. It will also help your organisation to strengthen the impact of Parliamentary Questions tabled on its behalf by exploring ways of engaging with key policy makers in the Government, and in Parliament, around the questions, and the potential tie-ins with media opportunities.

Question Time in the House of Commons

The formal business in the House of Commons commences on sittings days, after Prayers have been held, with 'Question Time'. This offers backbench MPs opportunities to ask Government ministers oral questions on issues falling within the remit of the Government department for which they are responsible. The ministers for these departments answer questions on a rota basis, which is called the 'Order of Oral Questions'. Question Time takes place in the House of Commons for an hour, Mondays to Thursdays, and Prime Minister's Question Time is held every Wednesday. The procedures in the House of Commons provide that oral questions must be tabled by MPs at least three days prior to Question Time. The questions tabled for Question Time can be viewed in the House of

Commons' Questions Book, which can be accessed on the Parliament's website.[1]

Question Time also includes opportunities for MPs to ask 'Topical Questions' on any issue falling within the Government department for which the minister is responsible. Topical Questions can be asked during the last 15 minutes of the Question Time with ministers where one hour has been allocated for questions, and during the last ten minutes of the Question Time with ministers where a 40 minutes time slot is available for questions.

The procedure followed for Question Time in the House of Commons is that, when the Speaker calls an MP to ask a question, the MP calls out the number of the question. The Government minister then replies to the question, and the MP is entitled to ask a supplementary question. This generates a short 'question and answer' session with the minister in which other MPs can also ask supplementary questions on the subject raised by the initial question.

Prime Minister's Question Time (PMQs)

Prime Minister's Question Time takes place every Wednesday from noon for 30 minutes. The format for PMQs is that an MP will ask the Prime Minister an 'open question' about his or her engagements, and follow up with a supplementary question that can relate to any issue. The MP will use this to raise a specific issue, which can, for example, be a high profile political issue of national importance, or one which concerns matters specifically relevant to their constituency. Once the MP has asked their question, the Leader of the Opposition is entitled to press the Prime Minister on the original question or to follow up with another issue. The procedure followed by the House of Commons is that only the Leader of the Opposition is able to raise further questions.

---

1   This section draws upon information provided by the UK Parliament about 'Question Time' in both Houses, and those seeking more detailed information about the structure and procedure for oral questions in both Houses should refer to the following source: UK Parliament, 'Question Time', UK Parliament's website, www.parliament.uk.

Question Time in the House of Lords

Question Time in the House of Lords, as in the House of Commons, offers an opportunity to raise issues with Government ministers on the public policy areas falling within their remit. Peers are able to ask oral questions, or 'Starred Questions' as they are known in the House of Lords, at the start of business on sitting days on Mondays to Thursdays. One significant difference between Question Time in the two Houses, is that Starred Questions in the House of Lords are addressed to Her Majesty's Government (HMG) rather than to specific Government departments, which is the practice in the House of Commons.

There are four Starred Questions per day, and details of these questions can be found in the House of Lords' Order Paper. Starred Questions can be tabled at any time up to 24 hours in advance. This will depend upon the availability of spaces for Starred Questions on a particular day when the House of Lords is sitting. The exception is the slots reserved for a 'Topical Question' on Tuesdays, Wednesdays and Thursdays. These questions are chosen by ballot, and must be tabled two days in advance. Once Starred Questions have been tabled they will be published in the House of Lords' Business Paper, which can be accessed on the House of Lords section of the Parliament's website.

Approaches to Question Time

Oral questions in the House of Commons and in the House of Lords can make a useful contribution to your organisation's public affairs strategy, and you should consider ways to use oral questions as a key component of its influencing strategy. There are, however, a number of preliminary issues you will need to address in developing your approach to using oral questions to progress the aims of this strategy. These include, for example, deciding which issue you want to raise, and to prioritise. Is your organisation, for example, seeking to raise a major issue of national importance and likely to gain widespread media coverage? Alternatively, is the issue relevant to a specific nation but falls within the competence of the UK Parliament? Or does it relate to developments/events within a certain geographical area or parliamentary constituency?

Consideration should also be given to the strategic importance of the question within, and to, your organisation's public affairs strategy. In this respect, do you wish the question to be lodged to raise the profile of a specific issue and to potentially gain some short- to medium-term, high profile media coverage? Or is it part of a wider, long-term campaign designed to deliver significant policy changes with the question being used to clarify the Government's position on a particular issue?

Your organisation should also identify the outcomes that you are hoping the question will deliver. Will your organisation achieve its objectives if the question raises the profile of an issue with the Government and other key policy makers, and generates some media interest? Or has the question been tabled to secure an announcement from the Government that it will introduce specific policy changes around the issues you are highlighting, possibly in direct response to your organisation's question? Alternatively, is your organisation hoping that the Government will, in response to a question lodged on its behalf, clarify its intentions in a specific policy area?

Once your organisation has addressed these preliminary issues, it should decide whether it wants an MP or Peer to lodge the question. There are a number of factors which your organisation will need to carefully weigh up in deciding which of these options will deliver the most advantageous outcomes. It is worth noting, for example, that oral questions in the House of Commons are generally more likely to attract media coverage. On the other hand it may be that, at least on certain policy issues, the chances of your question securing a positive response from Government ministers is greater in the House of Lords, especially if the sponsoring Peer has a long standing interest in the issue being raised, and the issue is one which can potentially command cross-party support. Other considerations would be the respective levels of interest in the question in both Houses, and on whether your organisation's main support lies with specific MPs or Peers and on their parties or groupings. Timing and the urgency with which you require the issue to be raised would also be major considerations, especially if the question relates to a current development on the political landscape.

When your organisation has addressed these issues, it will then be in a position to approach an MP or a Peer to lodge an oral question on its behalf. Careful thought should be given to whom you approach. Ideally, you should choose someone who has a strong association with your organisation, and who will be able to raise the issues on your behalf with a good knowledge and understanding of the key issues, and of your organisation's aims in seeking to lodge the question. This would be a good opportunity to call on an MP or Peer whom your organisation has engaged with previously, possibly attending one of your events or supporting a fringe event hosted by your organisation at one of the party conferences, and who has indicated a willingness to be supportive of your work. If your organisation is unable to identify an MP or Peer falling into this category, it should approach an MP or Peer who has an interest in the policy issues raised by your question, and who will be an effective advocate in the question and answer session with the Government minister generated by your initial question.

Style and format of questions

MPs and Peers are generally very busy, and your chances of persuading them to table a question on behalf of your organisation will improve if they have an interest in the policy issues raised by your question, and if the question is presented to them in the correct style and format. It is, therefore, important that you get a feel for the style and format of oral questions in both Houses. It has already been noted above that Starred Questions in the House of Lords are addressed to Her Majesty's Government, whereas questions in the House of Commons are addressed to ministers with responsibility for specific departments. To gain further insight into the format of oral questions in both Houses, and the style and format you should follow, it is recommended that you look at the House of Commons' Question Book, and at the House of Lords' Business Paper.[2] These sources will provide guidance on how to draft questions in the style employed in each House.

Significance of supplementary questions

When you approach an MP or Peer to table an oral question on behalf of your organisation it is strongly advised that you provide a briefing paper in support of the question. This should outline the background to the question, the importance of it being asked and the key issues you are seeking to raise. The briefing paper should also include

2   UK Parliament website, www.parliament.uk.

suggested supplementary questions which the MP or Peer can ask after the minister has answered your initial question. The supplementary questions will provide an important opportunity to raise further points around the issues you wish the MP or Peer to raise on your behalf. It will also enable the MP or Peer to concentrate on the specific areas you wish to raise and, if necessary, to put the minister under a bit of pressure on issues which require further clarification. Providing a range of supplementary questions will support the MP or Peer to take a flexible approach by providing different potential options for how to respond to the minister's initial answer.

Maximising the impact of oral Parliamentary Questions

Organisations can maximise the impact of oral questions tabled on their behalf by taking an integrated approach to Question Time in the House of Commons and in the House of Lords. The way to approach the question and answer session with the minister generated by Question Time is to view it as a mini-debate, which will potentially provide your organisation with important opportunities to raise awareness of major issues and to influence policy makers. To make the most of these opportunities you should focus on briefing the MP or Peer who has agreed to table your question, but also focus on briefing the minister, and on briefing the MPs or Peers who are most likely to participate in the question and answer session initiated by your question. To increase the likelihood that the minister will engage effectively in the question and answer session and to provide answers that are useful to your organisation, make sure that you provide the minister with a briefing about the question tabled on your behalf. This should outline the issues you are seeking to raise, and on which you want the minister to specifically respond.

Briefings should also be circulated to those MPs and Peers that are most likely to seek to participate in the question and answer session generated by the initial question. This briefing should include suggested supplementary questions. To ensure that your approach is co-ordinated it is strongly advised that, with high profile questions, you follow up any briefings with phone calls to request meetings with the MPs or Peers as appropriate, and allocate specific supplementary questions to individual MPs or Peers. This will help to ensure that the question and answer session with the minister, generated by your initial question, is effective, lively and meets your organisation's aims and objectives in seeking to have the question lodged.

Personalising the questions for individual MPs or Peers will help to stimulate the mini-debate by encouraging more MPs and Peers to participate. It will also minimise the risks of duplication. There is nothing more likely to turn MPs or Peers off if they have received a briefing with a list of questions, are poised to intervene to ask one of the questions on the list of supplementary questions only to then see someone else intervening immediately before them to ask a question from the same list. Taking an integrated approach will require a bit more effort to ensure that the supplementary questions are personalised for individual MPs and Peers, but it will be worth it if it leads to a series of informed interventions being made which lead the minister to give serious consideration to the issues being raised, and to a subsequent intervention by the Government to address these issues.

Media tie-ins: oral Parliamentary Questions

Another way in which your organisation can strengthen the effectiveness of any oral questions lodged on its behalf in the House of Commons or in the House of Lords is to ensure that the questions are supported by media tie-in activities. When planning how you will approach your strategy around the oral question you should factor in media activity. Not all questions are likely to gain media interest, and assessing the likely media interest in your question should be an important part of developing your public affairs strategy around the question. Where the question is likely to generate media interest you should provide the media with an alert through the Press Association on when the question will be answered by the minister, and on the issues you are seeking to raise. This, and using your existing media contacts, will help to improve the prospects that the question gains media coverage. You should also use social media to publicise the question, and to raise its profile with as wide an audience as possible. Taking a dual approach to publicising your question through TV, radio and newspapers, and through social media will maximise the impact of your question, and improve the chances that the minister will take the action, or make the type of statement, your organisation is seeking in response to your question.

Written Parliamentary Questions in the House of Commons

MPs are entitled to submit questions for written answer in the House of Commons. 'Ordinary Questions' do not have to be answered by a specific date, although MPs can normally expect an answer within seven days of the question being tabled. By contrast, 'Named Day Questions', which are unique to the House of Commons, confirm the date by which the MP expects an answer. In addition, oral questions which are not answered at Question Time are submitted to the relevant departments as Named Day Questions. All written questions tabled in the House of Commons, and in the House of Lords, and the answers they receive, are available on the searchable database of Written Questions and Answers on the Parliament's website. Details of Written Questions in the House of Commons are also published in the House of Commons' Questions Book.[3]

Written Parliamentary Questions in the House of Lords

Peers are also entitled to table written questions in the House of Lords, and can table a maximum of six questions for written answer per day. Answers are usually received within 14 days of the question being tabled. Written questions and the answers received in the House of Lords can, as with written questions and answers in the House of Commons, be found on the 'Written Questions and Answers' section of the Parliament's website. Details of written questions in the House of Lords can also be found on the 'House of Lords: Cumulative list of Unanswered Questions for written answer' on the Parliament's website.

How to use written Parliamentary Questions in your public affairs strategy

The opportunities presented by written questions, and their potential contribution to an organisation's public affairs strategy on a number of

---

3   Further information about written questions in the House of Commons and in the House of Lords can be found on the 'Written Questions and Answers' section of the Parliament's website, www.parliament.uk.

levels, should not be underestimated. Organisations can, for example, use written questions to obtain information from the Government. This information can then be used by your organisation to strengthen the evidence base of its public affairs strategy. Basing a specific public affairs campaign, or 'policy ask', on information provided by the Government in response to a written question offers significant advantages, and could increase your organisation's chances of securing concessions from the Government if your overall arguments are persuasive and your policy aims are realistic.

The information provided by the Government, in its response to written questions, can sometimes also help to clarify the direction of political travel around specific issues. In this respect, organisations often find that they have taken their public affairs strategy so far on a particular issue, but need to 'smoke-out' the Government's policy position before deciding on how to take their strategy forward. Approaching an MP or Peer to table a written question on behalf of your organisation is a good way of providing that clarification. Your organisation can then take a view on the tactics and approach your public affairs strategy should employ going forward to best meet your organisation's policy aims and objectives, and to secure concessions from the Government.

Media tie-ins: written Parliamentary Questions

Written questions often work particularly well for organisations when combined with a media strategy. Organisations should, therefore, scope out the potential media story and strategy they will progress if the information secured through a written question (or through a Freedom of Information request) proves significant to a specific policy campaign or 'policy ask' they are pursuing. Issuing a news release highlighting the main aspects of the answer provided by the Government can help your organisation to generate media interest in the issues you are seeking to raise.

Working in advance with a preferred media partner will often increase the chances that the story will attract good levels of media attention. Social media should also be used to strengthen the impact of the news story, and to increase awareness in Parliament and amongst the general public about the issues you are seeking to raise. It is strongly recommended that, if your organisation does undertake media activity on the back of the written answer, you work closely with the sponsoring MP or Peer. There might, for example, be tactical or strategic reasons for not seeking publicity on a specific occasion where a question has been tabled, and the appropriateness or not of seeking publicity is one of the discussions which you should have with the MP or Peer. Such considerations will be particularly relevant if there is a risk that the publicity could have an adverse effect on the Government's likely answer to the question, and on future relations between the Government and your organisation.

Apart from ensuring that you maintain good relations with the MP or Peer, which you can then develop and take forward, this approach offers a number of other major advantages. Where it is agreed that securing publicity would be advantageous working closely with the sponsoring MP or Peer will, for example, help to increase the level of coverage for the news story, and social media interest, around the written answer. Moreover, it will ensure that the news headlines and articles are more likely to be translated into the political action that will be necessary to deliver positive outcomes for your organisation's campaign, rather than just short-life headlines.

Summary of key points

The key points from this chapter can be summarised as follows:

- The opportunities around Parliamentary Questions in both Houses of Parliament should be a key component of organisations' influencing strategies.
- Organisations should consider approaching an MP or Peer with a long association with the organisation, or interest in a particular topic, to ask a question relating to this topic.
- Organisations can maximise the impact of oral questions by approaching the question and answer session with the minister as a 'mini-debate', which will potentially provide their organisation with important opportunities to raise awareness of key issues, and to influence policy makers.
- The opportunities to use written questions to deliver tangible outcomes will be significantly increased if combined with an effective media strategy.

15

Parliamentary Debates

Parliamentary debates in the House of Commons

Debates often represent the main daily business in the House of Commons. These debates are frequently high profile, set-piece debates in which the Government and the opposition parties will debate the key issues and developments of the day. The purpose of debates in the House of Commons includes calling attention to issues of national importance requiring the attention of Parliament, and raising awareness of such issues. Other purposes include holding the Government to account in the case of debates initiated by the opposition parties, and for the political parties to submit each other's policies and policy positions to parliamentary scrutiny. Debates in the Chamber are chaired by the Speaker, and the debate usually concludes with a Division on whether or not the question for the debate (the Motion) is agreed.

These debates can, for example, focus on legislation such as the Second Reading debates on a Bill, or on a topic chosen by the Government, or by the Official Opposition or by one of the other opposition parties. Examples include the 2016 Second Reading of the Scotland legislation devolving further powers to the Scottish Parliament,[1] the Government's debate on ISIL in Syria,[2] and Opposition emergency debates on the UK Steel Industry[3] and on the refugee crises

---

1 *Hansard*, House of Commons Debates, 8 June 2015, Col.916, UK Parliament website, www.parliament.uk.
2 *Hansard*, House of Commons Debates, 2 December 2015, Col.323, UK Parliament website, www.parliament.uk.
3 *Hansard*, House of Commons Debates, 12 April 2016, Col.188, UK Parliament website, www.parliament.uk.

in Europe.[4] Other categories of debate include those held on committee reports such as the House of Commons' 2012 debate on the Culture, Media and Sport Select Committee's report on News International and phone-hacking,[5] and debates selected by the House of Commons' Backbench Business Committee such as the debate on Diversity in the BBC.[6] Another category of debate are the debates which take place on the emergency recall of Parliament such as the 2013 debate on Syria and the use of chemical weapons,[7] and the 2014 debate on developments in Iraq.[8]

One of the most frequent types of debate is the adjournment debate. Examples include the adjournment debates on care for childhood cancers,[9] on investigations of deaths in mental health settings[10] and on the effects of mining in Goa by UK-listed companies.[11] An adjournment debate enables the House of Commons to consider the policy issues of the day without requiring a Division at the end of the debate. MPs can use adjournment debates for a number of purposes. These include raising a general policy issue focusing on a specific aspect of Government policy in which they have an interest, or to highlight a constituency matter relevant to their constituency and to their constituents. The structure followed in these debates is that the sponsoring MP will speak in favour of the Motion, other MPs can then contribute to the debate, and the minister will provide a response at the end of the debate. Half-hour adjournment debates take place in the Chamber at the end of each sitting day. Adjournment debates, and other short debates, are also held in Westminster Hall. On Tuesdays and

---

4   *Hansard*, House of Commons Debates, 8 September 2015, Col.245, UK Parliament website, www.parliament.uk.

5   *Hansard*, House of Commons Debates, 22 May 2012, Col.990, UK Parliament website, www.parliament.uk.

6   *Hansard*, House of Commons Debates, 14 April 2016, Col.566, UK Parliament website, www.parliament.uk.

7   *Hansard*, House of Commons Debates, 29 August 2013, Col.1425, UK Parliament website,www.parliament.uk.

8   *Hansard*, House of Commons Debates, 26 September 2014, Col.1255, UK Parliament website, www.parliament.uk.

9   *Hansard*, House of Commons Debates, 25 February 2015, Col.434, UK Parliament website, www.parliament.uk.

10   *Hansard*, House of Commons Debates, 27 February 2015, Col.649, UK Parliament website, www.parliament.uk.

11   *Hansard*, House of Commons Debates, 24 February 2015, Col.593, UK Parliament website, www.parliament.uk.

Wednesdays two one-and-a-half-hour debates are held in Westminster Hall, along with three half-hour debates. The focus of the one-and-a-half-hour debates tends to be on more general topics and policy areas. The Speaker chooses the topic for those adjournment debates held on a Thursday, with the topics of the adjournment debates for the other sitting days being decided by ballot.[12] Transcripts of all adjournment debates held in the Chamber of the House of Commons, and in Westminster Hall, are available in *Hansard*, and on Parliament's website.[13]

Parliamentary debates in the House of Lords

In the House of Lords there are general debates, short debates and debates on committee reports. Each political party in the House of Lords, as well as the group of Crossbench Peers, are entitled to table Motions for debate, and backbench Peers can also enter a ballot to hold a general debate on a topic of their choice. These general debates usually take place on a Thursday, and consist of either one long debate or two shorter debates. General debates look at key policy issues including aspects of UK Government policy, such as the debates on the availability and quality of apprenticeships,[14] and on the Chilcot Inquiry.[15] Debates in the House of Lords, as with debates in the House of Commons, can also focus on legislation through Second Reading or Third Reading debates on Parliamentary Bills. Examples include the Second Reading debates on the Consumer Rights legislation,[16] on the Deregulation legislation[17] and on the Modern Slavery legislation.[18]

Short debates lasting an hour, or an hour and a half, also take place

---

12 UK Parliament, 'Adjournment debates', UK Parliament website, www.parliament. uk.

13 UK Parliament website, www.parliament.uk.

14 *Hansard*, House of Lords Debates, 15 October 2015, Col.313, UK Parliament website, www.parliament.uk.

15 *Hansard*, House of Lords Debates, 12 July 2016, Col.129, UK Parliament website, www.parliament.uk.

16 *Hansard*, House of Lords Debates, 1 July 2014, Col.1645, UK Parliament website, www.parliament.uk.

17 *Hansard*, House of Lords Debates, 7 July 2014, Col.13, UK Parliament website, www.parliament.uk.

18 *Hansard*, House of Lords Debates, 17 November 2014, Col.238, UK Parliament website, www.parliament.uk.

in the House of Lords at the end of business, or during the dinner breaks. In addition, Peers can enter a ballot for the short debate (lasting one hour) held on Thursdays. The subject matter for these debates is wide ranging, and examples include the debate on the likely impact of Britain's vote to leave the European Union on farming,[19] on mental health,[20] on Government support for British exports[21] and on developments in the Ukraine.[22] Debates in the House of Lords also consider Motions relating to committee reports such as the report of the Trade Union Political Funds and Political Party Funding Committee,[23] and emergency Motions where Parliament has been recalled.[24] The Lord Speaker chairs debates in the House of Lords, but does not intervene, and the conduct of debates is self-regulating. Transcripts of all debates in the House of Lords can be found in *Hansard*, and on the Parliament's website.

Opportunities presented by debates

Parliamentary debates in both Houses of Parliament can present organisations with major influencing opportunities. It is, therefore, essential that you follow the advice in Chapter 4, and ensure that you closely monitor business in the House of Commons and the House of Lords to identify debates relevant to your organisation. Both responding to, and initiating, debates will offer your organisation the chance to influence key policy makers in both Houses. Furthermore, debates can provide organisations with strategic opportunities to raise the profile of major issues on which they are campaigning, and/or on which they are seeking to influence the Government and other leading policy makers. Another factor to bear in mind is that debates can

19 *Hansard*, House of Lords Debates, 21 July 2016, Col.783, UK Parliament website, www.parliament.uk.
20 *Hansard*, House of Lords Debates, 26 May 2016, Col.773, UK Parliament website, www.parliament.uk.
21 *Hansard*, House of Lords Debates, 29 January 2015, Col.759, UK Parliament website, www.parliament.uk.
22 *Hansard*, House of Lords Debates, 18 March 2014, Col.100, UK Parliament website, www.parliament.uk.
23 *Hansard*, House of Lords Debates, 9 March 2016, Col.769, UK Parliament website, www.parliament.uk.
24 UK Parliament, 'Checking and challenging Government', UK Parliament website, www.parliament.uk.

help organisations to strengthen contacts with the Government, with the Official Opposition party and other opposition parties, and with individual MPs and Peers. Developing and strengthening such contacts will be critical to the long term success of many organisations' public affairs strategies.

Moreover, responding to debates in a timely and effective manner will enable organisations to build support for their position on important issues. Intervening in a debate could, for example, reinforce internal support for an organisation's policy position on a particular issue or area from staff and/or trustees, or from members or from shareholders. It can also assist the organisation to generate support from other organisations and from the general public, which will be critical if it is seeking to develop a national campaign, or to secure wider support for its policy position, as part of its public affairs strategy. Social media can play a major role in this area, by engaging with supporters, and with potential supporters, around the issues raised by the debate, and by focusing on the organisation's intervention in the debate. Another use of social media in this area would be to keep your organisation's supporters updated on the key points highlighted in the debate, and on how the organisation intends to take forward the issues it raised during the debate. This will be essential if your organisation is seeking to progress a national campaign, and the debate was simply one stage in the campaign, which will then need to be further developed and progressed following the debate.

Responding to debates

Where your organisation has identified a debate relevant to its interests, it must consider if it is a debate in which it is essential to intervene. Alternatively, is it a debate where you could note the content of the debate and pick up any key issues with the Government, the opposition parties and individual MPs and Peers after the debate, or is it a debate in which your organisation can afford to sit out? This is a strategic decision that your organisation will need to make, and it is a decision which you would be well advised to thoroughly risk assess before taking. After all, there are some debates where it might not be absolutely vital to intervene and, to do so, could take up valuable staff time and resources. An example would be where an MP or Peer has tabled an adjournment Motion on behalf of a specific organisation, and the issues raised are closely identified with that organisation and, therefore, limit the opportunities for other organisations to mount a major influencing operation in response to the debate. By contrast, there are some debates which your organisation simply cannot afford to ignore, regardless of other conflicting priorities and capacity issues. These are the debates which focus on issues that are fundamental to your organisation, its aims and objectives and its work. For many organisations failing to engage in this type of debate could potentially present significant reputational risks, both internally and externally.

If your organisation identifies a debate which it believes will provide important opportunities to engage with the Government, with the opposition parties and with other policy makers on key issues, and to raise awareness of these issues, careful thought should then be given to how best to progress your influencing strategy effectively. It is important that your organisation should, as much as possible, prepare briefing material that is tailored for specific debates. Admittedly, with some debates it will be possible to use generic, 'off the shelf' briefings, and to adapt these as appropriate for the debate, but this type of approach will not work for all debates. In this context, the type of briefing your organisation circulates to leading policy makers for a particular debate will depend upon the subject matter of the debate. Other factors will also play a part, including the amount of notice your organisation receives about the debate, and its capacity to draft and circulate a concise, persuasive briefing in the time available.

To make your organisation's briefing stand out from those of other organisations seeking to brief ministers and MPs or Peers for the debate, it is recommended that you ensure any briefing material demonstrates that the policy issues it raises are based on a sound evidence base, and on the best practice of your organisation. Moreover, if your organisation delivers services it will strengthen the impact of your organisation's briefing if you can refer to any awards won by your services, or to any external evaluations of your services. Referring to Government endorsements, and/or to the endorsements of other key agencies, of your organisation, its work, or of its policy positions or campaigns, or services, will also reinforce the messages and themes presented in your briefing. These references will often make briefings stand out, and will make a positive impression on policy makers. In this context, you should always remember that the Government, the relevant Opposition spokespersons and those of the other opposition parties, and individual MPs and Peers will often receive dozens if not hundreds of briefing papers for debates (depending upon the subject matter of the debate). It is, therefore, vital that your briefing stands out for the right reasons, and makes a sufficiently positive impression on policy makers to persuade them to refer to your briefing during the debate. Ideally, you also want the impression made by your organisation to have been so favourable that the policy maker will be eager to pick up with your organisation after the debate, and to discuss ways in which the issues highlighted in your briefing can be taken forward if they are not dealt with satisfactorily by the minister in the debate.

Your organisation will also need to take a view on which policy makers it wishes to brief for the debate. An important consideration in that process will be what successful engagement will look like for your organisation? What outcomes are you hoping to achieve with your influencing work around the debate? Is your organisation looking, for example, for the Government, in response to your public affairs activities, to make a policy announcement that will benefit your organisation, or the sector in which it operates or to benefit those on whose behalf your organisation works? Alternatively, is your organisation looking for the Opposition and/or other opposition parties to take up a policy position recommended by your organisation? Or is your organisation simply looking to raise the profile of key issues, and to see the minister and as many MPs or Peers as possible refer to these issues and to your organisation in the debate? These are all potentially positive and achievable outcomes for your organisation as a result of undertaking public affairs activities for a specific debate, which are strategic and well thought-out.

To improve your organisation's chances of achieving any of the above outcomes, it is recommended that you approach the relevant ministers[25] and their civil servants to determine if the Government is sympathetic to all or some or any of the issues you are raising. The Government may wish to follow up with a meeting with certain organisations prior to the debate and in response to such contact, but most organisations will have to approach a debate on the basis that

25 For Second Reading debates on Parliamentary Bills, and for general debates, one minister is likely to open the debate, with another closing or 'winding-up' the debate.

the minister will be unable or unwilling to meet them, but may be open to considering at least some of the issues raised in their briefing for the debate.

For many organisations it will be essential to take a cross-party approach to their public affairs strategy. Where this is a critical factor for your organisation, you should also try to engage with the relevant spokespersons of the Opposition, and of the other opposition parties, and to seek their support for the issues you are looking to highlight in particular debates. Indeed, if the Government is unsympathetic to the issues you are attempting to raise in the debate, these parties are likely to be your organisation's first port of call in terms of seeking support for the policy positions in your briefing. In some cases organisations will achieve their outcomes by simply ensuring they are briefing the minister and the relevant spokespersons of the opposition parties or groupings. With adjournment debates in the House of Commons, or with short debates in the House of Lords sponsored by individual Peers, you should approach the sponsoring MP or Peer, as appropriate, and provide them with a copy of your organisation's briefing paper.

To maximise your organisation's impact in a debate, whether it is a general debate or an adjournment debate, it is recommended that you take a targeted approach to briefing MPs or Peers. In this respect, you should give consideration to contacting the local MP or MPs in constituencies in which your organisation is based, to seek a meeting to discuss the issues you wish to raise in the debate or to provide them with a personalised briefing. Alternatively, you could contact MPs or Peers with a firm interest in the issues you want to highlight in the debate, or who are known to be strong supporters of your organisation and its work. Indeed, with some of the high profile, set-piece debates, where the focus will often be on political point scoring rather than on raising awareness of the issues, some organisations may find it is more productive to target individual MPs or Peers to raise issues on their behalf in the debate. Another approach would be to work in alliance with other organisations to collectively brief the minister, the Opposition and the other opposition parties, MPs or Peers. This type of approach would be particularly advantageous for the high profile, set-piece debates where the parties will normally be approaching the debate on strict party lines. With these debates little time will be available for interventions, and the opportunities, therefore, for individual organisations to influence the debate could be limited.

Initiating debates

The above section addresses situations in which organisations are responding to debates in the House of Commons and in the House of Lords, and are seeking to take advantage of the influencing opportunities these debates potentially offer. The influencing opportunities presented by debates your organisation has initiated will, however, generally be far greater than those debates to which you are simply responding. After all, with the latter your organisation may be competing with various other organisations seeking to influence policy makers participating in the debate, and in these circumstances it might not always be possible to ensure you are able to raise key issues. You also have to remember that if it is a high profile, set-piece debate this will sometimes place further limitations on the opportunities available to influence the minister leading for the Government in the debate and the relevant spokespersons for the opposition parties.

Against this background, securing a general debate in the House of Commons or in the House of Lords would be a major achievement for many organisations. To attain this position you would need to persuade the Government or the Official Opposition or one of the other opposition parties or parliamentary groupings of the merits of the issues you are raising, and of the case for using scarce parliamentary debating time to focus on these issues. The benefits of doing so, however, make this a challenge which is worth facing. Securing a debate would, for example, raise the profile of the issues you are seeking to raise, and of your organisation. It would also potentially provide significant media opportunities, including increasing support through social media for your organisation and the issues it is raising in the debate.

The first step would be to approach the Government, the Official Opposition party and the other opposition parties to determine what support, if any, there is for the issues you are seeking to raise. You should build upon any support expressed from these quarters, in response to your organisation's approaches, to make the case for the issues being debated in Parliament. If the Government agrees to the debate you should work with the minister to influence the issues and areas to be covered in the Motion for the debate, and to ensure that the Government has all of the information it needs for the debate. This would include robust evidence in support of the issues, and any examples of best practice that are relevant. The Government will also be able to advise your organisation of which, if any, of their backbench MPs or Peers they would like you to brief for the debate, and on what issues. In this context, you should follow up by circulating a general briefing to the Opposition and to the other opposition parties, as well as to individual MPs or Peers. Where the Government is unsympathetic to a general debate, but the Opposition or one of the other opposition parties has indicated their interest, you should work with the relevant spokespersons to ensure they have enough information for the debate. The latter will be able to advise on those backbench MPs or Peers whom are likely to be sympathetic to the issues you are raising, and whom you should brief for the debate.

If the Government or the Opposition or one of the other opposition parties is unwilling to use one of their slots for a general debate to raise issues on your organisation's behalf, another option would be to seek an adjournment debate in the House of Commons, or a short debate in the House of Lords. These debates also offer significant opportunities to raise issues, and to promote your organisation's engagement with the Government, with the Opposition and other parties, and with MPs or Peers. With adjournment debates or short debates respectively you should approach a sympathetic MP or Peer as appropriate, and persuade them to table a Motion for debate. Once tabled, you should work with the MP or Peer to bring them up to speed on the issues you wish to see debated. Another option would be to approach a backbench MP in the House of Commons with a proposal for a debate on a specific issue or policy area, and to persuade them to approach the Backbench Committee with a request for a debate. If accepted, this would be one of the Backbench Committee's slots for a debate.

To maximise the impact of a debate on a Motion, tabled on behalf of your organisation, you should provide the relevant minister with a briefing, including confirmation of the action you are seeking the Government to take in response to the debate. Your organisation should also consider which MPs or Peers to brief for the debate. Ideally, you should arrange a briefing meeting for MPs or Peers, or meetings with individual MPs or Peers, to update them on the key issues for the debate.

Initiating a debate will potentially provide your organisation with more control over the subject matter for the debate, and over the ways in which the debate will be treated by Parliament. In this respect, once the Motion has been tabled, your organisation can try to make the debate as well informed as possible by working with the sponsoring MP or Peer on the issues you wish raised, and by ensuring that the relevant minister has early notice of these issues. This will help to improve the chances that the Government's response to the debate is detailed and well informed. Steps should also be taken to brief the Opposition and the other opposition parties to ensure that they understand the key issues. Securing a debate will also offer significant media, including social media, opportunities and your organisation will be in a unique position to work with the Government, or the opposition parties or the sponsoring MP or Peer, as appropriate, to maximise these opportunities.

Follow-up strategies

Once the debate has taken place, it is important that your organisation takes steps to follow up on the debate, and to exploit any opportunities it has presented. This should be a key factor in your organisation's public affairs strategy, regardless of whether or not the debate was one stage in, or a strategic activity within, a specific campaign your organisation is running. The follow-up strategy will support your organisation to identify, and to build upon, the tangible outcomes that its intervention in the debate has secured. You will be able to get a sense of the opportunities which can be followed up and exploited following the debate by early engagement with the Government, or with the opposition party which sponsored the debate or with the sponsoring MP or Peer as appropriate.

A detailed analysis of the report in *Hansard* should also be undertaken. You should take time to assess any key policy statements in the debate, as well as expressions of support for your organisation, and consider how your organisation can best capitalise on these developments. *Hansard* will confirm what commitments, if any, the Government has given, and the type of action it will take, in response to the debate. In addition, it will give your organisation a sense of whether or not the Opposition and/or the other opposition parties are willing to take the issues you have raised forward and, if so, an indication of how they will do so. Analysing *Hansard* will also confirm which MPs or Peers participated in the debate. This will be important intelligence in enabling your organisation to identify new supporters, and potential supporters, for your organisation and for the issues it has raised during the debate. These MPs or Peers can potentially offer significant support to your organisation and its interests going forward, and you should proactively cultivate these contacts following the debate.

One of the first steps your organisation should take after the debate is to formally write to the minister or opposition parties' spokesperson, or MP or Peer who has tabled the Motion for debate on behalf of your organisation, or to contact them through social media, and to thank them for their support. Furthermore, if the minister has made an announcement during the debate which will impact upon your organisation and its interests, you should consider raising this in correspondence. Your organisation's letter should either welcome the announcement, or express any concerns over its likely effects. If it would be strategically advantageous, the letter should include a request for a meeting to discuss the issues further. Equally, you should consider writing to the relevant opposition parties' spokespersons, or to contact them through social media, to respond to any major issues they have raised in their speeches, particularly where there would appear to be opportunities for working with them to develop ways in which the issues arising from the debate can be taken forward with the Government. Similar considerations would also apply to individual MPs or Peers whose contributions to the debate have raised issues for your organisation. As with the letter to the minister, you should suggest to the opposition parties' spokespersons, and to MPs or Peers, that you meet them to discuss ways in which the issues can be progressed. The key thing is that your organisation has a strategy in place to take forward the policy issues following the debate, and to increase support for your policy positions with ministers, the opposition parties and with MPs or Peers. This will be an important consideration in demonstrating that your organisation's contribution to the debate has delivered tangible outcomes.

Another aspect of your organisation's follow-up strategy should be an assessment of how the debate has strengthened, or can potentially strengthen, your organisation's policy position, or reinforce the impact of any campaigns it may be running. In this respect, it is important that your analysis of *Hansard* includes identifying any statements made in the debate which you will be able to use to reinforce the evidence base of your policy position or campaign. This can, in the right circumstances, be a powerful tool, especially where a minister or an opposition party spokesperson has made a statement which you are able to successfully challenge with robust evidence of your own. This is something which can be progressed in correspondence with the minister or opposition party spokesperson or, if this approach is inappropriate or proves unsuccessful, through a news release. Such interventions by organisations can sometimes lead to significant changes in policy and/or legislation on the part of the Government or of the opposition parties.

In this context, you may wish to provide a summary of the debate for your organisation setting out the key statements made in the debate, and flagging up the potential for further influencing work in your follow up strategy based on these statements. This could be set out in table form, highlighting the statement made and who made it, the key issues raised, the potential for follow-up action, and also confirming internally within your organisation who will be responsible for taking that follow-up action. An example is provided in the table below:

MP/Peer	Statement	Key issues	Follow-up action	Action taken by, and when

Providing this summary after each debate will both help to keep organisations updated on major developments arising from specific debates, but will also ensure that organisations are able to take full advantage of any opportunities for influencing key policy makers arising from the debates. It will also help organisations to plan how best to respond to any challenges presented by the debate, and by policy issues on the political landscape.

Use of media

It is important that organisations initiating, or responding to, debates in either the House of Commons or the House of Lords give consideration to undertaking media work in support of their contribution to the debate. Initiating a debate will present a number of media opportunities for raising the profile of key policy issues, as well as for raising the profile of your organisation and its policy positions and/or campaigns. As part of this process, you should explore the possibility of joint media work with the minister, opposition party spokesperson or MP or Peer that has lodged the Motion for debate in support of your organisation and/or its policy position. Securing media coverage where your organisation is responding to a debate can often be challenging, and your chances of success will depend upon a number of factors. These include the media interest in the debate, the number of organisations seeking to brief ministers, the opposition parties' spokespersons, and MPs or Peers, and the extent to which your organisation's briefing raises issues that are likely to capture the media's interest.

To maximise the impact of your organisation's contribution to the debate you should also use social media to call attention to the debate, and to highlight the issues you are seeking policy makers to raise on your behalf during the debate. Social media could also be used to energise supporters to call on the minister and other leading policy makers to take a particular action prior to the debate, or after the debate, as appropriate. In addition, following the debate, you should look at ways in which you can use social media to increase levels of support for your organisation's policy positions on the issues on which the debate focused, and to keep pressure on the Government and the opposition parties to follow through on any commitments made during the debate.

Summary of key points

The key points from this chapter can be summarised as follows:

- Using robust evidence and best practice examples will help your organisation to ensure that its briefing for a debate stands out for the right reasons.
- To maximise your organisation's impact in a debate, take a targeted approach to briefing the ministers, the opposition parties' spokespersons, MPs or Peers.
- Organisations should take steps to follow up on debates, and to exploit any opportunities they present.
- Organisations should give careful consideration to undertaking media work in support of their contribution to debates, including the use of social media.

16

Early Day Motions

Early Day Motions (EDMs) are formal Motions lodged for debate by MPs in the House of Commons. EDMs, however, rarely lead to debates, with EDMs tabled against statutory instruments being one of the few types of EDMs that normally lead to a debate. There are different types of EDMs, and these are generally used by MPs to secure the backing of other Members for their policy stance on a specific issue, or to obtain their support for a particular cause, event or campaign.[1]

Other types of these Motions include internal party groups EDMs that are tabled by MPs with a different viewpoint to their party on a particular issue, all-party EDMs which seek to attract support on a cross-party basis, and critical EDMs which aim to criticise another MP or Peer.[2] EDMs can also be used to highlight a constituency matter, or to criticise the policies or conduct of other political parties. Some EDMs call attention to specific events an organisation or agency is holding and which the MP wishes to support or to publicise, including national policy or campaign events, or fundraising events.

The subject matter of EDMs covers a wide range of policy areas, and issues. Examples include EDMs focusing on public service pensions,[3] on youth services,[4] on wildlife crime,[5] on Iran and nuclear

---

1   House of Commons Information Office, 'Early Day Motions', Factsheet P3, (June 2010), UK Parliament website, www.parliament.uk.
2   UK Parliament, 'What are Early Day Motions?', UK Parliament website, www.parliament.uk.
3   House of Commons, EDM 586, Session 2016 – 2017, 24 October 2016, UK Parliament website, www.parliament.uk.
4   House of Commons, EDM 488, Session 2014 – 2015, 6 November 2014, UK Parliament website, www.parliament.uk.
5   House of Commons, EDM 189, Session 2014 – 2015, 30 June 2014, UK Parliament website, www.parliament.uk.

weapons[6] and on Holocaust Memorial Day.[7] Once an EDM has been tabled by an MP, other members can confirm their support by signing the EDM. Copies of tabled EDMs can be found on the EDM database on the House of Commons section of the Parliament's website.

Purpose of EDMs

EDMs can provide useful opportunities to influence the Government, the opposition parties, MPs, Peers and other key policy makers, and can play an important role in your organisation's influencing strategy. EDMs can be used for many different purposes, some of which are outlined below:

Examples of different uses for EDMS

Type of EDM	Purpose	Outcomes	**Measurement of success**
EDM to raise awareness of a policy issue or campaign.	To raise awareness of a specific policy issue or campaign on which your organisation is seeking support from the Government, the opposition parties, MPs, from other organisations and agencies, and from the public as appropriate.	The EDM raises the awareness of the Government, of the opposition parties, of individual MPs and of other stakeholders about your organisation, and about the policy issue or campaign it is seeking to progress.	• Triggers positive response from the Government and/ or from the opposition parties. • Secures support from significant numbers of MPs. • Secures support from other stakeholders, including the public. • Obtains media coverage. • Stimulates interest in your organisation, its work and campaigns on social media.

---

6   House of Commons, EDM 342, Session 2014 – 2015, 12 September 2014, UK Parliament website, www.parliament.uk.
7   House of Commons, EDM 927, Session 2015 – 2016, 7 January 2016, UK Parliament website, www.parliament.uk.

Type of EDM	Purpose	Outcomes	Measurement of success
EDM to raise profile of your organisation by highlighting the significance of its work, its contribution to a specific sector or part of the economy or to society as a whole.	To raise your organisation's profile with the Government, with the opposition parties, with MPs and with other stakeholders.	The EDM raises the profile of your organisation, of its work and of its contribution to the economy and to society.	• Raises awareness of your organisation within the Government, and helps to promote positive engagement with the Government. • Secures support from the opposition parties and from significant numbers of MPs, and raises awareness of your organisation amongst MPs. • Increases awareness of your organisation amongst other key stakeholders, including the public. • Secures good levels of media coverage. • Results in increased social media interest in your organisation and its work.
EDM to celebrate an organisation's success.	To raise the profile of your organisation, to increase awareness of its work, and of its best practice including any recognition it has received such as a national award.	The EDM raises the profile of your organisation and increases awareness of its work, including any awards it has won or received.	• Raises the profile within the Government, with the opposition parties, with MPs and with other stakeholders of your organisation, and leads to positive engagement going forward. • Secures significant recognition from MPs, and from other stakeholders for your organisation and its work. • Secures increased recognition for your organisation from other key stakeholders. • Generates good levels of media coverage. • Leads to increased levels of interest in your organisation on social media.

Type of EDM	Purpose	Outcomes	**Measurement of success**
EDM to raise national profile of an event.	To raise the profile of your organisation, and of a national event, including fundraising events or activities, it is holding or supporting.	The EDM raises the profile of your organisation, and of the event it is holding or supporting.	• Raises the profile of your organisation, and of the event within the Government and with the opposition parties, and leads to a positive response from the latter, e.g. the minister or an Opposition spokesperson attends the event. • Raises interest in the event and leads to MPs deciding to attend the event. • Increases interest in the event amongst other stakeholders, including the public. • Stimulates media interest in the event. • Increases interest in the event on social media.
EDM to raise profile of a local service or business.	To raise the profile of your organisation, its work and of its local services or business.	The EDM raises awareness within the Government, with the opposition parties and with MPs, of your organisation, its work and of its services or business.	• Leads to positive response from the Government, e.g. greater awareness of your organisation, and a ministerial visit to the local service or business, and from the opposition parties. • Raises awareness amongst MPs of your organisation's work, and helps to secure visits by MPs to your local services or businesses. • Increases awareness amongst other key stakeholders, including the public, about your organisation, its work and its services or businesses. • Secures good level of media coverage. • Generates interest in social media about your organisation and its work.

Your organisation should consider each of the different set of objectives that can potentially be delivered through EDMs on their merits, and identify the EDMs above which will best assist your organisation to secure the outcomes it is hoping to achieve, and at which stage in your organisation's public affairs strategy. Key factors in your organisation's decision making around EDMs will be whether or not you are hoping to use the EDM as part of a specific campaign you are progressing within your organisation's public affairs strategy. If so, an EDM could be a useful means of providing your organisation's campaign with a parliamentary focus. This would help your organisation to raise awareness of the campaign amongst MPs, and get them to confirm their support for the campaign by signing the EDM. Moreover, the EDM could offer opportunities to engage the Government on issues around the campaign, and to keep the campaign on the Government's radar, and help to trigger a formal response to the issues your organisation is seeking to progress through the campaign.

Alternatively, using an EDM as a stand-alone initiative within your organisation's influencing strategy can offer important benefits. An EDM could, for example, be used to raise the profile of your organisation and its work, or of your organisation's support for specific policy issues or developments or events. In this respect, one potential scenario would be for your organisation's local MP to lodge an EDM in support of your organisation where it is celebrating a landmark anniversary, or one of its services, or part of its business has received a national award. Once your organisation has decided if it wishes to use the EDM as part of a wider campaign, or as a stand-alone initiative, within its influencing strategy, it will also need to consider how to ensure the EDM tabled on its behalf delivers the desired outcomes.

How to make the most of EDMs

To make the most of the EDM your organisation should work with the sponsoring MP to ensure that the EDM presents the issues, you are seeking to raise or to campaign on, in a concise and persuasive manner. Your aim here should be to try and secure a positive response from the Government, to maximise the support for the EDM amongst the opposition parties and individual MPs, and to ensure that the EDM attracts a good level of media interest. If you are using the EDM as part of a campaign, an important consideration will be capturing the essence of the campaign and presenting its headline issues and themes. Securing cross-party support from MPs will depend upon the subject matter of your campaign, and what the campaign is seeking to achieve. For some campaigns there will be natural limits to the extent to which they will attract support from the members of specific political parties, due to the key campaign messages reflected in the EDM cutting across the policies of specific political parties.

EDMs which celebrate an organisation's achievements, including the success of its local services or business, would normally stand the best chances of securing cross-party support, providing of course that there is no controversy involved. If the organisation is a charity, and fundraising is a key part of the organisation's work, EDMs can be helpful in raising the organisation's profile for fundraising purposes. An EDM focusing on an organisation's fundraising events or funding pressures would generally also fall within the category of EDMs most likely to attract cross-party support. This, however, would depend upon the type of charity involved, and with the proviso that its fundraising events or funding difficulties have not led it into areas of political controversy.

Where there is scope for an EDM to secure cross-party support, getting the right tone and balance for the EDM, and choosing the policy issues strategically, will help to improve the chances of securing good levels of support from MPs of all parties, and of attracting media interest including on social media. Looking at the EDM data base on the UK Parliament's website will give your organisation a good insight into the content of EDMs. It is recommended that you pay particular attention to those EDMs which have attracted the most support from MPs in the parliamentary session, and have generated high levels of cross-party support. Following these steps will give your organisation a sense of what issues will have the best prospects of securing good levels of support amongst MPs. It will also provide practical examples of how those issues could best be presented in EDMs to maximise the backing they are likely to attract from MPs of all parties.

To make the most of EDMs, and to maximise the impact for your organisation, you should use them sparingly, and not overdo your organisation's reliance on EDMs. After all, once an EDM has been tabled on your organisation's behalf it will remain current for the remainder of the parliamentary session. This means that MPs will be able to add their name in support of the EDM until the end of the parliamentary session.[8] Having a number of EDMs tabled on your organisation's behalf at the same time could, therefore, prove confusing, and blunt the effectiveness of your organisation's influencing work on the back of the EDM.

Taking a strategic approach to progressing a small number of EDMs in each parliamentary session will provide your organisation with the best opportunities for maximising the impact of a specific EDM for your organisation. This is particularly true where you are seeking to use an EDM to raise awareness of specific policy issues, or campaigns, your organisation is seeking to progress. There will be more leeway if your organisation is attempting to use an EDM to increase the profile of its services or business within local areas or to celebrate a particular success such as a national award, and the EDM has been tabled by the local MP for this purpose. By contrast, frequently using EDMs to raise your organisation's profile, and to generate support for its policy positions and campaigns, could have unintended consequences. You could find, for example, that MPs are less likely to be interested due to the volume of EDMs your organisation has had tabled on its behalf, and fail to support the EDM. This could be humiliating, and runs the risk of reputational damage to your organisation. There is also the danger that overuse of EDMs will make the media less likely to run stories about the issues you wish to promote through the EDM. These are significant risks. Use EDMs in a strategic, targeted way, on the other hand, and the benefits can potentially be significant.

Getting EDMs tabled

Careful thought should be given to which MP your organisation approaches to table an EDM on its behalf. Please note that parliamentary protocol debars Government ministers, Government whips and ministerial private secretaries from sponsoring or supporting EDMs. Against this background, a good starting point, particularly if the EDM is to raise the profile of your organisation, would be your organisation's local MP. In this respect, the latter should be approached to see if they would be willing to table an EDM on your organisation's behalf. Their

---

8   House of Commons Information Office, 'Early Day Motions', Factsheet, UK Parliament website, www.parliament.uk.

response is likely to depend upon a number of factors including the subject matter of the EDM, the MP's interest in your organisation and its work, and the extent and strength of any existing links between the MP and your organisation.

One initiative you should consider developing as a key part of your public affairs strategy is to invite the local MP to visit your organisation, and to suggest they table an EDM following any visit made by the MP to your organisation's services or business. The EDM would focus on areas such as your organisation's best practice, the evidence of its effectiveness and its contribution to the economy and/ or to society. If, on the other hand, your organisation is seeking to have the EDM tabled as part of a campaign or to highlight a specific policy issue or position, it might be that there would be other MPs whom it would be more appropriate or productive to approach. In this context, you should consider asking an MP to sponsor the EDM who has been supportive of your organisation in the past, or who has an interest in the policy areas on which the EDM will focus.

Ideally, you are looking to enlist the support of an MP who will be able to secure good levels of support for the EDM, and in particular who will be able to potentially generate cross-party support. Each EDM can have a maximum of six sponsoring MPs, and ideally you should try and secure sponsors from as many different parties as possible. This, however, is not always practical or realistic. An EDM will have limited cross-party support, if any, where, for example, the EDM focuses on a policy issue or position which does not have the policy support of all of the parties at Westminster. In these circumstances, you would have to rely on the willingness of individual MPs to go against their party's Whip on a specific policy issues or policy position. The EDM is more likely to attract sponsorship from MPs from different parties if it is a cross-party issue, or if the aim of the EDM is to seek recognition of the work of your organisation and/or to celebrate its achievements. Organisations which are not associated with any political partisanship or controversy will generally have a better chance of securing cross-party backing for an EDM tabled on their behalf. Getting the tone and substance of the EDM right will also improve its chances of generating cross-party support.

Building up support for an EDM

Once the EDM has been tabled by a sponsoring MP you should liaise with the MP to consider how best to secure support from other Members for the EDM. The sponsoring MP will usually be able to use their contacts within their own party to encourage support from that quarter. Where there is more than one sponsoring MP for the EDM, and they are from different parties, this will be helpful in building up cross-party support. As well as using their personal contacts within their own party, the sponsoring MP will be able to employ any personal contacts they may have in the other parties to secure backing for the EDM. The sponsoring MP will also be able to use their party's weekly Whip, which includes details of forthcoming business, to highlight the EDM in their name, and to seek support from their parliamentary colleagues.

It is also suggested that, with the sponsoring MP's prior agreement, your organisation should send an e-mail to key MPs calling their attention to the EDM, explaining why it has been tabled and highlighting the importance of their supporting the EDM. Once the e-mail has been circulated, it is strongly recommended that you phone around the MPs' offices to find out if they have received your organisation's e-mail, and to confirm if they are willing to sign up to support the EDM. This exercise offers several important advantages. Apart from helping to increase the number of MPs willing to support the EDM, contacting the MPs' offices can play a useful intelligence gathering and relationship building role. Phoning MPs' offices to secure their support for the EDM will give your organisation useful opportunities to introduce itself and its work to MPs, and to develop good working relationships with MPs, and with their staff. It will also help your organisation to build up a picture of the policy issues and areas which individuals MPs are most interested in progressing. These are areas which can help to support your organisation's influencing strategy by ensuring that it is based on the support of a good network of MPs and their staff who your organisation knows would be interested in raising issues on its behalf. Such approaches can also present other opportunities. In this respect, if the MP is keen to find out more about your organisation, and to take their support beyond signing the EDM, seize the moment and arrange a meeting with the MP or arrange a visit for the MP to one of your services or businesses.

Using the media to publicise EDMs

Since few EDMs lead to debates in the House of Commons, often the most effective use of EDMs is to use them for publicity purposes. Approaching an MP to table an EDM, and then working with the Member to generate media interest in the EDM, and in the issues it is seeking to raise, can be highly effective. It has been used by a number of organisations to generate significant levels of publicity. Examples include EDMs on climate change, and on the need to reinstate the Access to Elected Fund which was designed to help people with a disability to stand for elected office.

Against this background, your organisation will need to take a view on whether it would be more productive to target the national media or the local media or both. This will depend upon the subject matter of the EDM, and on whether it is part of a campaign or a stand-alone initiative to recognise or celebrate your organisation and its work. With high profile policy issues and campaigns, it is probably more likely that your organisation will want to focus on the national media, while EDMs celebrating the success of your organisation's local services or business would normally be of most interest to local media.

Your organisation should issue a media release to coincide with the EDM being tabled, and to generate interest in the EDM. Prior to it being tabled you should also have used your media contacts to trail the news that the EDM was to be tabled. If the EDM is part of a long-term policy campaign, it is recommended that further consideration should be given to the next stages of the campaign, and in particular to how your organisation intends to generate media interest in the campaign beyond the media activity around the EDM. The EDM will also provide your organisation with an opportunity to identify the media most interested in the policy issues being raised in the EDM, and a concerted effort should be made to cultivate the journalists associated with any coverage of the EDM. This will help to increase the likelihood that the next stage of the campaign will secure a good level of publicity, and deliver major outcomes. The same considerations would apply for an EDM which is covered by local media. In these circumstances efforts should be made to build up relations with the local media to make sure that they retain an interest in your organisation, and in its work.

Social media

Publicising EDMs on social media offers significant potential to raise the profile of your organisation, and of the policy issues and themes of the EDM. Once the EDM has been tabled you should work with the sponsoring MP to publicise the EDM on Twitter, Facebook and through other social media. This will help to generate interest in the EDM, and encourage more MPs to sign up in support of the EDM. You can also use social media to build up interest in your organisation, and in any policy issues raised in the EDM, from other agencies and organisations. In addition, profiling the EDM on, for example, Twitter and Facebook can help to increase support for your organisation amongst the general public. For organisations with a focus on campaigning and on fundraising this will be an important consideration, as it can potentially increase public support for the organisation's campaigns, and for its fundraising activities. The level of interest in these areas could make it more likely that the minister will respond positively to any policy issues highlighted in the EDM. Social media can also play a potentially important role where the focus of the EDM is on raising awareness of your organisation, and of its service or business. In this respect, you can use your organisation's Twitter and Facebook accounts to keep its followers updated on the progress of the EDM, and in particular about the number of MPs who have signed up to support the EDM. This would include encouraging your organisation's followers to use social media and correspondence to persuade other MPs to sign up to confirm their support for the EDM.

Follow-up action

Once the EDM has been tabled, and it has secured a good level of support from MPs, your organisation should formally write to the sponsoring MP or MPs and to all the MPs who signed up to support the EDM. The letter should thank them for their support for your organisation, and for the issues the EDM is raising, and also follow this up on social media. Thanking those MPs who have helped your organisation should become best practice for your organisation, and expressing your organisation's gratitude to those MPs who have supported an EDM recognising your organisation's work, or supporting one of its campaigns would be no different. The MPs will appreciate the gesture, and this is likely to have a positive bearing on your future relationships.

In terms of other follow-up action you should also consider with the MP who sponsored the EDM, and with key supporters, how you take things forward. Is there any other action which can be advanced in the parliamentary context, such as, for example, securing a parliamentary debate on the issues? If so, how should this be progressed? By whom and when? Equally, has the EDM raised issues which merit an attempt to secure an early meeting with the relevant Government minister, or are there issues which you wish to progress in correspondence? If the EDM was part of a specific policy campaign, your organisation will need to consider the next stages of the campaign, and what part, if any, Parliament will play in that process. For EDMs designed to raise an organisation's profile, and to increase interest in its services or business, you need to consider how to build upon the interest generated by the EDM, and how best to take things forward to the next level in raising your organisation's profile.

Summary of key points

The key points from this chapter can be summarised as follows:

- EDMs, if used strategically, can provide useful opportunities to influence the Government, the opposition parties, MPs, and other leading policy makers.
- To maximise support amongst MPs you should attempt, as much as possible, to try and progress EDMs with a cross-party appeal.
- You should work closely with the media to ensure that the EDM generates good levels of media interest.
- Your organisation should review the scope for taking follow-up action with the Government, with the opposition parties, with MPs, and with other policy makers to build upon the support it secured for the EDM.

17

Petitions

Over the centuries petitions have often been used in Great Britain by individuals, communities, and interest groups to seek the Monarch's or Parliament's or the Government's intervention, as appropriate, on a wide range of issues, and to request that they take a specific action or steps in response to these issues or related developments. The use of petitions in Parliament can provide a useful means of influencing the Government, MPs and Peers. There are two types of petition to Parliament – the public petitions (also referred to as paper petitions) presented to the House of Commons or to the House of Lords, and e-petitions submitted through the Parliament's website. It is the role of the House of Commons' Petitions Committee to consider, and to respond as appropriate to, public petitions and to e-petitions in relation to the House of Commons. A separate procedure applies to petitions presented in the House of Lords.

Public petitions in the House of Commons

The public petition is a written request addressed to Parliament, signed by at least one person, calling for Parliament to take action in a specific area, or in response to a particular development or event, or calling on Parliament to encourage the Government to take action. Public petitions must be presented by an MP. High profile examples of public petitions include the Ambulance Dispute petition which was presented in 1989 with an estimated 4.5 million signatures.[1] Public petitions can be a particularly effective option for voluntary

---

1   House of Commons Information Office, Public Petitions, Factsheet P7 Procedure Series, (August 2010), Parliament's website, www.parliament.uk.

and community organisations, including charities and their supporters, seeking to raise awareness of major issues, and to secure action from the House of Commons, and/or the Government, in response to those issues. Public petitions are also an option which local voluntary and community organisations may wish to consider for the same reasons.

Procedure for submitting public petitions in the House of Commons

In general, anyone can present a public petition to the House of Commons. A public petition will be accepted for consideration by the House of Commons provided it has the signature and address of at least one person, and has been set out in the correct format. The petition must be addressed to the House of Commons, and not to the Government, and call on the House to take specific action, or state that the House of Commons should demand the Government take such action. In contrast with an e-petition, the public petitioner must also secure the agreement of an MP to present the petition on his or her behalf. Detailed information about public petitions, including the procedures for presenting public petitions, and the content and style of public petitions, can be accessed on the Parliament's website.[2] Guidance and advice for individuals and organisations wishing to submit a petition are also available from the Clerk of Public Petitions in the Journal Office.

MPs will normally present public petitions they receive from constituents to the House of Commons, although they are under no obligation to do so. Moreover, the fact that an MP presents the petition does not imply that they support its content or aims. Against this background, the MP will either formally present the public petition by making a short statement in the House of Commons about the petition, or informally present the petition by placing it in the Petition Bag behind the Speaker's Chair.

Once the public petition has been presented, the daily Votes and Proceedings (a publication available on Parliament's website[3]) will provide details about the subject matter of the petition, confirm the

---

2   UK Parliament, 'Public Petitions to the House of Commons', UK Parliament website, www.parliament.uk.

3   UK Parliament website, www.parliament.uk.

petitioners and if it was presented formally or informally. The text of the public petition will be published in *Hansard*, and a copy of the petition will be sent to the Government department with lead responsibility for the subject matter of the petition. A further copy will be sent to the Select Committee which scrutinises the work of the Government department in question. With substantive public petitions, the Government department, with responsibility for the policy areas covered by the petition, would normally provide a response to the petition, known as an 'observation' within two months of the petition being presented. A copy of the response will be published in *Hansard*.[4] The Petitions Committee will consider a petition once the Government has responded, or if it raises a highly topical issue.

Public petitions in the House of Lords

Public petitions can also be presented to Peers in the House of Lords. The procedure for petitions in the House of Lords is that the Peer, once he or she receives a public petition and agrees to present it, will make a brief statement to the House of Lords confirming who the petition is from, and what action he or she is seeking the House of Lords to take. It should be noted, however, that Peers are under no obligation to present a petition they receive to the House of Lords. Furthermore, the procedure usually leads to no action being taken, and is, therefore, seldom used. As a result, it is more usual for public petitions to be presented in the House of Commons rather than in the House of Lords.[5]

E-petitions

The other type of petition which can be submitted to the House of Commons is the e-petition. E-petitions which secure 10,000 signatures will be guaranteed a response from the Government, while those attracting 100,000 signatures will be considered for debate. E-petitions that receive 100,000 signatures are generally likely to be debated unless

---

4   UK Parliament, 'Ask your MP to present a petition', UK Parliament website, www. parliament.uk.

5   UK Parliament, 'Ask your MP to present a petition', UK Parliament website, www.parliament.uk.

the petition covers a topic that has recently been debated, or a debate is already scheduled.

Significantly, e-petitions must raise issues which fall within the competence of the Government or the House of Commons.[6] The procedure for e-petitions stipulates that the petition must request that the Government, or the House of Commons, take a specific action or steps. Any member of the general public can initiate an e-petition, but a total of six people must support the petition before it can be published on the House of Commons' petitions website for other people to sign. The e-petition will then remain open for six months, during which period other people can add their signatures in support of the petition.

Role of the Petitions Committee

The role of Parliament's Petitions Committee is to consider public petitions presented to the House of Commons, and e-petitions submitted through Parliament's website. The Petitions Committee has the power to request that action should be taken by the Government, or Parliament, or by another relevant person or organisation. This committee reviews the merits of individual petitions, and can respond to an individual petition in a number of ways. The Petitions Committee can, for example, reject an e-petition because it does not comply with the prerequisite Standards for Petitions. These standards stipulate that a petition must be submitted by a British citizen and UK resident, and that the purpose of the e-petition must be clear and avoid being party political. The standards also confirm that the petition must not raise a purely personal issue, or contain offensive or defamatory statements.[7]

Alternatively, the Petitions Committee can, in response to an e-petition, ask the petitioner, or the Government, or other relevant person or organisation to provide more information in writing or in person. Another option for the Petitions Committee would be to write to the Government to request that it, or another body, should take action in response to the issues raised in the e-petition. Other options for the

---

6 UK Parliament, 'Find out more about e-petitions', UK Parliament website, www.parliament.uk.

7 For further details about the Standards for Petitions see UK Parliament, 'How petitions work', UK Parliament website, www.parliament.uk.

Petitions Committee would include referring the e-petition to another parliamentary committee for further consideration, or recommending that the issues raised in the e-petition be debated.[8] Where the Petitions Committee concludes that the e-petition should be debated, it can recommend that the e-petition be debated in Westminster Hall or in the Chamber of the House of Commons. If the Petitions Committee recommends that the e-petition should be debated in the Chamber, it will forward this request to the Backbench Business Committee for its consideration.

Strategy for progressing petitions

For individuals, or groups of people with a common interest on a particular policy issue or area, or for voluntary and community organisations, wishing to progress public petitions or e-petitions in Parliament, there are a number of factors which should be considered. These include the subject matter and policy areas covered by the public petition or e-petition, and whether or not these will generate sufficient interest and support from the public, and persuade large numbers of people to sign the petition. It is also recommended that, prior to the submission of the petition, your organisation should have already taken soundings from MPs and Peers about the level of support the petition is likely to receive in the House of Commons and in the House of Lords. You also need to ensure that your public petition or e-petition includes a request for action or intervention which is within the competence of Parliament. In this respect, it is important to bear in mind the policy and legislative areas devolved to the Scottish Parliament, to the Northern Ireland Assembly and to the National Assembly for Wales, and to ensure that the petition avoids these areas.

Consideration must also be given to the aims and objectives of the public petition or e-petition. What are you looking to achieve? Could this be achieved by other, more effective means? If your organisation is a voluntary and community organisation it is important that you assess how a petition will fit into your overall public affairs strategy. Will the petition, for example, be part of a much wider, long-term campaign? Is the petition designed to persuade Parliament, or the Government

---

8   UK Parliament, 'Find out more about e-petitions', UK Parliament website, www. parliament.uk.

or another agency to take a specific course of action, or to make an intervention? Or are you primarily seeking to use the petition to raise awareness of a particular national or local policy issue? These are all areas which should be addressed before presenting a public petition, or submitting an e-petition, to Parliament.

Another factor to consider is whether you want to send a petition to an MP and request that he or she present it to Parliament. Conversely, would you find it more effective and beneficial to launch an e-petition and to aim to encourage large numbers of on-line signatories to support the petition. Both options could potentially provide influencing opportunities for your organisation, but it is suggested that using an e-petition might offer longer-term opportunities to influence key policy makers. In this context, the process of sending a public petition to an MP could end with the relevant Government Department providing a response to the MP, and publishing this in *Hansard*. You would then need to take a view on whether or not this response meets your organisation's aims, or if further action would be required and, if so, how you would take this forward with the Petitions Committee. By contrast, a long-term campaign could be progressed with the focus being on the e-petition, and on securing enough on-line signatories for the e-petition during the six months it will stay open on Parliament's website. An e-petition could provide your organisation with a strong focus for its campaign on specific issues, which would include the tangible outcomes that the online campaign could potentially deliver. In this respect, your organisation could help to galvanise on-line support for your e-petition by highlighting that securing 10,000 signatories will ensure the Government responds to the e-petition,[9] while 100,000 signatories would lead to the petition being considered for a debate either in Westminster Hall or in the Chamber of the House of Commons.[10]

---

9   Examples of petitions which secured 10,000 signatories and received a response from the Government include: *Put a VEGAN meal on every school, college, university, hospital and prison menu; Set up Independent Pump-Watch body to monitor and regulate vehicle fuel pricing;* and *Support Live Music Venues by preventing inappropriate complaints being actioned.* House of Commons, Decisions of the Petitions Committee, Tuesday 13 December 2016, UK Parliament website, www.parliament.uk.

10 Examples of petitions which secured 100,000 signatories, and led to debates include: *Force child cancer to the forefront of the NHS and government funding schemes,* Decisions of the Petitions Committee, Tuesday 15 November 2016, UK Parliament

You should also take into account, in the context of public petitions, that seeking to secure your aims and objectives through sending a public or paper petition to an MP is generally less likely to make heavy demands upon your organisation's resources and upon its staff's capacity. Seeking to progress an e-petition through an on-line campaign, on the other hand, could potentially involve significant demands being made upon your organisation's capacity and resources. After all, securing the prerequisite 10,000 signatories or 100,000 signatories for the e-petition to trigger a response from the Government, or to be considered for a parliamentary debate respectively, could be a major logistical challenge. Allied to this is the risk of reputational damage by failing to secure the prerequisite number of signatories. The level of the challenge involved will depend upon a number of important considerations, including the subject matter of the petition, and the capacity of your organisation to secure this level of support from its supporters and from the wider public.

Support from key policy makers

Careful thought should be given to how best to build up support for the public petition or e-petition amongst key policy makers. Enlisting the support of MPs will be critical if a public petition is to progress. In this context, you will require at least one MP to present the public petition either formally or informally to Parliament. In addition, you should bear in mind that the Petitions Committee, in deciding whether or not a specific public petition or e-petition should be debated, will want to gauge the level of support for the public petition or e-petition amongst MPs. It is, therefore, vital that if your organisation does have a public petition presented on its behalf, or if it submits an e-petition, it engages with MPs to brief them about the issues raised by the public petition or e-petition, and to enlist their support. The more MPs your organisation can persuade to support the petition or e-petition, the

---

website, www.parliament.uk; *Debate in the House the Local Government Pension Scheme Investment Regulations*, Decisions of the Petitions Committee, Tuesday 11 October 2016, UK Parliament website, www.parliament.uk; *Stop retrospective changes to the student loans* agreement, Decisions of the Petitions Committee, Tuesday 28 June 2016, UK Parliament website, www.parliament.uk; *Revoke Article 50 and remain in the EU*, February 2019, UK Parliament website, www. parliament.uk

better chance that it will be debated in Westminster Hall or in the Chamber.

Any MP can present a public petition to Parliament, but you should approach your constituency MP first. Alternatively, if they are unable or unwilling to present the petition, you should approach an MP or MPs with whom either you or your organisation has existing strong links, or who you know has an interest in the subject matter and issues raised in the petition. With e-petitions you should also, once the e-petition has been presented to the Backbench Business Committee, seek to engage with the individual members of the committee through briefings and meetings. Gaining their support will be vital if the committee is to be persuaded that the issues raised in your petition merit a parliamentary debate. Steps should also be taken to brief the minister and their officials about issues you are raising in a petition or in an e-petition. This will help to improve the chances that the Government will respond positively to the petition.

Working with the media

To maximise the impact of your petition it is vital that you work with the media to ensure that the petition receives good levels of coverage. This area should not be neglected, because in many cases raising awareness of the issues raised in the petition, by using the media, is the most tangible outcome that a petition will achieve. A campaign focusing on, for example, securing 100,000 signatories in favour of an e-petition to secure a parliamentary debate on a particular issue could also offer important opportunities to obtain media coverage. Indeed, the success of an organisation in securing this level of signatories will rely heavily on its ability to secure media coverage to raise awareness of the e-petition, and to attract signatories. Key opportunities to secure media coverage are most likely to be when the petition is first presented to Parliament, and when the Government responds to the petition. E-petitions remain open on the Parliament website for six months so it is important that your organisation has developed a media strategy, as part of its campaign, to try and raise the profile of the e-petition throughout this period and to maximise the number of signatories.

Social media can also play a major role in promoting public petitions and e-petitions in Parliament. Organisations seeking to progress petitions should, therefore, consider ways in which social media can be used to publicise the issues being raised in the petition, and to energise their supporters and the general public to support the petition. Providing regular updates on progress, including the number of people supporting the petition, is just one way in which social media could be used to develop links with your supporters, and to keep them interested in the campaign. Furthermore, social media should be used to raise awareness of these issues with the general public, and to encourage members of the public to sign up to support the petition. Many politicians use social media as an integral part of their every day political activities, and your organisation should use social media to generate support amongst MPs and Peers for its petition. Demonstrating significant levels of support on social media for the petition will also make it more likely that the Government will respond positively to the petition, and that there will be support amongst the members of the Petitions Committee and other MPs for the petition to be debated. These outcomes, however, will depend upon factors such as the subject matter of the petition, its aims and 'policy asks'.

Summary of key points

The key points from this chapter can be summarised as follows:

- A petition should only request that Parliament, and/or the Government, take action which falls within their competence.
- Consideration should be given to whether an organisation's aims and objectives can best be supported by submitting a public petition to an MP for presenting to Parliament, or by progressing an e-petition.
- To maximise the impact of a petition steps should be taken to ensure it receives good levels of media coverage, particularly as this will often be the most tangible outcome that a petition will achieve.
- Social media can play a major role in increasing support for a public petition or e-petition.

18

All-Party Parliamentary Groups

All-Party Parliamentary Groups (APPGs) are informal cross-party structures, and membership is open to all MPs and Peers. Individual APPGs are run for, and by, the MPs and Peers in membership. Backbench MPs and Peers tend to dominate membership of APPGs, although membership is also open to Government ministers.[1] APPGs cover a wide range of topics and subject matter. Examples include the APPGs on Africa, on Animal Welfare, on Disability, on Energy, on Football, on Health, on Manufacturing and on Poverty to name but a few. A full list of APPGs is available on the Register of All-Party Parliamentary Groups. This register, which confirms the APPGs recognised by Parliament, can be found on Parliament's website.[2] It is only by looking at the Register that you will get a full sense of all the policy areas and subject matter covered by the APPGs.

The secretariat of individual APPGs is often provided by organisations or agencies, which share the aims and objectives of the APPG. The role of the secretariat is vital to the day-to-day running of APPGs. The organisation providing the secretariat will liaise with the MPs and Peers who have been elected as the officers of the APPG, and will help to plan a schedule of meetings and activities for the group. This will include agreeing a timetable over the parliamentary session of speakers to provide presentations at meetings of the APPG. The secretariat will also generally have responsibility for publicising meetings of the APPG, and promoting its work. Meetings of the APPG will be attended by MPs and Peers, but also by organisations

---

1   UK Parliament, 'All-Party Parliamentary Groups', UK Parliament website, www. parliament.uk.
2   UK Parliament, Register of All-Party Parliamentary Groups, UK Parliament website, www.parliament.uk.

which wish to support and participate in its activities, as well as by individuals who share that commitment. These organisations will often be classified as 'affiliate' or 'associate' members by certain APPGs, but only MPs and Peers can be members of an APPG registered in Parliament.

The role of APPGs in public affairs strategies

Organisations should give serious consideration to the role which APPGs can play in their public affairs strategies, and to the ways in which their involvement in APPGs can help to progress these strategies. One of the first issues for organisations to consider is the outcomes they wish to achieve through participation in an APPG or APPGs. Involvement in APPGs can potentially deliver significant outcomes for your organisation in terms of shaping policy debates, and influencing policy makers. APPGs can, for example, provide organisations with important opportunities to increase awareness of key issues and campaigns, and to engage with policy makers from both Houses of Parliament. Participation in meetings of APPGs can also assist organisations to raise their profile with MPs and Peers, and to brief the latter on policy issues of mutual interest.

To ensure that your organisation's participation in APPGs achieves its objectives, it is recommended that you should first review the Register of APPGs, and identify those APPGs which are most relevant to your organisation's work. The range of APPGs is wide, and the number in which your organisation may have an interest could be large. This will depend upon the type of organisation concerned, and the policy areas and issues that relate to its work. In this respect, if there are more than a few APPGs which are relevant to your organisation, then you will need to prioritise your organisation's involvement according to their importance to your organisation, and its work. Ideally, you should seek to contribute to those APPGs that are most directly connected with, and relevant to, your organisation and its work, and which are best suited to assisting your organisation to meet its own goals and objectives. If, upon reviewing the Register of APPGs, you discover that there are no APPGs covering the issues or policy areas or countries on which your organisation wishes to focus, you should consider trying to establish a new APPG to address this gap.

Establishing a new APPG

Establishing a new APPG would provide your organisation with a parliamentary forum in which to increase awareness of key issues and policy areas relevant to its work, and/or to the sector in which it operates and/or to the people on whose behalf it operates or campaigns. For some organisations the focus might be on a specific country or global region. Apart from raising awareness of different policy issues and areas or countries or regions, the APPG could also provide opportunities to raise the profile of your organisation. Once your organisation has identified the need for a new APPG, it should consider if it would be in a position to provide the secretariat for the proposed new APPG.

This will be an important consideration when you approach MPs and Peers with your proposal to establish the APPG, because being able to confirm that you can support the APPG in this way will make the proposal more attractive to MPs and Peers. It will be one less thing for them to worry about with their busy schedules. Remember, persuading an MP or Peer to attend a meeting of an APPG will depend upon the many competing demands upon their time. Against this background, being able to reassure the MPs and Peers you approach that your organisation will provide the secretariat, and that the demands upon their time and that of their staff will, therefore, be kept to a minimum, could make their backing for the proposal to establish a new APPG a more realistic proposition.

If your organisation is seeking to establish a new APPG, it should assess what other organisations and agencies would support the proposal, and would be willing to play an active role in the proposed APPG. This is vital because it will demonstrate to the MPs and Peers, whom you will be approaching, that the APPG is likely to generate good levels of interest in its work, and will be sustainable and well attended throughout the lifespan of the Parliament. Securing the support of other organisations and agencies will increase the authority of the APPG, especially if these organisations and agencies are well respected in their field. It will also confirm to the MPs and Peers that the APPG will receive high quality support, and that its work will be likely to generate media interest. A further benefit is that increasing the supporter base of the APPG will help to ensure that it receives inputs and presentations from a wide range of speakers, and benefits from informative updates on relevant research, evidence and best practice from various sources. These factors will potentially create a powerful dynamic for the APPG, and ensure that it has a committed membership of MPs and Peers, and is well supported by external organisations and agencies.

Once your organisation has addressed these preliminary issues it will then need to decide which MPs and Peers to approach about establishing the APPG. This is critical because only MPs and Peers can establish APPGs, which can be included on the Register of APPGs. The best starting points would be your local MP, and/or MPs and Peers with whom your organisation already has close ties. If these approaches are unsuccessful, you should then engage with MPs and Peers with an interest in the policy issues and areas, or country or global region, on which the proposed APPG will focus. Important sources in this respect would be the Register of Members' Interests in the House of Commons,[3] and the Register of Lords' Interests in the House of Lords.[4] Other useful sources would be the MPs' and Peers' membership of any organisations which support your organisation's proposal for an APPG. You should also consult *Hansard* to see which MPs and Peers have intervened in parliamentary business relating to policy issues or areas, or countries or global regions relevant to the proposed APPG. A parliamentary debate, or proceedings on a Bill, would be particularly helpful as this will clearly identify which MPs and Peers intervened, and what they said. You can then target these MPs and Peers, highlighting that you are approaching them on the basis of their interest in the subject matter of the proposed APPG, and of their recent parliamentary intervention in this area.

You should telephone the offices of MPs and Peers who could potentially support the APPG, and follow up by letter or by e-mail or use social media as appropriate, to request a meeting to outline the proposal to establish the APPG. Where other organisations support the proposal, you should try and involve them in this meeting to highlight to the MPs and Peers that the APPG would be well supported, and that there would be strong interest in the subject matter and issues on which it will focus. When the proposal to establish the APPG receives

---

3   House of Commons, Register of Members' Interests, UK Parliament's website, www.parliament.uk.

4   House of Lords, Register of Lords' Interests, UK Parliament's website, www. parliament.uk.

support from MPS and Peers, the latter will need to take this forward if an APPG is to be set up that can be registered on the Register of APPGs. The MPs and Peers who agree to the proposal, and to establish an APPG, must comply with the appropriate rules and procedures outlined in the Parliamentary Commissioner for Standards' Guide to the Rules on All-Party Parliamentary Groups, which is available on the parliamentary website.[5]

Opportunities to influence

The opportunities for organisations to influence policy makers through supporting MPs and Peers to establish a new APPG, or by seeking to contribute to the activities of an existing APPG or APPGs, are potentially great. Such opportunities are presented by many of the diverse range of activities undertaken by APPGs. These include parliamentary breakfast briefings, meetings, seminars and conferences focusing on particular policy issues or areas. Some of these activities and events will concentrate on updating the members of the APPG about key policy themes and developments. This could include briefings on the main provisions of new legislation, and on identifying the major issues that the APPG may wish to progress on a collective basis in response to the legislation. One of the types of events favoured by APPGs is the roundtable discussion, such as the APPG for Education's roundtable events to help inform its inquiry into how well British schools are preparing young people for their future careers.[6]

Another aspect of the information exchange aspect of the APPGs' work is undertaking study visits to other countries, and hosting meetings where the evidence and best practice of other countries and global regions are shared by guest speakers from these countries. Examples include the visit of African agribusiness entrepreneurs to the APPG on Agriculture and Food for Development.[7]

Apart from concentrating on information exchanges between the

---

5   Parliamentary Commissioner for Standards' Guide to the Rules on All-Party Parliamentary Groups, UK Parliament website, www.parliament.uk.

6   All-Party Parliamentary Group for Education's website, www.parliament.uk.

7   All-Party Parliamentary Group on Agriculture and Food for Development website, www.parliament.uk.

parliamentarians and the external organisations and agencies active in the APPG, many APPGs will seek to actively shape and influence key policy debates, and to make a tangible contribution to policy development within the scope of their remit. The APPG on Dementia, for example, developed a manifesto focusing on dementia priorities for Government,[8] while others have undertaken inquiries such as the APPG on Children's inquiry into children and the police[9] and the APPG on Excellence in the Built Environment's inquiry into sustainable construction and the Green Deal.[10] Significantly, some APPGs will also provide collective responses to consultations launched by the UK Government and by other agencies.

If your organisation has supported MPs and Peers to establish a new APPG it will be in a strong position to engage with these policy makers to influence how the APPG will take forward its activities, and the issues on which it will concentrate. Your organisation's ability to do so will be greatly strengthened if it provides the secretariat for the APPG, and is in regular contact with the chair and other officers of the APPG. This type of role will provide opportunities to work with the office holders of the APPG to develop and agree agendas for meetings of the APPG, and to contribute to the thinking of the office bearers in these areas. By contrast, if your organisation is not in this position, it will need to engage with the chair and other officers of the APPG to persuade them to provide your organisation with an opportunity to, for example, deliver a presentation at one of the group's meetings. It is advised that your organisation should also engage with the organisation or agency providing the secretariat to the APPG to increase the chances of being offered such an opportunity. The importance of this type of activity to enable your organisation to engage with the APPG should not be underestimated because attendance at the APPG will often be on an invite only basis. Securing a presentation slot, or being invited to one of the APPG's roundtable discussion events or seminars, will provide your organisation with invaluable opportunities to raise the profile of your organisation and its work, and to raise awareness of key issues. Participating in an APPG will also afford major chances to

8   All-Party Parliamentary Group on Dementia's website, www.parliament.uk.
9   All-Party Parliamentary Group on Children's website, www.parliament.uk.
10 All-Party Parliamentary Group on Excellence in the Built Environment's website, www.parliament.uk.

network with MPs, Peers, parliamentary staff, and with representatives from other organisations and agencies. Developing contacts through this networking should be an important part of your organisation's public affairs strategy, as these contacts will assist your organisation to progress its aims and objectives going forward.

Making the most of presentations

As indicated above, securing a slot to provide an input at a meeting of an APPG, or even to be invited to attend the meeting, will not necessarily be guaranteed. If your organisation does secure a presentation at a meeting of an APPG it is, therefore, vital that it makes the most of the chance, particularly in view of the influencing opportunities it will afford. Your organisation should, therefore, liaise with the officers of the APPG and/or with the organisation or agency providing its secretariat, to get a sense of who will be attending the meeting, and how the input should be pitched. One aspect of this will be getting a steer on which policy topics and issues should be covered, and if the input should focus more on, for example, practice and service delivery than on policy issues, or on a combination of both areas. This will be invaluable in giving you a sense of who would be best placed from your organisation to provide the input.

Delivering this input will help to raise the profile of your organisation, and of its work, so it is essential that the input is delivered by a senior member of your organisation such as the chief executive or a senior manager. The person delivering the input may have as little as five or ten minutes, so you need to make the most of this time. You should provide a strong focus on the key issues, and draw upon the evidence and best practice of your organisation as much as possible. Case studies are also helpful in putting the issues in context for the audience, and should be considered for your input. To maximise the networking opportunities available you should make a copy of your input available to all those in attendance, and to ensure that your full contact detail are included in this document. You should also use any opportunities to contact the MPs and Peers after the meeting to offer follow-up meetings, or to provide them with additional briefing material, or to address any queries that may have emerged during the meeting of the APPG.

Media opportunities

In many cases the organisation which provides secretariat for the APPG will also be responsible for generating publicity for the APPG and its activities, and for increasing its profile through social media. If your organisation is working with MPs and Peers to establish a new APPG you will need to reach early agreement on who will be responsible for managing the APPG's media relations. In this respect, it is also important that a decision is made about who will be responsible for managing the APPG's website, and for maintaining and updating the APPG's social media presence. These will have a significant role to play in promoting the APPG, and it is essential that whichever organisation assumes responsibility for promoting the APPG has the capacity to do so.

If, on the other hand, your organisation is simply an 'associate' or 'affiliate' member, or an organisation that supports the work of the APPG, and which has provided an input at a meeting, you should liaise with the officers and with the organisation providing the secretariat about publicity. By doing so, you will be able to confirm how publicity for the meeting is to be handled, and by whom. This will also help your organisation to be part of any discussions about how your input will feature, if at all, in any activities to promote the event with the media. You should also ensure that your own organisation's social media activities focus on its input at the APPG, and seek to promote the event with MPs, Peers, with other organisations, with your supporters and with the general public. In this respect, the use of social media will potentially offer further opportunities to engage the Government, the opposition parties, MPs, Peers and parliamentary staff on the issues you will be raising at the APPG. This will be another useful means of increasing the profile of your organisation and its work. It is vital, however, that if you take this option that you provide regular updates on social media to ensure that you are providing information as up-to-date as possible.

Summary of key points

The key points from this chapter can be summarised as follows:

- APPGs cover a wide range of topics and policy issues, and the APPGs recognised by Parliament can be found on the Register of All-Party Parliamentary Groups.
- Participation in APPGs can raise the profile of organisations, and increase awareness of headline issues and campaigns.
- Priority should be given to participating in those APPGs most relevant to your organisation and its work, and which are best suited to assist your organisation to achieve its goals and objectives.
- If you are seeking to establish a new APPG, consideration should be given to identifying other organisations and agencies which share your commitment in this area, and to working with them to engage with MPs and Peers to achieve your common goals.

19

Maximising the Impact of Parliamentary Events

There are two main types of parliamentary events – briefing events, and receptions. Briefing events are used to update politicians on major policy developments including, for example, an organisation's response to a specific piece of parliamentary legislation or on policy issues it wishes to raise for a forthcoming parliamentary debate. These events can also be used to launch campaigns, or to brief MPs, Peers and parliamentary staff about ongoing campaigns. The other type of event is the parliamentary reception. These are used to showcase organisations, or to celebrate a landmark anniversary for the organisation or to highlight other significant developments. The distinctions between the two types of event are, however, often slight, given that both can be used to brief MPs, Peers and parliamentary staff on key policy issues, or to play a strategic role in their organisation's campaigns. The term 'parliamentary event' is, therefore, used throughout this chapter to include both parliamentary briefing events and parliamentary receptions (unless otherwise stated).

Events take place throughout the entire parliamentary session, and can be held in either House of Parliament. Organisations with the capacity and resources to hold such events have found that they can be a highly effective way of engaging with political parties in Parliament, and in developing their relationships with MPs, Peers and parliamentary staff. Many of these organisations have discovered that the potential benefits of holding a parliamentary event far outweigh the investment in time, resources and effort they require to make the event a success. Parliamentary events can, for example, provide organisations with important opportunities to raise their profile with key policy makers, and to build, or strengthen existing, relationships with politicians of all parties. This, in turn, can make it easier for the organisations to secure support for their policy positions and campaigns, and potentially help to shape and influence policy development with Government and in Parliament.

Apart from targeting the political parties, and their MPs, Peers and parliamentary staff, these prestigious events can also offer your organisation the chance to engage with partner organisations, and with agencies or other stakeholders with whom you wish to work more closely, and/or to develop your relationship. Businesses, for example, might want to consider inviting Board members, major investors and representatives from other companies with which they enjoy a close relationship or would like to develop such a relationship. Charities, on the other hand, should consider inviting trustees, leading supporters, donors and funders. While public bodies would want to give thought to inviting representatives from partner organisations and other key stakeholders such as funding bodies. This would include civil servants from Government departments, especially where the public bodies are in receipt of funding from these departments.

Aims and objectives

Holding a parliamentary event can provide strategic opportunities to raise the profile of your organisation and its work. If your organisation is interested in holding a parliamentary event, it is recommended that, as part of its initial planning, you set clear aims and objectives for the event. The main things to consider are what your organisation wants the event to achieve, and how this will be evaluated. Is it to raise awareness about your organisation and to strengthen its relationships with key policy makers? Or are you also seeking to shape and influence major parliamentary business impacting upon your organisation, its business and work? It is vital that these factors are addressed from the outset as they will have an important bearing on the nature of the event, as well as on how the arrangements for the event are progressed.

Organising a parliamentary event will be a major undertaking for most organisations. It is, therefore, essential that, if your organisation decides to hold one, it must be given high priority. This is particularly important because organising the event will potentially involve a number of different departments and sections within your organisation, including senior management, policy and public affairs, media, events, services, business and administration. Which parts of your organisation are likely to be involved will depend upon how your organisation is structured and on the nature of its work or business, and on how it approaches events planning and management. The main thing is that your organisation takes a co-ordinated approach to planning, managing and delivering parliamentary events.

Against this background, your organisation should establish a short-life, internal working group to oversee progressing the arrangements for the event, and to take key decisions relating to its management. Having this structure in place will help to ensure that the event is organised efficiently, and that a co-ordinated approach is taken to progressing and delivering all aspects of the event. It will also contribute to promoting the organisational buy-in that will be crucial if the event is to showcase your organisation for the right reasons, and to achieve all of its aims and objectives. Once your organisation has addressed these issues, it will need to consider various logistical factors to design and deliver the event. Given that the event will be a high profile occasion it is vital that you give these areas detailed consideration to guarantee that the event is as successful as possible.

Purpose of the event

One of the first issues your organisation will need to consider, and to decide, is the purpose of the event it wishes to hold. This will be an overriding factor in your organisation's decision making, and event planning. Do you want to hold a parliamentary reception to showcase your organisation, its work and successes? Examples include parliamentary receptions to launch or progress a campaign, to celebrate a major event, or to mark a keynote anniversary or other landmark or development. Alternatively, do you want the event to have a stronger policy focus, the aim of which is to brief MPs, Peers and parliamentary staff on your organisation's policy position in relation to specific issues, or to launch, or update the latter about, a campaign? Once the purpose of the event has been agreed, this will provide your organisation with the foundations on which to base the event, and to plan and manage the arrangements to deliver the event.

Key themes

It is also important that your organisation identifies an appropriate theme for the event, and has clear messages it wishes to get across to those attending the event. This would include headline corporate messages, as well as any policy positions or 'policy asks' you want to highlight at the event. Many organisations will only have the capacity and resources to hold a parliamentary event once every Parliament. It is, therefore, essential that your organisation, in order to make the most of the event, carefully considers and reaches a firm decision at the beginning of the planning process about the themes and issues on which the event will focus. This will help to provide the event with a clear identity, and make a positive contribution to promoting the event with MPs, Peers and parliamentary staff, as well as with other key stakeholders.

Consideration should be given to linking the event with, or to focusing the event on, current or forthcoming parliamentary business. Is your organisation seeking, for example, to brief MPs, Peers and parliamentary staff on legislation which has been introduced in Parliament, or is there a strong interface between the policy issues on which you wish to focus and the date for future parliamentary debates? Making these connections will strengthen the policy context of the event, and increase the chances that your event will secure a good turnout from MPs, Peers, and parliamentary staff and from other prominent stakeholders. MPs and Peers will often be looking for updates, and for new perspectives, on such business. Being able to go to an event which promises to quickly get them up to speed on a substantial piece of parliamentary business will increase the attractiveness of the event.

Approaching a sponsoring MP or Peer

Once your organisation has agreed fundamental issues, such as the purpose, and main themes and messages, it will need to approach an MP or Peer to sponsor the event. The MP or Peer will be able to book the venue in Parliament, and act as a first point of contact with the House authorities for any queries which may arise. The MP or Peer will also be able to advise about when the event should be held: generally lunchtime or evening, although other times may be available for briefing events.

In addition, they will be able to highlight any other events with which your event could potentially clash. This would include internal party meetings, committee proceedings and other high profile events being staged at the same time by organisations. This information will be invaluable in giving your organisation the best chances of securing a high attendance of MPs, Peers and parliamentary staff.

There are a number of options for your organisation to consider in choosing a sponsoring MP or Peer. One option would be to approach your local MP, or the MP or Peer most closely associated with your organisation, to sponsor the event. Alternatively, your organisation could contact an MP or Peer who has a high public profile, and/or has a proven track record of campaigning or advocacy on the issues on which the event will focus. This could help to boost the number of MPs, Peers and parliamentary staff likely to attend the event. It is, therefore, important that your organisation gives careful thought to which MP or Peer it decides to approach to host the event. The sponsoring MP or Peer might also have advice on which venue to choose. In this respect, consideration should be given to using venues such as the Terrace, or the Moses Room or the Pugin Room in the House of Lords. For a briefing event you might find that a House of Commons or a House of Lords committee room would suit your organisation's needs. The MP or Peer or their staff will be able to advise you on the availability of these rooms.

When you contact the MP or Peer and secure their agreement to sponsor the event you should try and get a sense of how active a role they would like to take in planning the event, and at the event itself. If it is an MP or Peer with particularly close ties with your organisation, or a long track record on the specific issues or themes for the event, they may wish to have a say in important aspects of the event such as its structure, the programme, choice of speakers etc. Most MPs or Peers, however, will be happy to leave the everyday planning to your organisation. Regardless of their input, if any, into the design of the event, you should have a discussion with the MP or Peer about how much they want to be involved in the event itself. Some will be content just to attend, others will be happy to chair the event or to give a formal welcome. An MP or Peer with a strong interest in the issues and themes on which the event will focus may want to be one of the formal speakers at the event. It is strongly recommended that you agree at the earliest stage with the MP or Peer on the role they will play at the event. This will help to ensure that the sponsoring MP or Peer is 'given their place'. It will also support your organisation to finalise the programme for the event at an early stage.

Identifying your target audience

Your organisation should identify the major policy makers it wishes to target for the event. Ideally, you want to ensure that the relevant Government minister attends the event, and provides a formal input such as the keynote speech or a welcome to the attendees. To influence the policy debate going forward, you also need to identify which MPs, Peers and parliamentary staff you want to invite to the event. The starting point should be your existing contacts within these groups, and those with whom you have the closest ties. As well as these groups, your organisation should target the MPs, Peers and parliamentary staff with an interest in the policy issues on which the event will concentrate. Once you have finalised your guest list, the above groups should be targeted by letter and by e-mail, and you should follow up with phone calls to the MPs and Peers, and also use social media.

If your organisation is uncertain about which MPs and Peers have an interest in the policy areas on which the event will focus, useful sources for this information would be the membership lists of relevant All-Party Parliamentary Groups, and the biographies of the MPs and Peers on the House of Commons and House of Lords sections of the UK Parliament's website, or in *Vacher's Quarterly*. Researching relevant debates in *Hansard* is another useful source of information, as this will confirm which MPs or Peers spoke in debates, or raised questions, on relevant policy issues and themes. You can then take a targeted approach to inviting those MPs and Peers. Apart from adopting a targeted approach to inviting the latter, your organisation should also send out a general invite to MPs and Peers.

Particular thought should be given to approaching MPs or Peers if your organisation is seeking to build a cross-party alliance in response to a Bill. In this context, apart from securing the attendance of the relevant Government Minister, your organisation should also target the relevant spokespersons of each political party to ensure the policy debate at the event, and stimulated by the event, is as wide ranging as possible. Your organisation should also target MPs or Peers with an interest in the policy issues raised by the Bill. You should try to have both MPs and Peers at the event focusing on legislation to generate cross-party support for your policy positions. This will maximise your organisation's ability to influence the legislation as it progresses through both Houses of Parliament. The interventions of the politicians at your event will give you a sense of which issues may generate cross-party support, and those where the parties will divide along party lines. This will be invaluable political intelligence for your organisation as it develops its response to the Bill. It will also help your organisation to develop or strengthen its relationships with MPs and/or Peers who will be willing to raise issues on your behalf, including taking forward your organisation's proposed amendments to the Bill.

Contacting specific MPs and/or Peers, as part of an overall, general approach, will hopefully secure the attendance of sufficient numbers at the event. You should keep a running total of responses received, and record who will attend, who has declined and who is a 'maybe'. This will give your organisation a sense of how well attended the event is likely to be. The guest list should be kept under constant review and, if the numbers of potential attendees look low, new names and organisations should be added to the guest list where others have already confirmed they are unable to attend.

Where MPs or Peers fall into the 'maybe' category it is important that you follow up with them and, where appropriate, their staff. As the date of the event approaches, your organisation should send out a final communication to those MPs and Peers who will be attending to confirm the details, and stating that your organisation looks forward to seeing them at the event. For those who remain 'maybes' you should send them a final reminder, and follow up with a phone call. In this context, remember that MPs and Peers are often extremely busy, and that your organisation's event will be just one of the many demands upon their time. Your priority is securing a high turnout of MPs, Peers and parliamentary staff at the event, so it is crucial that your organisation promotes the event amongst MPs, Peers and parliamentary staff, to maximise their attendance.

The sponsoring MP or Peer and, where appropriate, their staff can also play a vital role in promoting the event using their contacts across both Houses of Parliament. This would include publicising the event at the meetings of any relevant APPGs. Their parties will also be able to feature details for the event in the Party Whip which they will send out to their members in the House of Commons and in the House of Lords.

In the case of an event sponsored by a Crossbench Peer details can be circulated in the information sent out to the Crossbench Peers by their Convenor and by the resource centre for the Crossbench Peers. Most MPs will have parliamentary staff, and they can play an important role in publicising your organisation's event, and it is recommended that you copy them into any e-mails about the event sent to the MPs they work for. If a party has advisers or specialist researchers focusing on the policy issues on which your event will focus, you should ensure that they are invited. These staff members will often write the MPs' or Peers' speeches or briefings, and getting them to attend will, therefore, help to progress the policy debate within Parliament.

Developing the programme

The programme and format of the event should be as attractive as possible. Securing the participation of high profile speakers will be critical. As part of that process, you should make a determined effort to secure the participation of the relevant Government minister. To secure the participation of the minister you will need to ensure that you factor in enough time in your event planning for the minister's office to respond to your invite. It is suggested that you allow a minimum of three months for a ministerial reply to your invite, unless the minister has already given a strong indication that they will speak at the event. Ideally, you want the minister to be the keynote speaker at the event. It is recommended, however, that your organisation has a back-up plan for inviting other prominent speakers just in case the minister is unable to participate in your parliamentary event.

Assuming the minister agrees to attend the event as the keynote speaker, for a parliamentary reception you would probably want the sponsoring MP or Peer to welcome everyone to the event, and to outline the purpose of the event. This could be followed by a senior figure in your organisation – either the chair or the chief executive – providing some background about your organisation, and highlighting the headline issues on which the event is focusing before formally introducing the minister. With parliamentary receptions the Minister's speech would normally focus on the interface between the Government's policy positions and activities in specific areas, and your organisation and its work. The aim of a parliamentary reception would be to showcase your organisation. It is, therefore, recommended that you limit the number of speakers for this type of event. Ideally, you want to keep the speeches to a minimum, and for the speeches to be brief. You want to ensure that as much time as possible is available for your organisation's staff to network with leading policy makers, and to ensure this engagement delivers tangible outcomes. Examples of such outcomes would include the minister agreeing to a formal meeting with your organisation to discuss an issue of mutual interest, an MP agreeing to lodge an amendment to a Parliamentary Bill on your behalf or a Peer agreeing to raise issues for your organisation in a parliamentary debate.

Where your organisation is looking to hold a parliamentary briefing event, you should also seek to secure the participation of the relevant Government minister and other high profile speakers. The focus of these events is on policy issues, and on raising awareness of these issues and stimulating debate amongst key policy makers. Your organisation should, therefore, concentrate on securing the participation of influential speakers who will be able to help your organisation to meet these aims. As with parliamentary receptions, it is recommended that the MP or Peer who sponsors the briefing event says a few words to welcome everyone to the event. A senior representative from your organisation could then provide an input on the policy issues and themes your organisation wants to raise. This would set the scene for the minister, and for any other prominent speakers who have agreed to participate in the event, to provide their inputs. You want high quality speakers who will help to inform discussions at the meeting, but it would be best not to have too many speakers as ideally you will want to leave time for questions, and to promote a discussion after the speeches in which all attendees will have an opportunity to participate.

Promoting the event

Once you have the venue booked, secured speakers and developed the programme for the event, your organisation will need to actively promote the event to ensure it is well attended by MPs, Peers and parliamentary staff, and to raise the profile of your organisation. The sponsoring MP or Peer will be able to use their networks within Parliament to raise awareness of the event. Apart from including details of the event on their Party's Whip, it is strongly recommended that you request that the sponsoring MP or Peer highlights the event on social media. You should also work with the sponsoring MP or Peer to prepare a news release to try and generate publicity for the event. The extent to which it is realistic to expect to secure national or local media coverage will largely depend upon the subject matter of the event, the newsworthiness of the issues on which it will focus and the profile of the speakers and other attendees. Securing a good level of publicity for the event is vital on a number of levels. Apart from maximising attendance at the event, and raising awareness of your organisation and its business or work with key policy makers, a well attended event will be invaluable if the event is part of a campaign to influence policy development or legislation at Government level and within Parliament. In this context, demonstrating to the Government and to the opposition parties and other groupings in Parliament that your organisation has significant support for its policy position in a specific area will strengthen your capacity to influence leading policy makers, and the direction of policy travel. Part of that process will be your organisation's ability to show that there is strong media interest in the issues it is raising.

Summary of key points

The key points from this chapter can be summarised as follows:

- Parliamentary events can be a highly effective way for organisations to engage with the Government, and the opposition parties, and to develop or strengthen their relationships with MPs, Peers and key parliamentary staff.
- These prestigious events can also offer your organisation the chance to engage with partner organisations, and with agencies or other stakeholders with whom you are seeking to work more closely.
- Organising a parliamentary event will be a major undertaking for most organisations, and it is important that your organisation takes a co-ordinated approach to planning, managing and delivering parliamentary events.
- Careful thought should be given to which leading policy makers your organisation wishes to attend the event, including securing the agreement of the relevant Government minister to provide a formal input at the event.

20

Making the Most of Party Conferences

The main political parties represented in Parliament generally hold spring and autumn conferences. These high profile events usually take place over a few days, with the length of conferences varying from party to party. The conferences represent major political events in each party's political calendar, and will be attended by the respective parties' leaderships, MPs, Peers, councillors, as well as by their activists and supporters. The conferences provide a forum in which the full membership of the different parties can meet to progress a wide range of activities. This can include discussing and agreeing their party's manifesto or other internal business, electing party members to senior party positions, debating and deciding their party's policy positions and launching and progressing campaigns. Above all, these major political gatherings provide each party's membership and supporters with a chance to hear from the party's leadership about the latter's vision and plans for the future, including key policies and campaigns that the party is, or will be, prioritising. The conferences also afford excellent opportunities for the party's membership and supporters to network with each other. Most conferences will generate significant media coverage.

Good party conferences can be dynamic, exciting events, which can see a party emerge stronger and strategically better equipped for the parliamentary and electoral challenges ahead. A poor conference, on the other hand, played out under the full glare of the media spotlight, can prove extremely costly to a party in terms of its public profile and reputation. Over the years, there have been a number of occasions in which political parties have paid the supreme electoral price for conferences that have created, or perhaps reinforced, a public perception that the party in question is unelectable or otherwise cannot be trusted. By contrast, other parties have been able to use their conferences as launch pads to improve their electoral fortunes by demonstrating to the public that they are strong, united and 'fit to govern'. These factors, combined with the dynamic of the comparative weaknesses of their rivals, will often lead to success at the ballot box.

Significantly, the parties' conferences are also attended by various non-party organisations seeking to engage with the respective parties' key policy makers in discussions around policy issues of mutual interest, and trying to influence the parties' policy positions and campaigns. Against this background, it should come as no surprise that the party conferences can offer organisations major opportunities to engage with the political parties, and with their leading policy and decision makers. This includes the respective parties' leaderships and other main spokespersons, their MPs, Peers and councillors. It can also offer significant chances to engage with the parties' political staff, including their advisers, and their parliamentary researchers and assistants who, as we have seen in previous chapters, are an important group of contacts in their own right.

Building up your organisation's contacts with these different groups of political contacts can offer a wide range of advantages, and opportunities. It can, for example, help to raise your organisation's profile, and to increase awareness of its work, with the political parties, and within Parliament. This would include potentially providing your organisation with openings through which to engage with the parties' respective senior policy makers on the main policy issues and debates your organisation is seeking to influence, or on campaigns your organisation is progressing. It would also ensure that the respective parties are fully up-to-speed on the issues and concerns on which these campaigns are based, and on your organisation's 'policy asks'. In addition, attending these conferences will give your organisation opportunities to engage with ministers, MPs and Peers on parliamentary business relevant to your organisation and its work. This can be particularly useful where your organisation is seeking to have issues raised in a debate, or to help shape and influence legislation which is going through Parliament, and you are seeking support to amend the legislation.

Furthermore, attending the conferences will offer your organisation strategic opportunities to strengthen its existing connections with key policy makers, and to develop new relationships with a range of senior policy makers. Progress in these areas will be vital to the long term effectiveness of your organisation's public affairs strategy in influencing Government ministers, the opposition parties and their main spokespersons, MPs, Peers and councillors. A successful conference could present various new opportunities, and also help your organisation to successfully manage (on an early intervention basis) any challenges it may face reputationally, or in the policy development sphere in areas where there could be policy tensions with a particular party or parties. These are all important, positive outcomes which give some insight into the potential benefits that can arise from ensuring your organisation has an active presence at the political parties' conferences. The type of outcomes outlined above highlight the need for your organisation, when it considers the case for attending these conferences, to clearly identify from the outset, and to base its planning for the conferences on, the goals and results it wishes to achieve through its attendance at the conferences.

Key considerations

Once your organisation has decided in principle it is going to attend the parties' conferences, it will need to take a view on whether or not it is going to attend the conferences of all of the main parties, or to prioritise the conferences of those parties which it considers most relevant and strategic to the aims of its public affairs strategy. After taking a view on these matters, your organisation should determine if it will attend both the spring and autumn conferences of the individual political parties. It will also have to consider if it wishes to manage its presence at a particular conference by sending representatives to the conference as observers, and/or by hosting an exhibition space and/ or by holding a 'fringe' meeting. Alternatively, your organisation may wish to have a conference presence which is a combination of all, or some, of these elements.

Ideally, your organisation should take a cross-party approach to the political parties' conferences, and try and attend as many of the different parties' conferences as possible. For most organisations, however, these issues will probably, by necessity, be driven by, and decided on the basis of, cost, resources and capacity. In this respect, many organisations will need to prioritise those conferences which they believe are most likely to assist their organisation to meet the main aims of their public affairs strategy, and to give the organisation the greatest return in terms of their influence with the different parties, and with the latter's senior policy makers. For some organisations that would mean focussing on the conferences of the party or parties of Government, and of the Official Opposition party, while for other organisations budgetary and capacity constraints might limit their conference presence to attending the conferences of the party or parties of Government. If acting on a cross-party basis is a major consideration for your organisation, it is important that you have a clear policy in place to explain any decisions taken which result in your organisation not having a presence at all of the political parties' conferences. This is particularly important to avoid such an approach being called into question within your organisation, or publicly. The last thing you want is for your organisation's credibility, and its public affairs strategy, to be undermined by allegations of bias, where being seen to act in a non-partisan, cross-party way is an important part of your organisation's character and identity. Not all organisations are likely to be sensitive to such allegations, and this will depend upon their remit, campaigns and political associations or relationships.

Another key consideration for your organisation, once it has addressed the above issues, will be to decide which members of your organisation's staff will attend particular conferences. A number of factors will contribute to your organisation's decision making in this area. The first thing is to take a view on who will lead your organisation's presence at a specific conference. These conferences can present major influencing opportunities for your organisation. It is, therefore, important that your organisation is represented by staff that have a sound knowledge of your organisation, and are able to speak knowledgeably and articulately about its work, policy priorities and campaigns. As part of your organisation's internal discussions and decision making about its conference presence, serious consideration should be given to the need for, and appropriateness of, your organisation's chair and/or chief executive and/or other members of the senior management team attending the conference.

You will also want to take into account your organisation's policy positions, and any high profile campaigns it is prioritising at the time of a particular conference, in your organisation's discussions and decision making about attending a specific party conference, as this may have a bearing upon who represents your organisation at the conference. It would also be helpful to have literature about your organisation, its policy positions and campaigns available at the conference.

Another factor will be how your organisation wishes to be represented at the conference. If, for example, it is running a fringe event or hosting an exhibition space, then serious thought should be given to ensuring that your chair and/or chief executive and/or other members of the senior management team will be available to attend at least those parts of the conference most critical to your organisation's public affairs strategy. Some organisations, however, are content to be represented at the political parties' conferences by their policy and/or public affairs staff, especially if the organisation has decided to attend the conference with observer passes, and will not be holding a fringe event or hosting an exhibition space which would, in particular, merit consideration being given to members of the senior management team attending. Your organisation should weigh up very carefully how it wants to manage its presence at specific conferences to maximise its impact, and to ensure the organisation's presence delivers positive outcomes. Your organisation can then take a view on who should represent it at the different conferences.

Planning and managing your organisation's conference presence

Once your organisation has decided which conferences it wishes to attend, and what type of presence it wants to have at these conferences, you should start planning for the conferences. In this respect, you should, ideally, start planning in October for conferences in the following March, and commence planning in April for conferences in September/October.

As part of this process, you need to contact the conference organisers to process the necessary booking forms. Some of the political parties will require your organisation's representatives to have photo IDs to attend their conferences, so it is vital that you allow enough time to provide the information necessary to complete your applications for photo IDs, and for these to be processed. It is essential to get this right, because without the prerequisite ID (usually in the form of a photo pass) you will not be allowed access to the conference venues. This could lead to a major reduction in the time available at the conference for your organisation to engage with senior policy makers. This, in turn, could be extremely costly in terms of limiting the tangible outcomes your organisation's 'reduced' presence at the conference will be able to deliver. Against this background, it is recommended that, while recognising that the paper work may be the least of many organisations' worries in the busy run up to the conference, it is important you do not neglect this area. You want to put your organisation in the best possible position of having completed the necessary paper work, and of being able to turn up at the conference ready to immediately start your influencing work with each party's senior policy makers, and with its wider membership.

Many organisations, regardless of which sector they are principally based in, will have a limited budget for the political parties' conferences, and will want to make this budget stretch as far as possible. Attending the different conferences can be very expensive, because once you have paid for the main elements of your organisation's conference presence, i.e. observer passes and/or exhibition spaces and/or fringe meetings, you will also have to pay for additional costs such as staff time, transport costs, courier costs, publications, entertainments costs, staff subsistence costs and possibly accommodation costs. These can all mount up quite quickly, so it is strongly advised that when you contact the organisers you ask for their best price, and see if you can negotiate a lower price. The options to get a better deal will depend upon a number of factors, such as when you contact the organisers, and whether or not your organisation is a 'return' client which books every year. Being a charity can also sometimes be helpful in securing a discount, on top of those normally available at most conferences for third sector organisations. The demand for observer passes, exhibition spaces and fringe meetings from external organisations will also be influential factors. In effect, the lower the levels of take-up in these areas, the better chance you have of securing a discount. There is no exact science to this process, but the main thing is that you at least try and negotiate a better deal for your organisation's conference package if costs are likely to be an issue for your organisation.

To maximise the time available for your organisation to influence senior policy makers at a party's conference, careful thought should be given to the accommodation your organisation books for any staff attending the conference. This will be an important consideration where the conference is taking place a considerable distance from your organisation's normal place of business, or if there are evening events which will be central to your organisation's influencing strategy for the conference. Booking your accommodation early will give your organisation the best chances of being near the main 'political action' at the venues for the keynote events and meetings, many of which will take place in the evening. These conferences are flagship events for the different parties, and you will need to make the most of your organisation's presence at the conferences if this is to deliver the best outcomes. In this respect, being based near the main conference centres will be helpful in accommodating any meetings you have arranged with the party's senior policy makers, and will support your organisation to manage its conference presence as efficiently as possible. It will also ensure that your organisation's staff are able to attend any evening receptions or events with the minimum inconvenience.

Political 'prep'

Even organisations with excellent political contacts, and which enjoy high levels of engagement with Government, with the opposition parties and with other key policy makers, will attend the main political parties' conferences. Indeed, most of these organisations will remain sensitive to the impact of political change either through a change in policy by Government or by a specific opposition party, or through a change in minister or Government itself. They are, therefore, still likely to attend the conferences as an important forum in which to engage with policy makers. Many of these organisations will attend the parties' conferences, or at least attend the major conferences, to try and insulate themselves against any adverse effects arising from such wide governmental and political changes.

Some organisations with powerful brands will generally be able to secure high levels of engagement at the parties' conferences. By contrast, the majority of organisations will not be in this position, and will need to carefully consider how they can best maximise the impact of their presence at the parties' conferences to secure good levels of engagement with key policy makers. For many, this will hinge on the pre-conference political preparation or 'political prep' they undertake before the conference. Getting this right can be the difference between an organisation having a highly successful conference, or experiencing a conference washout. One of the main aspects of your organisation's pre-conference 'political prep' should be deciding the key outcomes you wish to secure through the conference. Are you hoping, for example, to use the conference to strengthen your existing political contacts with specific ministers or leading policy spokespersons as appropriate, with MPs or Peers or councillors? Or are you seeking to use the conference to develop new contacts, or a combination of both? Alternatively, are you aiming to use the conference to generally raise awareness about your organisation and its work including specific areas of its business or services with prominent policy makers, or to lobby the latter about particular policies or campaigns you are prioritising? In this respect, part of your 'political prep' should be agreeing which headline messages you will be emphasising to the policy makers at the conference, or what aspects of your business or services you wish to promote.

An important part of your 'political prep' should be undertaking research into the key policy makers you wish to engage with at the conference. First of all, who are they, and will they be attending? Secondly what contact has your organisation had with the individual policy makers to date, and what are you hoping to achieve through engaging with them later at the conference? Thirdly, what policy areas are the policy makers interested in, and what issues are of mutual interest? Once your organisation has undertaken this 'political prep', it can use the information gained to develop a programme of meetings with the policy makers at the party conference. The main thing is to get in touch with the Government ministers or lead spokespersons for the different parties, and with the MPs, Peers and councillors with whom you wish to engage. You should let them know that your organisation will be attending their conference, and provide an outline of what your organisation will be doing at the conference, particularly if you are running a fringe event or hosting an exhibition space. You should also use this contact to try and fix up meetings with the different policy makers at the conference. Taking this approach, rather than just turning up and hoping that you will be able to meet all of your main contacts, will strengthen your organisation's engagement with senior policy makers at the conference. Securing such meetings will help your organisation to increase its impact at the conference, and to ensure that its presence delivers tangible outcomes.

Another major part of your 'political prep' for specific party conferences will be ensuring that you have publications and briefing materials which will enable your organisation to best promote itself to the Government ministers, party spokespersons, MPs, Peers, councillors and to the wider party membership attending the conference. If you are generally seeking to raise the profile of your organisation, and to increase awareness of its work, you should ensure that you have some general information which will tell the policy makers about your organisation, its work and the policy areas and issues on which it focuses. In addition, you should consider making more specialist briefing material available if you have launched a campaign on which you are seeking the support of the different political parties and of their senior policy makers. Specialist briefings would also be helpful if you are seeking to engage with the party on parliamentary business such as a piece of legislation impacting upon your organisation, and on its business or services. Getting the right tone and balance in your briefing material will be an important consideration if you are holding a fringe event or hosting an exhibition space. It is important not to lose sight of the fact that you are attending the conference to 'sell' your organisation, its 'policy asks' and campaigns to the political party hosting the conference, and to the policy makers attending.

Exhibition spaces

Many organisations will focus their presence at party conferences through hosting an exhibition space. Typically, this will be a space in the exhibitors' area (sometimes referred to as the exhibitors' 'market place'), which will use their organisation's large banner, or smaller 'pop-up' banners, featuring their logo and branded messages as a backcloth, with tables for the display of their briefing material. Exhibition spaces will normally be sold as packages and include observer passes, the number of which will vary from party to party. Subject to the number of observer passes available with the exhibition space, these passes may enable organisations to staff their exhibition space and also to attend key parts of the conference programme without purchasing separate observer passes. For some organisations having an exhibition space and the attendant observer pass package will be enough to meet their needs for particular conferences.

There are a number of significant advantages for hosting an exhibition space. One of the key advantages is that the exhibition space will provide your organisation with a base for the duration of the conference. It is a strategic area where you can profile your organisation, and advertise its work, 'policy asks' and campaigns. The exhibition space can also provide your organisation with a base, where it can arrange to meet key policy makers. This can be particularly useful if any of your pre-arranged meetings with MPs or Peers or councillors fall through, and you are looking to reschedule with the policy maker concerned. After all, you need to be mindful of the conference dynamics, and that the conference is for the political party and for the party faithful, and the focus is on the political party's conference business. It is important not to forget that your organisation, and the other external organisations attending, are there as guests, and have to fit in with the conference dynamic, which means that arrangements with policy makers may sometimes be overtaken by, for example, internal party politics or conference business. Against this background, you need to take a flexible approach to managing your organisation's conference presence, and an exhibition space is a good way of maintaining that approach because it will give your organisation a strong focus for the conference even if its pre-arranged meetings fall through.

Hosting an exhibition space will also give you a base at which you can take various publicity photographs with senior policy makers against the backcloth of your banner and logo. Such photographs can be a helpful form of engagement with policy makers, and can potentially provide a useful record of the conference for your organisation. MPs will also often be keen to use the photographs through social media to highlight their association with your organisation and its work. You should also use these photographs on your organisation's own social media to highlight its presence at the conference, and its engagement with policy makers. In addition, the photographs can provide your organisation with an excellent stock of publicity material for the future. Such materials can make an invaluable contribution to your organisation's influencing strategy going forward.

The main disadvantage of an exhibition space is that it can be very expensive. Booking a space also assumes that there will be a steady stream of policy makers to it. There can, however, be a significant variance in this experience across different conferences. Best practice is that the organisers of the conference will make a concerted effort to ensure that Government ministers or the opposition parties' leaders and key spokespersons as appropriate, as well as the party's MPs, Peers, parliamentary staff and councillors visit all of the exhibition spaces. This is not always the case, and is an area in which your 'political prep' will come into play. In this respect, the more effort you have made prior to the conference, including using social media, to make sure that the party's leading policy makers know that your organisation will have an exhibition space at the conference, the better. This will help to promote interest in your organisation's exhibition space, and assist your organisation to maximise its engagement with senior policy makers during the conference.

The exhibition space area at party conferences is usually one of the busiest areas at a conference, and your exhibition space is likely to be just one of many. Your organisation, therefore, needs to make sure that its exhibition space stands out for the right reasons. Some key policy makers will be drawn to exhibition spaces by an organisation's brand and logo alone, but others may take a bit more persuasion to visit, and to spend any time at, your exhibition space due to their busy conference diaries and prior commitments. Apart from your organisation's 'political prep', you need to think about what else can be done to make your exhibition space one which your target policy makers will definitely visit. Making sure that your banners are eye-catching, and that your exhibition space is best suited to promote your organisation will be important considerations. It is also recommended that you have a good selection of briefing materials, and 'freebies' e.g. branded pens, notebooks, or sweets, which can be given away to those who visit your organisation's exhibition space.

To attract key policy makers to your exhibition space, you might want to consider making the exhibition space as interactive an experience as possible. Examples would include getting the policy makers to sign a 'pledge board' on which they write their names, and confirm their commitment to work for a particular political and/or policy objective either within Parliament or generally at the national level. This works well if it is combined with a photo opportunity. This type of initiative provides your organisation with a chance to brief the policy maker on the issues you are prioritising, and on the 'policy asks' you wish them to progress. Other examples which work well are where businesses give policy makers an opportunity to undertake an exercise, or to try out some product, which demonstrates the value of their business. By way of further example, many health charities have enjoyed excellent engagement with policy makers by providing health checks that demonstrate their policy priorities and work. For busy politicians, the lure of receiving free health checks to prove they are in rude health without taking time out of their intense schedules to visit the doctor or dentist often proves irresistible.

Observer passes

Not all organisations will focus their presence at the party conferences on hosting an exhibition space or on holding a fringe event. Some will choose to manage their presence at these conferences by purchasing observer passes only. This decision could be based on cost, capacity, or simply because the organisation has found this approach to be the most effective for its purposes. The advantages of focusing on observer passes is that logistically there is less to organise in certain areas prior to the conference. With the observer pass option you will be spared any worries around the transportation of your organisation's banner and briefing materials to the conference, and the setting up of the exhibition space, prior to the start of the conference. The risk, however, is that, by focusing on this option alone, your organisation could be placing significant limits on its likely impact at the conference. The conference, after all, will be busy and organisations will often be in intense competition with each other to engage with key policy makers. Exhibition spaces and fringe events can offer important advantages in these areas, as both will distinctly advertise your organisation's presence at the conference in ways that an observer pass will be unable to match.

It should be emphasised that organisations relying on the observer pass option can still have highly successful conferences, and enjoy a high level of engagement with senior policy makers. The effectiveness of this approach will ultimately depend upon being focused, well organised and upon ensuring that your pre-conference political prep will deliver meetings and contacts with all of the key policy makers your organisation wishes to target. One aspect of this will be reviewing the conference programme, and taking a view on which events and meetings will offer the best opportunities for your organisation to contribute to the main policy discussions at the conference relevant to your organisation and its work. To assist this process your organisation should map the main networking opportunities presented by the conference. This would include attending any civic receptions, which can sometimes offer important opportunities to engage with senior policy makers in what is sometimes a less pressurised environment than the often intense main exhibition space area.

Your organisation also needs to consider why it is attending the conference, what outcomes it wants to achieve and which Government ministers, opposition party leaders or spokespersons, MPs, Peers, parliamentary staff or councillors you will have to engage with to secure these outcomes. This is where your 'political prep' will prove critical. Prior to the conference you should contact these policy makers to update them on your organisation's work, to confirm you will be at their party's conference and to make arrangements to meet them. If you do not host an exhibition space, or hold a fringe meeting, at the parties' conferences such pre-conference approaches to key policy makers will be essential if you are to ensure that your organisation's presence at the conferences secures significant engagement with senior policy makers, and delivers tangible results. To maximise the success of these pre-conference approaches you should try and link these approaches with parliamentary business in which the minister or opposition party key spokesperson, or MP or Peer has an interest, and would be interested in discussing issues around the business.

Ideally, you want to put in place a programme of meetings with leading policy makers at the conference, which has been arranged well in advance of the conference. Without such a programme, it could be difficult for your organisations to secure the conference outcomes it is hoping to achieve. Turning up to take 'pot luck' on which policy makers you bump into would be a risky strategy for most organisations. If you opt for the observer pass option, it is strongly recommended that your organisation does its 'political prep' well in advance of the conference, and can approach the event safe in the knowledge that it has a clear strategy and a full programme of activities and meetings planned and in place for the conference. Attending conferences can be expensive, and you need to make the most of your observer pass. 'Political prep' can deliver value for money for your organisation, and ensure that it has highly effective engagement with senior policy makers that deliver major benefits to your organisation.

Fringe meetings

Fringe meetings can offer organisations excellent opportunities to brief senior policy makers on high profile policy issues, and to engage the different political parties in significant policy debates. Fringe meetings are showcase events, and a successful fringe event can potentially help to strengthen your organisation's relations with the political parties. Following up with Government ministers or a party's spokespersons as appropriate, and with the specific party's MPs, Peers, parliamentary staff and councillors can deliver major benefits in terms of raising your organisation's profile, and in helping to shape and influence national policy debates.

There are, however, certain disadvantages with holding fringe events which your organisation will also need to consider in its assessment of whether or not to hold such events. The first disadvantage is that holding fringe events can be very expensive, and will often require a significant amount of expenditure, organisation and staff time if they are to be successful. Another potential disadvantage is that, regardless of all of the hard work and effort your organisation puts into organising a fringe event, there is still no guarantee that the event will be well attended by the specific policy makers you are seeking to influence. There will, after all, usually be major time pressures upon each party's leadership and main spokespersons to attend events and functions at their conference. You may also find that the party's MPs, Peers, parliamentary staff and councillors are often preoccupied with internal party business. These circumstances could mean that attending your organisation's fringe event could be a major time commitment for the policy makers in their busy conference schedule, and one that many will be unable to fulfil. Against this background, competition amongst fringe events will be fierce, and it will take a major effort by your organisation to maximise the attendance of senior policy makers at its fringe event. Success will depend upon the approach you take to planning the event.

Given the level of competition that your fringe event is likely to face, it is important that you make your event as attractive as possible. To support this process, it is essential that your organisation is very clear about the aims and objectives of the event, and what it is hoping to achieve through the event. In this respect, it is strongly recommended that your organisation chooses a theme for the fringe event which will be attractive to the policy makers you are seeking to influence. Your organisation will improve its chances of securing the attendance of senior policy makers if your fringe event has a focus on current parliamentary business, such as a piece of legislation which has recently been introduced in the Parliament. Holding an event to brief policy makers on the main provisions of the Bill, and on the key issues it presents for your organisation, could help to increase interest in the event. With such events it is important that your organisation tries to secure the participation of the relevant Government minister or the opposition party spokesperson as appropriate, depending on which party conference you are attending. This will automatically raise the profile of the event, and highlight to organisations and individuals seeking to find out more about the legislation that they simply cannot afford to miss your fringe event.

To further develop interest in its fringe event your organisation should choose prominent speakers, and ask them to provide inputs on policy areas and themes that will prove interesting to policy makers and to conference delegates. It is advised that you spend time getting the programme for the event right, and securing the involvement of prominent, keynote speakers. Well known experts, and speakers from other countries sharing best practice and evidence in their areas of expertise can often help to generate interest in a fringe event. If your organisation is a business, or a charity which provides for example health and social care services, it is recommended that the fringe event includes a focus on the best practice and evidence from your business or services. For those attending, the impact of the event will be strengthened by sharing tangible examples of what works in practice. For policy makers searching for best practice and evidence to help shape political solutions your fringe event, by providing such examples, could potentially make a significant contribution to their party's policy development in a particular area. If the conference is being hosted by the governing party this could have major benefits for your organisation.

Given the level of competition between fringe events, serious consideration should be given to the potential benefits of holding a fringe event with partner organisations. This might not be an option for all organisations, but where partnership working is a realistic option for your organisation the benefits could be considerable. Apart from sharing costs, and the work necessary to organise the event, by holding a partnership event your organisation will also be able to draw upon your partner's/partners' contacts to support the event. This could include their contacts with Government ministers or the opposition parties' leading spokespersons, and with MPs, Peers, parliamentary staff, and councillors. This could be highly significant in terms of helping to maximising attendance at the event amongst those policy makers you are seeking to influence. Holding a fringe event with a partner organisation or as a consortium will also underline the strength of the policy issues and 'policy asks' you are seeking to make at the event. It will be a powerful message for the policy makers attending the fringe event if you can demonstrate this level of unity across your particular sector in support of specific policy issues and 'policy asks'.

You should also liaise with the conference organisers to identify the best options for when to hold the event, with the main options being a lunchtime or evening event. An informal chat to try and get a sense of which time slots will put you in direct competition with other high profile fringe events and party events is also recommended. Careful thought should be given to choosing an appropriate venue. You want to hold the fringe event in a venue which will promote your organisation to the best effect. If you cannot do it well, do not do it! In this context, if the organisers cannot offer such a venue, and there are no other venues available, you might wish to consider other types of events to get your key messages across. An alternative would be to have a parliamentary event at Westminster once the party conference season is over. The fringe event should also provide refreshments, because ensuring that the participants and audience will be 'fed and watered' will be an important consideration for policy makers faced with an array of conflicting invites. Knowing that they can pick up some refreshments, while working their way through their list of conference events and functions, will definitely be a consideration for many policy makers in deciding which events to attend, especially as they will often be seeking to attend various events over the same lunchtime or evening.

Promoting the fringe event

As previously mentioned, your organisation's fringe event will face stiff competition from many other organisations in terms of attracting Government ministers or key party spokespersons, MPs, Peers, parliamentary staff and councillors to attend the event. To give your organisation the best possible chance of securing a good level of attendance from these leading policy makers it is vital that you organise early to raise awareness of your organisation's event. The parties' conference programme will provide some opportunities to publicise the event, but this will not be enough given the level of competition your organisation is likely to encounter during the conference for the attention of senior policy makers. It is, therefore, imperative that your organisation starts the process of maximising attendance at your fringe event well in advance of the conference. This approach can offer significant advantages if undertaken effectively, and if you have chosen the right speakers and themes for the event.

Against this background, it is recommended that you get a date-in-your diary e-mail/letter out to your organisation's target groups as soon as you have a date, time and venue for the event. Having a draft programme, or even being able to confirm the themes on which the event will focus, and at least some, if not all, of the speakers, will be helpful in this respect. Prior to the conference you should also follow up with policy makers by phoning them to confirm the event, and to 'sell' it to them. There will be a lot of demands upon their time at the conference, so you need to persuade the policy maker and/or their staff that your event is the one to attend during the conference.

You will need a sponsoring MP or Peer to host the event, and you should ask them and their staff to help your organisation to publicise the event, and to increase support from leading policy makers. The sponsoring MP or Peer can play a critical role by publicising the event through their internal party networks, and through their party's internal communications. If you are running the event in partnership your partners can also play an active role, and can use their networks to raise awareness of the event amongst the key policy makers. In terms of protocol your organisation should ensure that, when it initially approaches an MP or Peer to sponsor the event, its discussions with the latter include deciding with the MP or Peer about the role they will play at the event, and how involved they want to be. Some policy makers will be happy to host the event, and to provide an introduction and to leave all of the arrangements to your organisation. Other MPs and Peers might seek a more active role in organising the event, particularly if the fringe event will focus on an issue or theme with which they have a long association. The main thing is to decide early in your discussions with the MP or Peer about how much they will be able, and will want, to be involved in progressing the event, and in what areas.

Social media should also be exploited to raise awareness about the fringe event, and to publicise the themes and issues it will be tackling. You should also liaise with the MP or Peer about the use of their social media to highlight the event. Using social media will allow your organisation to advertise the event to the key policy makers who will be attending the conference, and to the particular party's wider membership. It will also enable your organisation to keep these audiences up-to-date as the arrangements for the fringe event fall into place, and are confirmed. In addition, using social media will enable you to start the debate on the policy issues and themes on which the fringe event will focus. This is particularly important where the fringe event will give your organisation an opportunity to make specific policy asks or demands. Social media will help your organisation to build up support for these asks, and the different political parties will be mindful of the levels of support you are building up in favour of these asks.

Use of other networking opportunities

In preparing for each party conference it is important that your organisation puts in place effective planning to take forward the arrangements to manage its presence at the different conferences. Apart from securing appointments with leading policy makers, and putting in place the arrangements for your organisation's exhibition space and/or fringe event, it is important that you do not overlook other influencing opportunities which could potentially be very productive. This would include attending other organisations' fringe events or functions. Apart from the networking opportunities these present which can be significant, attending will also offer your organisation's representatives the chance to contribute publicly to major policy debates. Such interventions can be followed up by then engaging with those policy makers in attendance. Other important occasions to influence key policy makers are the civic receptions which are usually hosted by the local council which is hosting the conference. These functions are often well attended by senior policy makers, and will provide organisations with further chances to engage with the party's policy makers. Such opportunities should not be overlooked, especially as the atmosphere is usually relaxed and less frenetic than the main body of the conference.

Follow-up action

A successful conference will usually take up a lot of your organisation's policy and public affairs budget for the year, and the demands upon your organisation's staff time and capacity will have been significant. The demands on the staff attending the conference, and representing your organisation to Government ministers the opposition parties' main spokespersons, and to MPs, Peers, and councillors can be intense. The efforts of the entire staff team involved is considerable, and ranges from booking the conference package to setting up the exhibition space right through to managing the fringe event and drumming up support from amongst the policy makers you wish to target. It is only when the conference has finished, and your banners and any residual briefing material returned to your organisation, that arguably the most important phase of the conference begins.

This is the follow-up action your organisation should take in response to what happened at the conference. The follow-up action makes the difference between an average and great conference. Following up the conference properly gives you the chance to deliver high profile, tangible outcomes. To ensure that your organisation capitalises on its conference presence it is, therefore, important that your staff record each contact with a policy maker, and the outcomes of that contact and what follow-up action, if any, was promised to the policy maker. This exercise is vital as it will support your organisation to build upon the contacts it made and/or strengthened at the conference. The follow-up action can be wide ranging. It could, for example, be contacting a Government minister's office to arrange a meeting between the minister and your organisation regarding policy issues you may have over aspects of a new piece of legislation which is about to be introduced in Parliament. Alternatively, it could be contacting your local MP to arrange a visit to your business or services within their constituency. Other potential outcomes could be to contact a Peer you engaged with at the conference to follow up on a discussion about their lodging a Motion for a short debate in the House of Lords on issues of mutual interest. You might also find it helpful to have meetings with key figures in the local government community to continue your discussions about aspects of councils' policies in relation to areas such as business regulation, licensing and planning etc. Regardless of what type of follow-up action is required with the policy maker, the main thing is that there is follow-up. This will help your organisation to secure tangible outcomes from the conference. It will also strengthen your organisation's ties with policy makers relevant to its interests. These are significant factors and, if done in an effective and timely fashion, will enhance the impact, and success, of your organisation's public affairs strategy.

Summary of key points

The key points from this chapter can be summarised as follows:

- Attending political parties' conferences offers major opportunities to engage with the political parties, and to shape and influence their policy positions.
- Organisations should ensure they are represented at party conferences by staff who can speak knowledgeably about their organisation's work, its business and/or services, its policy priorities and campaigns.
- For many organisations the effectiveness of their pre-conference 'political prep', will have a major bearing on the success of their impact at the parties' conferences.
- The follow-up action your organisation takes, in response to commitments given to policy makers at the parties' conferences, can deliver significant outcomes for its influencing strategy.

21

Developing Effective Partnership Working

When your organisation is developing its public affairs strategy, you should consider whether or not there are public affairs activities and campaigns within the strategy which could best be progressed through partnership working. This type of working could provide major advantages to many organisations, and your organisation should explore the possibilities it might offer. Such an approach, however, will not be appropriate for all organisations. In this context, some organisations may enjoy such high levels of influence with the Government, and with the opposition parties, that a partnership approach would be unnecessary, and possibly counter-productive. It should also be recognised that some organisations may have formal restrictions on the type of activities they can undertake in partnership, and even on those whom they can work with in partnership. For those organisations that do not have close relationships of influence with the Government and with the opposition parties, or which do not operate under any constraints that would exclude partnership working, it is recommended that you should remain open to the possibility of taking a partnership approach where this will help your organisation to achieve the aims and objectives of its public affairs strategy.

Approaches to partnership working

Partnership working can offer a number of significant benefits, and these should be explored in the context of the appropriateness of such an approach to the specific activities and campaigns within your organisation's public affairs strategy. One of the main advantages of partnership working is that it will demonstrate to the Government, and to the opposition parties, that your organisation has wider support from other organisations for its policy positions and campaigns. This will often, subject to the policy issues and 'policy asks' you are raising, increase the likelihood that your organisation will secure backing from leading policy makers for its policy positions and campaigns. Another benefit of partnership working is that it will increase the partner organisations' capacity to lobby through their individual networks, and to potentially influence leading policy makers. Working in partnership could, for example, enable the partner organisations to maximise the impact of their influencing work by sharing the engagement with key policy makers. This could be particularly helpful where the partners' influencing work will rely on various meetings with different policy makers, and it is essential to engage with a wide range of target audiences and there are significant time pressures involved.

There are different levels of partnership working, and types of partnership approaches, to progress public affairs strategies, and to support your organisation to take forward specific aspects of these strategies. If your organisation wishes to adopt a partnership approach to progress its public affairs strategy, or to develop particular aspects of this strategy, it is important that your organisation has a clear idea of the policy issues and 'policy asks' it wishes to raise. This will have a direct bearing on the level, and type, of partnership working you decide to adopt. It will also influence your organisation's decision making around which organisations you wish to work with in partnership, as the effectiveness of the partnership working will be strengthened if the different partners share the same policy aims and objectives, and have a common shared view of how these should be achieved. With these aims and objectives in mind, your organisation should give careful thought to the organisations, or to the type of organisations, it would like to work with in partnership. Ideally, you want to seek partnerships with organisations that have a significant track record in service delivery, or in policy development, and which complement the work and policy positions of your own organisation.

Types of partnership working

One of the main types of partnership working is to progress policy positions and campaigns with partners through umbrella organisations. These organisations are membership organisations established to represent the interests of their members with the Government, the opposition parties, individual MPs and Peers and with other key policy makers. Examples include the Confederation of British Industry; the Law Society of England and Wales, which represents solicitors in England and Wales; the Local Government Association, which represents local authority bodies in England and Wales; and the National Council for Voluntary Organisations, representing voluntary organisations in England and Wales. These organisations can be highly effective in representing their members' interests to Government and other policy makers. The members will generally look to the umbrella organisation to engage with these policy makers on their behalf on issues impacting upon the members generally, and upon the sector or sectors in which they operate. The outcomes achieved will depend upon the effectiveness of the umbrella organisation in question, which, in turn, will usually depend upon the contribution of the member organisations and their support for any issues or campaigns being progressed by the umbrella organisation.

Working through an umbrella organisation can offer organisations good opportunities to work with partners on issues of mutual interest and concern. Indeed, such organisations are likely to be at their most effective where they are advocating and campaigning on issues that are affecting all of their members and the sector or sectors in which they operate. It will often be the case, however, that individual member organisations will only get out of their membership what they are prepared, and are able, to contribute to the work of the umbrella organisation. To maximise the effectiveness for your organisation of partnership working through the umbrella organisation, it is recommended that your organisation should try and be as active in its governance, and in its policy development and campaigns work as possible. Being active within the umbrella organisation will help to raise the profile of your organisation both within the umbrella organisation, and externally. By way of further example, if the umbrella organisation is progressing a campaign and is looking to develop campaigns material it is more likely to draw upon the best practice and evidence of your organisation and its services or work if it is an active member and is, therefore, a well-known quantity to the umbrella organisation. The same would apply if the umbrella organisation was issuing a news release in support of a policy position, and was looking for quotes from senior officers from some of the member organisations to be included in the release. This would offer a good opportunity to support the 'policy asks' being raised, and also to increase the profile of your organisation. Against this background, it is recommended that your organisation should play an active role in any umbrella organisation to which it belongs.

The opportunities for organisations to progress their public affairs strategies through supporting APPGs relevant to their work, policy interests and campaigns. have already been considered in Chapter 18. The point to highlight here is that these groups can provide extensive networks of organisations with which your organisation can engage, identify common policy ground and develop policy positions and campaigns based on your mutual interests or concerns. This can be done both through the APPG itself, or by engaging with other organisations which are 'affiliate' or 'associate' members of the group outside the APPG structure.

These groups will potentially provide the foundations for highly effective alliances which your organisation can build up and take forward to secure significant policy and legislative outcomes. In many respects this will be a very productive option to pursue, particularly as not all of the APPGs will have a focus on delivering tangible outcomes in influencing policy development and legislation at UK level. Indeed, some will lack the capacity to do so. In this context, it will be difficult for many of these groups to secure the levels of cross-party support for specific policy positions necessary to deliver such outcomes. In addition, even where there is cross-party agreement on a policy position it might prove more difficult to secure agreement on how best to take action to progress the policy position, and to ensure that it achieves major outcomes. Against this background, your organisation may find that the most effective form of partnership working around the APPGs is to target those other 'affiliate' or 'associate' members you can work with, and with whom you enjoy common interests, and to take things forward with these organisations as partners outside the structure of the APPG.

It is recommended that your organisation, in scoping and mapping out its options for partnership working, should carefully consider all of the networks it is involved in, or in which it has membership. This would include policy development networks such as, for example, the Scottish Council for Voluntary Organisations' Policy Officers' Network, where organisations regularly meet to discuss policy issues, as well as other networks focusing on issues relating to practice and service delivery. Engagement in such networks will provide your organisation with invaluable opportunities to identify where there are common policy grounds with other organisations, or where it has similar practice and/or service delivery issues with these organisations. This will support your organisation to identify and to develop collective 'policy asks' with members of these networks which can then be progressed with the Government and with other key policy makers. Such engagement will also enable your organisation to get a strong sense of which organisations it will be able to work with on common policy issues and campaigns, and with which it can build productive partnerships.

Taking the initiative

To try and keep as much control as possible over the aims and objectives of a particular public affairs campaign or activity (which would lend itself well to a partnership approach) it is recommended that your organisation should try to take the initiative in progressing and leading such campaigns and activities. Your organisation's ability to do so will depend upon a number of factors, including its internal capacity to take a lead role with other external organisations, its reputation and track record on running campaigns, the excellence of its business, or services and the type of policy positions for which it is seeking support. Being able to 'tick' at least some of these 'boxes' will put your organisation in a position where it can give serious consideration to recruiting partners to collectively progress a particular policy position or campaign.

To increase the chances that a partnership approach will deliver success, your organisation should clearly identify the 'policy asks' it is seeking the Government and other key policy makers to respond to, and the type of action which will be necessary to give effect to these 'policy asks'. It should also identify the strategy it is proposing to take with partners to achieve these 'policy asks'. Once your organisation has taken a view on these issues, it should then engage with potential partners to find out if they would be prepared to sign up to a partnership approach to progress the 'policy asks', and to the strategy for achieving these 'policy asks'. Your negotiations with potential partners may result in changes both to the 'policy asks', and to the means of achieving them. The extent to which your organisation is prepared to compromise will depend upon various issues, including the extent to which you want a particular organisation to work with your organisation as partners. On a note of caution you need to consider that compromising with one organisation, may lead to losing another organisation as a potential partner. The key is to try and identify the common ground in terms of 'policy asks', and agreement over tactics and strategy, which will ensure that the organisations you have identified as the main partners you want to work with are more likely to agree to work with your organisation and the other partners to take things forward.

Once your organisation has constructed a partnership in support of a specific policy position or campaign, it needs to work with its partners to engage with the Government, the opposition parties and with other key policy makers. It is recommended that your organisation should take the lead in progressing this engagement, including the arrangement of any meetings with the relevant Government ministers, the opposition spokespersons or with individual MPs and Peers. It should also take the initiative in undertaking any media work, including the use of social media. These steps will support your organisation to ensure that the focus of the partnership remains on the agreed 'policy asks', and employs tactics most likely to ensure that the partnership delivers its aims and objectives.

Opportunities for partnership working

There are many aspects of an organisation's interaction with the Government which will lend themselves to partnership working. Examples include where your organisation and its partners are seeking to raise policy issues, and have approached the relevant Government minister to discuss these issues. Meeting requests from alliances will often stand a better chance of securing meetings with Government ministers, and with opposition leaders and key spokespersons. Meeting the minister on a collective basis could make a significant difference in how the Government responds to your lobbying, as it will demonstrate that you are raising issues which are of wider concern and impact rather than just affecting your organisation.

The success of such meetings can often be increased where the organisations concerned are high profile, and are well known by key policy makers, across different sectors and by the general public. Ultimately, however, a lot will depend upon the policy issues and concerns your organisation and its partners are raising, and the amount of 'wriggle' room available to the Government to meet your 'policy asks'. Similar considerations would apply where the chief executive or other senior representative from your organisation, and their counterparts in partner organisations, write to the Prime Minister or to the relevant Government minister about a particular policy concern. This can be particularly effective if it is combined with a news release. You would, however, need to risk assess such an initiative in terms of the outcomes you are hoping to achieve, and the appropriateness of this route to achieve such outcomes compared to other routes, because such initiatives have been known, by creating adverse publicity, to embarrass governments and to overshadow future relations.

That said, for some organisations securing publicity might have been the purpose of the exercise in the first place in order to force concessions from the Government. While it is important to recognise that the public letter from organisations working in partnership can, in certain circumstances, be a highly effective public affairs tool, it is important to ensure that the case for employing this tool is properly risk assessed before this form of collective action is pursued. By doing so, your organisations can help to keep your relations with key policy makers positive and productive. Good communications are at the heart of successful public affairs strategies, and the last thing an organisation should want to do is to close down the channels of communication with leading policy makers for what could prove to be limited, short-lived gains provided by transient media coverage. Effective communications, and a willingness to engage constructively with a wide range of policy makers on a non-partisan basis, offer the best way of ensuring that your organisation can consistently help to shape and influence policy development at Government level, and legislation in Parliament. It is strongly recommended that you bear this in mind in any risk assessments of aspects of your organisation's public affairs strategy, including any public affairs initiatives or activities which it seeks to progress in partnership with other organisations.

There are also many types of business in Parliament which can be approached on a partnership basis. Debates in the House of Commons and in the House of Lords can offer excellent opportunities for your organisation to work with partners to collectively brief Government ministers, the opposition parties and individual MPs and Peers. These policy makers will often be inundated with briefings for high profile debates, and it will be a challenge for most organisations to ensure that their briefing stands out from the policy 'crowd', and for positive reasons. In this context, you will need to overcome a situation in which your organisation and its briefing could be in competition with various other organisations across the sector, as well as from other sectors. While some organisations will thrive in such competition, the reality for many organisations is that they will often find it more difficult to influence the debate.

Against this background, the policy makers, under significant time pressure to finalise their policy lines for the debate, could receive a bewildering array of briefings, often with conflicting messages from organisations within the same sector or across different sectors. Unity is strength in such situations. By preparing a joint briefing with partners, for example, your organisation will improve its chances of being able to engage constructively with the different policy makers, and to influence the debate. In this respect, a joint briefing will help to present a coherence of messages to key policy makers. It will also help to demonstrate to the latter that the issues your organisation is raising, and the 'policy asks' it is making, have significant support within the sector in which it operates. These factors will make it more likely that the policy makers will rely on your briefing for the debate, and will be willing to engage with your organisation and its partners prior to the debate.

A partnership approach can be especially effective and productive where your organisation is seeking to respond to, and to influence, legislation in the House of Commons and/or in the House of Lords. As with parliamentary debates, the Government, opposition parties and individual MPs and Peers will often receive a wide range of briefings in relation to legislation. Some of this briefing will include suggested amendments, i.e. changes, to the legislation. Securing support for your organisation's proposed amendments from other organisations is a good way of taking the initiative to lead a response to the legislation, and to ensure that your organisation can secure changes to the legislation. An example of where effective partnership working helped to secure important concessions on a 'flagship' Government piece of legislation, was the UK-wide alliance of organisations led by Action for Children Scotland and by One Parent Families Scotland, in response to the Welfare Reform legislation during its parliamentary passage in 2011-2012.

Action for Children Scotland and One Parent Families Scotland were concerned by a number of issues presented by the Welfare Reform legislation, including the use of sanctions against vulnerable claimants. The two organisations identified and drafted amendments to address these issues in the legislation. The amendments were designed to ensure that vulnerable claimants, who were unable to access work or the work-related activities introduced by the Welfare Reform Bill, due to a lack of accessible and affordable childcare, would not face sanctions, and a loss of benefits. Action for Children Scotland and One Parent Families built up a UK-wide alliance of over 50 organisations, including children's charities, churches, trade unions, advice agencies, and anti-poverty campaign organisations. The amendments were tabled in the House of Commons, and subsequently in the House of Lords where the Government made the concession that claimants with dependent children would not face sanctions where they were unable to access work, or work-related activity, due to a lack of suitable childcare. The Government confirmed that this issue would be addressed in the regulations and statutory guidance which would accompany the implementation of the Welfare Reform Act 2012.

The concessions to the Welfare Reform legislation, in response to the amendments tabled in the House of Lords by Baroness Lister of Burtersett, Lord Kirkwood of Kirkhope and the Lord Bishop of Ripon and Leeds on behalf of this UK-wide alliance marked some of the few concessions made by the Government during the passage of the legislation. The success of the alliance can be attributed to its strong focus, and to the conscious attempt to maximise support for the amendments from organisations across the UK. It can also be explained by the diverse range of organisations which supported the campaign, and the amendments that were progressed in the House of Commons and subsequently in the House of Lords. These factors, and the strength of the networking which built up the alliance and was then used to engage with the Government, the opposition parties and with individual MPs and Peers, were major strengths. The public affairs campaign in support of the amendments helped to secure concessions which have benefitted thousands of vulnerable claimants across the UK.

Another legislative area where there is scope for partnership action would be in progressing a Private Member's Bill. The key factor would be to identify a policy area where a number of potential partners share the same policy position as your organisation, and there is a legislative gap which a Private Member's Bill could address. It is recommended that your organisation, if it is interested in pursuing this option, should work through its networks to identify potential partners. Private Member's Bills are considered in Chapter 13, and can provide organisations with a strong focus for their long-term public affairs campaigns. Progressing a Private Member's Bill can be very challenging, and only a few make it onto the Statute Book. Working with partner organisations can, therefore, help you to secure a sponsoring MP or Peer to take forward the legislation. It can also be a useful way of raising awareness of the issues raised by the Private Member's Bill and to increase support for the Bill. These are the type of factors which can help to increase the chances that the Private Member's Bill will be successful, and pass all of its stages in the House of Commons and House of Lords.

Partnership events

Another way in which an organisation can work with partners to engage with key policy makers is to host joint events. This can include parliamentary events to raise the profile of the organisations, and their policy positions or campaigns. Examples would include arranging a joint briefing to engage with leading policy makers about the provisions in a new piece of legislation, or to update the policy makers about campaigns that you are running with partner organisations. Joint fringe events at the different political parties' conferences would be another option. Holding joint events can present a powerful message to the Government, the opposition parties and to individual MPs and Peers. Such events can demonstrate to the policy makers that there are strong, unified messages from the partner organisations, which has produced clear 'policy asks'. This can have a major impact upon target audiences. Logistically the advantages of sharing costs, and duties to organise the event, can also offer significant advantages. It is, therefore, recommended that when your organisation is seeking to organise events to engage with leading policy makers it gives consideration to the appropriateness, and the advantages and disadvantages of organising such events with partner organisations.

Summary of key points

The key points from this chapter can be summarised as follows:

- Consideration should be given to whether or not there are public affairs activities and campaigns which could best be progressed through partnership working, as this could offer major advantages.
- One of the main advantages of partnership working is that it will demonstrate to key policy makers that your organisation has wider support for its policy positions and campaigns.
- To increase the chances that a partnership approach will deliver success, your organisation should clearly identify the 'policy asks' it is seeking the Government and other key policy makers to address.
- A partnership approach can be particularly effective and productive if your organisation is seeking to respond to legislation in the House of Commons, and/or in the House of Lords.

22

Maximising Media Impact

Securing high levels of positive media coverage will be a major goal of many organisations' public affairs strategies, alongside the aims and objectives of influencing leading policy makers and policy development at Government level, and in Parliament. It is worth bearing in mind, however, when developing your organisation's public affairs strategy, that the House of Commons will generally attract more media interest than the House of Lords. There are few occasions when the media focus on the House of Lords will be stronger than on the House of Commons. Examples include when members of the House of Lords defeat the Government on a key vote in a debate or on a Bill, or when major political developments arise or attention turns on specific Peers. Such situations are the exception rather than the rule, and the House of Commons will normally attract much greater levels of media coverage. It is important that your organisation takes these factors into account when developing its public affairs strategy, and plans appropriate media activities to support the main stages in this strategy. Against this background, it is important to assess and decide whether or not your particular policy issue will be more newsworthy in the House of Commons or in the House of Lords.

Setting clear aims and objectives

The media can play a vital role in ensuring that your organisation's public affairs strategy, and the specific activities within this strategy, are effective and deliver tangible outcomes. It is, therefore, important that your organisation has a clear approach in relation to how its media work and public affairs activities should complement and support each other to deliver the organisation's aims and objectives. When developing this strategy, it is important, however, to recognise that not all public affairs activities have to be undertaken in the full media spotlight. Indeed, in certain situations your organisation may actively seek to avoid publicity. This would be especially true where your organisation is involved in sensitive negotiations with the Government or with the opposition parties, or with individual MPs or Peers over a specific policy issue. One example would be an organisation attempting to secure support from the Government, or from one of these other sources, for amendments it believes are necessary to improve a piece of Government legislation. Seeking publicity in these circumstances could be counterproductive. In this context, chasing relatively short-term media headlines could potentially undermine your organisation's negotiations with the relevant policy makers, and deprive your organisation of an opportunity to secure concessions on the legislation, and to improve it in ways which would benefit your organisation and its interests. As part of your organisation's public affairs strategy, you should carry out a robust risk assessment of the need for any media activities to accompany specific aspects of, or activities within, this strategy. For the purposes of this chapter, it is assumed that your organisation will be actively seeking to maximise media coverage of its public affairs activities, and that it will be appropriate to do so.

Good media coverage can raise the profile of your organisation, and promote its engagement with key policy makers. In addition, the media can play a critical role in helping your organisation to increase awareness of the policy positions on which its public affairs activities are focusing, and on any public affairs campaigns it is running. Intensifying the political spotlight on your organisation's policy positions and campaigns through media coverage could potentially help to build up support from leading policy makers, from other organisations and from the general public for its 'policy asks' and campaigns. Such backing could, in turn, increase the chances that your public affairs strategy will be successful, and deliver tangible outcomes that meet the aims and objectives of this strategy.

Achieving high levels of media coverage can also be used by organisations as one of the criteria in evaluations to demonstrate the effectiveness of their public affairs strategies, especially where it is taking the initiative in leading a campaign with partner organisations or in launching a public debate. In this respect, the extent to which an organisation has maximised its media profile through public affairs activities will be an important indicator for measuring and evaluating the overall success of its public affairs strategy, and of particular activities within this strategy. These factors highlight the major contribution which the media can make to delivering the aims and objectives of your organisation's public affairs strategy. It is recommended that your organisation should work closely with the media, and cultivate its contacts with individual journalists both at the national and local levels. Social media also provides major opportunities for organisations to raise their profile, and to showcase their work.

Developing an integrated approach

Your organisation, having set clear aims and objectives outlining what it is trying to achieve through its public affairs strategy, should decide internally what role working with the media will play in this strategy, and who will be responsible for leading this area of work. To maximise the profile of your organisation, and the media impact of its public affairs activities, it is recommended that you take an integrated approach in which the planning of public affairs activities and media activities are complementary, and are designed to mutually support each other to achieve these goals. The benefits of doing so, for this strategy, and for specific public affairs activities, can be considerable for an organisation, especially where all parts of the organisation work together to build and deliver effective public affairs strategies.

A useful way for organisations to develop an integrated approach, in order to maximise the impact of their public affairs strategies and of their organisation's media profile, is to establish an external affairs committee or working group.[1] The type of integrated planning structure your organisation puts in place will depend upon a number of factors. These are likely to include the size of your organisation, its structure, the capacity and skills set of its staff, the availability of resources, its geographical location and that of key staff, and whether or not it is a UK-wide organisation. The main thing is that the committee or working group has support from within the organisation at a senior level. Such support will enable the organisation to make decisions about its public affairs strategy in a timely and effective manner,

---

1   R. McGeachy and M. Ballard, Public Affairs Guide to Scotland, (Cardiff, 2017).

including how it should respond to developments at Government level or in Parliament, and to work with the media to maximise publicity for its public affairs work.

Ideally this structure should involve a member of the organisation's senior management team, and the lead persons or other representatives from its public affairs, policy, media and business or service delivery functions as appropriate. Third sector organisations would also want a senior colleague from their fundraising section to attend meetings of this group. Where the organisation has a UK-wide focus it is advised that the group should seek to include representatives from each nation. It is recommended that the group meets regularly to review opportunities and any reputational risks, and to plan appropriate action in response to all aspects of its external relations work, including public affairs, media work and fundraising.

Publicising public affairs activities

There are various public affairs activities which could potentially benefit from organisations undertaking media work in support of these activities. Using the media, including social media, can raise awareness of public affairs activities, and also strengthen the impact of such activities. Areas in which the media can play an important role include the use of news releases and social media to help publicise visits to your organisation by Government ministers or opposition parties' spokespersons or by individual MPs or Peers. These visits, which can provide your organisation with major influencing opportunities with key policy makers and to raise issues and concerns with them on a face-to-face basis, are considered in more detail in Chapter 5. Such visits can also generate good levels of publicity, and raise the profile of your organisation and its work through the media, including social media. Where your organisation is planning such visits it should assess whether a specific visit will be of most interest to the national or local media, and/or to social media. The type of publicity your organisation can secure for such visits will depend upon which policy maker is visiting your organisation, the purpose of the visit, its likely outcomes and the current issues dominating the political landscape either at the national or local level.

It is important that your organisation gives careful consideration to ways in which it can maximise the publicity around such visits, including highlighting their profile on social media by publicising the visits on, for example, your organisation's Facebook page and on its Twitter account. Part of this process will be working closely with the office of the visiting Government minister, or other visiting policy maker as appropriate, to agree a media strategy for the visit, including whether or not your organisation or the office of the policy maker will lead on arranging media activities in support of the visit. Working collaboratively has a number of potential benefits, not least of which will be the minister's, or other visiting politician's, media team using their networks and capacity to generate media interest in the visit.

Similarly, organisations should consider how they can undertake media activities in support of their contribution to major debates in the House of Commons or in the House of Lords. As previously mentioned, the media spotlight will predominantly focus on debates in the House of Commons, with only the most high profile debates in the House of Lords likely to attract media coverage. The likelihood of your organisation securing media coverage for its contribution to a debate in the House of Commons will depend upon a number of factors, including the subject matter of the debate, the level of media interest the debate attracts and the extent to which your organisation is raising relevant issues, and in ways that make these issues newsworthy. Circulating briefings for the debate that are based on strong evidence and on the good practice of your organisation, to highlight key themes in the debate will all help in this regard. Significantly, organisations will often face stiff competition from other organisations keen to raise their profile, and to grab media coverage for their policy demands. It is, therefore, recommended that you identify an MP to raise issues on your behalf during the debate, and then work with their office to brief specific journalists on a targeted basis. These steps will help to improve the chances that your organisation will be able to secure publicity for the issues it is seeking to raise in the debate. You should also make the most of opportunities presented by social media to raise awareness of the issues your organisation is seeking to raise during the debate.

Many organisations will consider approaching MPs to lodge Early Day Motions (EDMs) on their behalf, and EDMs are considered in more detail in Chapter 16. The main value of an EDM is the publicity it can potentially generate, and the contribution it can make to raising awareness of your organisation and of its work. Large numbers of EDMs are lodged each parliamentary session, so if you wish your EDM to fulfil these aims it is important that you choose a subject which is topical, and likely to be of interest to the media either on a national or local basis as appropriate. It is also recommended that you take a targeted approach to deciding which MP you approach to lodge the EDM. High profile MPs with a known interest in the policy issues raised in the EDM, your local MP and/or an MP with good links to your organisation, would all be strong options, and will improve the chances of securing media interest. As soon as you have secured the agreement of an MP to lodge the EDM, you should brief journalists about the EDM in order to ensure it secures media coverage. The type of coverage secured, if any, will depend upon the issues raised in the EDM, and whether or not the EDM raises policy issues of a national or local nature. Another factor which may have a bearing is what current issues are dominating the political landscape. Your organisation should also use social media, and in particular Facebook and Twitter, to publicise the EDM, and the policy issues it raises.

Some organisations have been highly successful in using oral questions in the House of Commons to raise awareness of, and to publicise, issues on which they are campaigning. The use of questions is considered in more detail in Chapter 14. This is another area where there is a much greater chance of securing media interest in the House of Commons than in the House of Lords. The key is to persuade an MP to lodge a question on your behalf, and to ensure they are fully briefed for the relevant Question Time, and to agree beforehand how any media relations will be handled. One issue to be determined is whether or not the issues being raised through the question are of national interest, or will be of particular interest to a geographical area with which your organisation is associated. With both options it is important that you work with the MP's office to consider ways in which you can maximise the media impact of the question. One option would be to brief a specific media contact, and to work with them to develop a feature focusing on the issues raised in the question, and to circulate a news release to ensure it is picked up as a news item. Social media will also offer significant opportunities to publicise the question, and to promote discussion on how these issues can be taken forward.

Organisations which are invited to give evidence to a committee in the House of Commons or in the House of Lords should try and generate media interest in the evidence session. Media interest will generally be greater in the House of Commons. The likelihood of the evidence session securing national publicity, however, will depend on a number of factors, including the subject matter of the evidence session, the issues currently dominating the political landscape and whether or not the committee proceedings are dealing with controversial matters. Given that some of the most high profile evidence sessions have been steeped in controversy, seeking this level of publicity could be a mixed blessing for your organisation, depending upon the specific circumstances of, and surrounding, the committee's inquiry. On the other hand, it should be emphasised that many committee inquiries deal with significant issues, which attract little, if any, media interest.

Being invited to give evidence to a committee can be a major opportunity for organisations, and this is dealt with in Chapter 9. Where your organisation is invited to give oral evidence it should try and secure media interest, notwithstanding the challenges involved. Subject to the type of parliamentary inquiry you have been asked to submit evidence to, and the policy issues involved, you may find, if there is likely to be limited national media interest, that the main opportunities for publicity are likely to arise in the local media and/or in the trade press. You should also use your organisation's Facebook and Twitter pages to highlight the evidence session, and the issues you will be seeking to raise in the evidence session. Following the committee proceedings, your organisation should use Facebook and Twitter to promote debate and publicity around the key issues that emerged during the evidence session.

Legislation

Prime Ministers' Question Time and departmental Question Times, and debates, in the House of Commons will generally attract much greater levels of publicity and coverage in the national media and in social media than legislation. The exceptions are where the legislation deals with high profile issues that generate significant political debates within Parliament, and high levels of interest from the general public. These circumstances will stimulate the media's interest in issues around the legislation. This interest will intensify if the legislation is controversial and/or there is a chance that the Government will face major defeats on the legislation, particularly if these are likely to occur in the House of Commons. This is another area, however, where the publicity is generally likely to be greater in the House of Commons, but there are occasions when legislation in the House of Lords will attract strong media interest, and may overshadow media interest in the House of Commons' stages of the legislation. Such occasions are normally where the legislation is controversial and the Government faces potential defeats in the House of Lords on Divisions on specific provisions within the legislation.

Bills, especially those including provisions which have generated significant political debate and wider public interest, offer media opportunities for organisations wishing to respond to the legislation as it goes through the different stages of the legislative process. It is recommended that organisations seeking to publicise their response to a Bill should engage with the media at the earliest possible stage in the legislative process. In this respect, it is worth bearing in mind that legislative provisions can be complex, and highly technical. Furthermore, for journalists and media commentators working to tight deadlines the challenge will often be trying to identify the headline issues presented by the legislation, and to translate these into news stories which will appeal to wide audiences in national media and in social media. This highlights the importance of getting the legislation on your media contacts' radar at an early stage, and to give your organisation enough time to get across the key issues you are seeking to raise in response to the legislation. It is also recommended that your organisation should consider ways in which it can use social media to raise awareness of its public affairs activities in response to the legislation as it goes through the legislative process in both Houses of Parliament.

Outlined below are some of the options your organisation should consider for raising awareness of issues around legislation through the media, including social media. Given the predominant media focus on the House of Commons, these approaches to generating media interest focus on the House of Commons, but could equally be used in the House of Lords where the legislation under consideration is high profile, and likely to produce wider political debate. Briefing the media, and using social media, will help to increase MPs' awareness of the policy issues your organisation is raising in response to the legislation.

You can try and gain some media coverage for these policy issues by briefing journalists and media commentators, and getting them up to speed on the main issues. Cultivating your media contacts on issues around Bills will improve your organisation's chances of gaining media coverage for its public affairs activities in response to a specific piece of legislation. A lot will depend, however, upon how high profile the legislation is in the Government's legislative programme. Is it, for example, a 'flagship' Bill which was a key aspect of the Government's manifesto, and in which a lot of the Government's political 'capital' and authority has been invested? Or is the Bill largely a technical measure which will generally be non-controversial, and produce little, if any, political debate? These factors, and the political environment in which the Bill is introduced, will have a direct bearing on the level of national media and social media interest the legislation attracts.

If a Bill raises major policy issues for your organisation you should engage with the national and local media to raise awareness of these issues, once the Bill has been introduced in the House of Commons or in the House of Lords, and before its Second Reading debate. You should approach your media contacts, and brief them on the key issues presented by the Bill, on its importance for your organisation and its work, and on why it is seeking to amend the legislation. In this respect, it would be useful to provide case studies which illustrate the likely impact of the legislation on, for example, those on whose behalf your organisation works or on the economy or on society as a whole. Providing such case studies will help to put the legislation in context. Organisations should also brief their existing media contacts about the public affairs activities they will be undertaking in response to the legislation. For organisations with a wide range of media contacts it is recommended that you try and secure interest in the issues you will be raising in response to the legislation from both your national and local media contacts, and seek to brief both. Organisations, on the other hand, which have had limited contact with the media may wish to focus on their local media contacts, particularly if they have case studies which illustrate how the legislation will impact upon local people, on local communities and on the local economy. It should also be pointed out that many local newspapers have major circulations that in some cases outstrip those of national newspapers, and that local radio and TV stations are often vibrant and well supported. These can offer significant means to raise awareness of your organisation's response to a Bill, especially if your organisation has provided case studies highlighting local circumstances and conditions.

Apart from providing media briefings you should also issue news releases at strategic points in the Bill's progress through its stages in the House of Commons or in the House of Lords. The key stages would be the introduction of the Bill, prior to its Second Reading debate or, if your organisation is pursuing amendments to the Bill, prior to the parliamentary stages at which the amendments will be debated. The news release should highlight your organisation's response to the legislation, the main issues it will be campaigning on and any amendments it will be pursuing. To help maximise the potential impact of coverage in national and local media, you should work closely with the MP or Peer who has confirmed they support your policy position on the legislation, and will be tabling amendments on your organisation's behalf. The MP and Peer will have media contacts who may be able to assist your organisation to gain coverage for the policy issues it is seeking to raise in response to the legislation. The MP, in particular, will usually have a parliamentary and constituency office, and their staff will be able to work with your organisation on joint media work, particularly in support of any major amendments the MP has agreed to table on your behalf. The same considerations would apply if the MP is able to secure concessions from the Government in response to any amendments they have tabled on your behalf.

Social media should also be used by your organisation to raise awareness of the issues it is raising concerning the legislation. You should use your organisation's Twitter account, Facebook page and other social media platforms to provide updates on the legislation's progress, and on the public affairs activities your organisation has undertaken in response to the legislation. This will help to increase awareness of your organisation's policy positions, and campaign, on the legislation. One way in which you could use social media in support of your campaign on a Bill would be to call on your organisation's followers to contact the Government and request that it agrees to the changes you are seeking to the legislation, including accepting specific amendments it believes are necessary to improve the legislation. Where your organisation is seeking amendments to legislation you should work with the MP, or Peer, sponsoring the amendments to publicise the amendments through their social media networks. These steps will help to maximise the impact and profile on social media of your organisation's campaign on the legislation.

Media briefings

One way in which organisations can secure media interest in their public affairs activities is to hold regular media briefings. These briefings can be used by organisations to update the media on their work, and on major aspects of the organisation's public affairs strategy. The regularity of such briefings will vary from organisation to organisation, and will ultimately depend upon the profile of your organisation and its capacity to raise policy issues and to progress campaigns which are of interest to the media, at a national and/or local level. Even if holding weekly or monthly media briefings is not an appropriate, or realistic, option for your organisation, it should nevertheless seek to hold briefings if it is seeking to raise high profile policy issues with leading policy makers at Westminster or has launched a campaign. In this context, your organisation should use media briefings to keep its media contacts up to speed on how it is taking forward the policy issues or campaign in question. It is also a useful way of taking a targeted approach to generating interest in your organisation's policy position or campaign from specific journalists. By providing a media briefing you can then have follow-up contact with these journalists to ensure they highlight key developments in your organisation's efforts to progress its policy position or campaign. The media coverage this can potentially generate, either at a national or local level, will help to raise the profile of your organisation's public affairs activities, and improve the chances that it will influence the Government and other prominent decision makers and deliver positive outcomes for your organisation.

Publicising events

A major aspect of many organisations' public affairs strategies will be holding headline events including, for example, parliamentary events or policy seminars. It is important that when your organisation does hold such events, it takes steps to ensure they are well publicised. These type of events will often attract media interest, and it is vital that you work with your organisation's media contacts to ensure the event secures good levels of media coverage. Whether or not this coverage is at the national and/or local level will depend upon the nature of the event being held, on the profile of the speakers, on who will be attending and on the policy issues that it will feature. More details about these events can be found in Chapter 19. To try and maximise the level of media coverage for these events it is important that your organisation ensures that as many of its media contacts as possible are invited to the event and attend. Parliamentary events, policy seminars and other high profile events including fringe events at the conferences of the different political parties should also be publicised through your organisation's Facebook page and Twitter account. Social media will provide important opportunities to increase the profile of your organisation's public affairs activities, and to build-up support for the 'policy asks' it is making to the Government, and to the opposition parties and groupings in both Houses of the Parliament.

Working with the political parties' media offices

Another area which can potentially offer invaluable benefits to your organisation, and to its public affairs strategy, is developing good contacts with the different political parties' media offices. These contacts can help to raise the profile of your organisation, and increase awareness of the policy issues on which you are seeking support from Government ministers, opposition spokespersons and other key policy makers. To take an example: if your organisation has been able to secure significant concessions on a piece of legislation you should seek to publicise this success through a news release, and through social media. It is recommended that you should work with the relevant media officers to ensure the news release includes quotes from the MP who secured the concessions on your behalf, and from the Government minister who agreed to the concession.

Your organisation should also take a cross-party approach to working with the political parties' media offices. In this respect, if an MP from the Government's party is progressing a Private Member's Bill on your behalf, and is supported by MPs from different opposition parties, it is recommended that any media work involves the different parties, and that their media officers are all on board. Taking a cross-party approach will help to increase support for the Private Member's Bill, and improve the prospects that it will become law. Working with the different parties' media officers on a cross-party basis can also pay dividends where your organisation has secured the participation of a Government minister, and of your local MP who represents one of the opposition parties, in an event your organisation is hosting. By working with the minister's and the MP's media officers, you will usually be able to draft a news release which features input from both parties, and can be circulated with their active support. This will be helpful in ensuring the coverage of the event is as wide as possible.

Summary of key points

The key points from this chapter can be summarised as follows:

- Securing good levels of media coverage can be a significant outcome for public affairs strategies by raising the profile of your organisation, and its campaigns.
- Organisations should take a cross-party approach to generating publicity for their public affairs strategies.
- To maximise the media impact of your organisation's public affairs activities, it is recommended that you take an integrated approach to the planning of public affairs activities and media activities.
- Social media can offer major opportunities for organisations to raise their profile, and to showcase their work, and public affairs activities.

Conclusions

This guide provides advice and insights into how organisations across different sectors can use public affairs strategies, campaigns and activities to effectively and ethically influence leading policy makers, including Government ministers, the opposition parties, individual MPs and Peers, and key members of the local government community to achieve their policy aims and objectives.

Organisations should set clear aims and objectives, and 'policy asks', for their public affairs strategies. This will help to increase the chances that these strategies will deliver tangible results.

Once your organisation has identified the main issues and 'policy asks' which will form the focus of its public affairs strategy, it needs to then consider the type of activities which will be most likely to maximise the impact of this strategy, and to secure its aims and objectives. Your organisation will know which of the activities outlined in this guide will be the most appropriate to deliver its public affairs strategy, and when it would be most advantageous to undertake these activities. The key is to adapt these activities, and the timing of the different stages and activities within your strategy, to fit the relevant political, legislative and policy context and key developments in both Houses of Parliament as appropriate. Undertaking effective monitoring of parliamentary business, and political intelligence gathering, in both Houses of Parliament will help your organisation to keep abreast of the political, legislative and policy context, and of the key developments, at Westminster.

Furthermore, your organisation's ability and capacity to undertake effective partnership working with other organisations, and to build up cross-party alliances, on major issues could be critical to the success of its public affairs strategy and activities. The House of Lords, in particular, offers significant opportunities to work on a cross-party basis with the political parties, and groupings, represented in the Upper House to influence policy development and legislation.

You should also take a 'Two Chambers' approach to ensure your organisation secures tangible outcomes for its public affairs strategies and activities in both the House of Commons and in the House of

Lords. The public affairs strategies and activities recommended in this guide offer real opportunities, through progressing such an approach, to deliver major results for your organisation in its influencing work. Adopting a Two Chambers approach will strengthen the ability of your organisation to achieve the aims and objectives of its public affairs strategy and activities and to help shape policy development and legislation.

Above all else, organisations should take a confident approach to their public affairs work. It is important not to forget that organisations across different sectors make an important contribution to our society, and that Government ministers, the opposition parties, MPs, Peers and other policy makers are interested in their successes, as well as in the challenges they face. Your organisation should, therefore, approach its public affairs strategy with some optimism that the issues you are raising will often be considered on their merit, and with renewed confidence from reading this guide that it does have the skills and capacity to deliver a highly successful, cost-effective public affairs strategy to achieve its policy aims and objectives, and to influence policy development and legislation.

Bibliography

Books & Magazines

Dod's Parliamentary Companion 2017 (London, 2017)
Erskine May: Parliamentary Practice, 24th Edition, (London, 2011)
House Magazine
Public Affairs Guide to Scotland, R. McGeachy and M. Ballard (Cardiff, 2017)
Vacher's Quarterly, (London, 2017)

Websites

A Guide to the Rules on All-Party Parliamentary Groups, www.parliament.uk (March, 2015)
All-Party Parliamentary Groups, www.parliament.uk
Ask your MP to present a petition, www.parliament.uk
Checking and challenging Government, www.parliament.uk
Delegated Legislation, SN/PC/6509, R. Kelly, www.parliament.uk (December, 2012)
Devolution of powers to Scotland, Wales and Northern Ireland, www.gov.uk
Devolution Settlement: Northern Ireland, www.gov.uk
Devolution Settlement: Scotland, www.gov.uk
Devolution Settlement: Wales, www.gov.uk
Early Day Motions - Factsheet P3, www.parliament.uk (June, 2010)
English votes for English laws: House of Commons Bill procedure, www.parliament.uk
E-petitions - SN/PC/06450, www.parliament.uk
Find out more about e-petitions, www.parliament.uk
General Elections, www. parliament.uk
Glossary, www.parliament.uk
Governance of Wales: Who is responsible for what?, www.assembly.wales
Memorandum of Understanding and Supplementary Agreements

Between the United Kingdom Government, the Scottish Ministers, the Welsh Ministers, and the Northern Ireland Executive Committee, www.gov.uk

Parliamentary Stages of a Government Bill, Factsheet L1, www. parliament.uk (August, 2010)

Petition Parliament, www. parliament.uk

Pre-legislative scrutiny - SN/PC/2822, www.parliament.uk (April, 2010)

Private Members' Bills, www.parliament.uk

Public Bills in Parliament, www.parliament.uk (December, 2012)

Public Petitions - Factsheet P7 Procedure Series, www.parliament.uk (August, 2010)

Public Petitions to the House of Commons, www.parliament.uk

Question Time, www. parliament.uk

Scotland Act 2016, Explanatory Notes, www.legislation.gov.uk

Standing Orders of the House of Commons, www.parliament.uk (April, 2017)

Standing Orders of the House of Lords, www.parliament.uk (May, 2016)

Successful Private Members' Bills since 1983 – 84', SN/PC/04568, www.parliament.uk (June, 2014)

Taking part in Public Bills in the House of Lords: A Guide for Members, www.parliament.uk

Wales Bill: Explanatory Notes, www.parliament.uk

What are Early Day Motions?, www.parliament.uk

Index

Abortion Act (1967) 184
Action for Children Scotland 36, 284-5
All-Party Parliamentary Groups ix, 21, 24, 83, 109, 140, 188, 238-46, 252-3, 279-80
Assembly Member (AM) ix
Autism Act (2009) 184

Backbenchers ix, 3, 8, 14, 69, 79, 83, 88-92, 98, 166, 177, 179, 184, 193, 205, 212, 238; Backbench business 51; Backbench Committee (House of Commons) 204, 212, 233, 236; 'Backbench rebellion' 3, 171
Barnardo's 36
Baroness Lister of Burtersett 285
Bishops 82, 95, 165, 171, 177, 190
Brexit 16, 26
By-elections ix, 74, 93

Cabinet ix, 62; Cabinet Ministers 60-2, 65-9
Carer's Allowance 28
Census Act 1920 155 fn.
Citizens Advice Scotland 36
Command Papers 58, 112
Committees 17, 37-9, 44, 58, 78, 81, 97, 102, 104, 109, 111-28, 293-4; Chairs and Members of committees 19, 22, 81, 109, 119, 121, 139, 181; Debates on committee reports 125-6; Delegated Legislation Committee (House of Commons) 45, 156; General Committees 114-5; Grand Committee (House of Lords) 54, 115, 127, 146-7; Inquiries 23, 38, 102-3, 112-3, 117-28, 293-4; Joint Committees 113-4; Legislative Grand Committee 114, 149; Northern Ireland Grand Committee 27, 114; Northern Ireland Affairs Committee 37-9; Public Bill Committees xii, 14-15, 168, 177, 186; Scottish Affairs Committee 37-9; Scottish Grand Committee 114; Secondary Legislation Scrutiny Committee (House of Lords) 156; Select Committees 59, 112-3, 138, 231; Social media 116; Sub-committees 116; Websites 123; Welsh Affairs Committee 37-9; Welsh Grand Committee 27, 114
Confederation of British Industry (CBI) ix, 11, 279
Consultations ix, 20, 24, 98, 101-10, 137, 243
Cross-party approaches 3, 12, 22-4, 37, 70-2, 75, 77, 82, 94-5, 98, 100, 120, 126, 134, 141,164, 169, 171-2, 174, 179, 183-4, 188, 190, 217, 222, 224-5, 252, 260, 280, 299, 300-1

Delegated Legislation (Secondary legislation) x, 3, 45, 50, 52, 56, 59, 92, 114, 155-6, 179-81; Affirmative procedure ix, 59, 155; Commencement Orders 179; Negative procedure xi, 52, 59; Orders 3, 52, 55, 57-8, 156, 179; Super-affirmative procedure xiii, 52
Devolution xi, xvii-xviii, 1, 26-39
Disability Living Allowance 28
Divisions x, 3, 115, 143, 147, 164-5, 168-9, 171-3, 175, 177-8, 185, 203-4, 288, 295
Dods Parliamentary Companion 81, 83, 252

Early Day Motions x, 85-6, 217-28, 292-3
Electorate x-xi, 94
English Votes for English Laws xii, 27-8, 149-50

Erskine May 148 fn.,174 fn.
European Union 16, 24, 26, 206; EU law 26

Forced Marriage (Civil Protection) Act (2007) 184
Fixed-Term Parliaments Act (2011) 16 fn.
Freedom of information request 201

General Election ix, 16 fn., 69, 71, 74, 93, 98
Government of Wales Act (1998) 33
Government of Wales Act (2006) 33-4
Great Britain 229
Green Papers x, xiii, 135-7

Hansard xi, 58, 80, 83, 123-4, 163, 169, 175, 188, 204-6, 213-4, 231, 234, 241, 252
House Magazine 81
House of Commons xvii-xviii, xx, 1-7, 16 fn., 35, 37, 40, 44-52, 59, 63, 81-2, 85, 87, 89-90, 93-5, 97, 103-4, 111-5, 119, 122-3, 127-30, 134-5, 138, 139, 142-56, 158-83, 185-86, 188-9, 193-200, 203-6, 210-12, 215, 217, 226, 229, 230-4, 251-3, 283-8, 292-7, 299, 301; Public Information Office 159; Register of Members' Interests 241; Social media 104; Westminster Hall xiii, 45, 47, 49, 51, 112, 204-5, 233-4, 236
House of Lords xvii-xviii, xx, 1-7, 35, 37, 40, 44, 51-9, 62, 66, 70-1, 82-3, 86-7, 89-91, 93-5, 97, 103-4, 111-15, 119, 122, 127-30, 134-5, 138-9, 142-56, 158-83, 186, 188-90, 193, 195-200, 205-6, 210-12, 215, 229, 231, 233-4, 241, 251-3, 275, 283-8, 292-7, 299, 301; Government Whips' Office 55, 172; Lord Speaker 206; Opposition Whips' Office 172; Register of Lords' Interests 241; Social media 104;

Law Society of England and Wales 279

Legislation xx, 1-4, 7, 12, 15, 20, 23-4, 27, 49, 50, 62, 64-5, 77-8, 81, 83, 86-8, 90, 92, 94-7, 101, 108-9, 111, 116, 118, 120, 127, 129-83, 205, 252-4, 271, 280, 289, 294-7, 299; Act of Parliament ix, 114, 129, 179-80, 182; Amendments ix, 14-15, 37, 64, 66, 71, 86, 91, 95, 115, 164, 167, 175, 284-5, 297; Bill Team 92, 166-7; Draft Bills x, 113, 138-40, 143; Bills ix, xii, xix, 9, 27, 36, 50, 54, 82, 84, 90, 114, 255; Consolidation Bills 27, 113; Committee Stage of a Bill ix, 20, 23, 37, 54, 114-15, 165-73; Consideration of Commons Amendments 153-4, 177-9; Consideration of Lords Amendments 27, 151-3, 177-9; Directions 181-3; First Reading of a Bill x, 158; 'Flagship' Bills x, 143, 284, 296; Groupings of amendments xi, 144, 146-8; Legislative Consent Motions xi, 31, 145; Legislative process xix-xx, 1, 4-5, 50, 81, 84, 92, 158, 295; Marshalled List of amendments xi, 144, 146-8; Overview of the Parliamentary Process 142-56; Pre-legislative stage of a Bill xii, 18, 129-41, 143; Public Bill Office 144, 170, 189; Report Stage of a Bill xii, 20, 23, 37, 54; Report and Third Reading Stages (House of Commons) of a Bill 173-5; Report and Third Reading Stages (House of Lords) of a Bill 175-7; Royal Assent xii, 50, 129-30, 152, 154-5, 179; Scottish Bills 27; Second Reading of a Bill xiii, 20, 23, 158, 162-5, 296-7; Third Reading of a Bill xiii, 20, 23, 54, 114
Local Government 19, 21, 76; Council leaders 8, 11; Councillors 8, 11, 257-9, 264-6, 267, 269-70, 272, 275; Local Government elections 35, 93, 98; Local authorities 8, 12; Local Government community 8-11, 14-15, 17, 301; Mayors 11; Senior officials 8
Local Government Association 279

Lord Bishop of Ripon and Leeds 285
Lord Kirkwood of Kirkhope 285

Media 3, 6, 22-3, 38, 63-4, 72, 76, 79, 80, 85, 115, 127, 135, 189, 191-3, 199, 201-2, 207, 213, 215-16, 218-20, 222-3, 226, 228, 236, 240, 245, 256-7, 282, 288-300; Social media 22-3, 63, 72, 79, 85, 127, 135, 189, 199, 201-2, 207, 213, 216, 218-20, 222, 227, 236-7, 241, 245, 252, 256, 267, 274, 290, 292-5, 297-300
Member of the Legislative (Northern Ireland) Assembly (MLA) xi
Monarch xv, 129, 152, 154-5, 179, 229
Member of Parliament (MP) xiii, xix, xx, xxi, 4-6, 8-12, 14-15, 17-25, 29, 39-40, 46, 48-51, 61-3, 66, 69-71, 75-6, 78-88, 90, 92, 97-9, 113, 117-18, 121, 126-7, 130-2, 135, 138, 140, 143, 157, 160-2, 165-70, 173-6, 179, 181, 183, 185, 18-94, 196-202, 204, 207-10, 212-14, 216-27, 229, 233-47, 249-59, 264, 266, 269-70, 272-3, 275, 282, 284, 286, 288-9, 291-3, 295, 297, 299, 301-2
Member of the Scottish Parliament (MSP) xi, 37
Murder (Abolition of the Death Penalty) Act (1965) 184

National Council for Voluntary Organisations (NCVO) 279
National Health Service (NHS) xi, 11, 41
Northern Ireland 28-9, 35-7, 39, 114; Devolution 26-39; Good Friday Agreement (1998) 31; Northern Ireland Assembly xvii, 26-7, 29, 31, 145, 233; Northern Ireland Executive 26-7, 29; Secretary of State for Northern Ireland 31, 36
Northern Ireland Act (1998) 31

One Parent Families Scotland 36, 284-5
Opposition parties xi-xvii, xix-xx, 2, 9, 12, 14-15, 17-20, 22, 25, 39, 61-3, 66, 72, 84, 87, 95-6, 109, 131, 135, 140, 144, 157-8, 165-6, 170-1, 174, 181, 183, 187, 190, 192, 203, 207, 209, 211, 213-16, 218-20, 228, 256, 259-60, 263, 274-5, 278-9, 282, 284-5, 289, 291, 299, 301-2; HM Official Opposition xi, 19, 63, 109, 144, 194, 207, 209, 211, 213, 260; Working with the opposition parties 95-6

Parliament Act (1911) 152-4, 178
Parliament xvii-xix, 1-2, 5, 17, 20, 26-9, 31, 33-6, 38-42, 47, 51, 60-1, 77-8, 81, 83, 86-7, 89, 92, 94, 98, 113, 116-17, 125, 128, 130-1, 134, 137, 143, 181, 189-92, 195, 203-4, 211, 216, 228, 233-38, 240, 243, 246-50, 256-8, 267, 271, 283, 288, 299, 301; All-Party Parliamentary Groups 21, 24; Bicameral structure 1-2, 4; Legislative competence 2, 39; Motions 50-4, 56, 62, 84, 114, 151, 204, 208, 211, 214, 217, 275; Parliamentary session xi, 16, 178, 222-3, 236, 247; Parliamentary staff 61, 118-19, 121, 123, 243, 245, 247, 249-54, 256, 267, 269-70, 272, 297; Question Time 79, 82; Standing Orders xiii, 111, 145 fn., 185; Website 10, 51, 63, 83, 159, 194, 205, 222, 229-30, 232, 236, 242
Parliamentary debates 2, 5, 15, 24, 49, 51, 83-4, 86, 97, 135, 163, 203-16, 226, 228, 241, 283-4, 292, 294; Adjournment debates xi, 45, 49 204-5, 210, 212
Parliamentary events 21, 24, 247-56, 298-9
Parliamentary Monitoring 99, 103, 110; Exploiting Parliamentary Monitoring and Political Intelligence Gathering 40-59; Monitoring business in the House of Commons 44-51; Monitoring business in the House of Lords 51-9
Parliamentary Questions xi, xviii, 2, 5, 6, 42, 48-9, 56, 79, 83, 85, 97, 193-202;

Starred Questions (House of Lords) xiii, 52-3, 70, 82, 195, 294

Peers xii, xvii-xix, 4-6, 8-12, 14-15, 17-25, 29, 39-40, 53-4, 61-3, 66, 69-71, 82-8, 90, 92, 97-9, 113, 117-18, 125-7, 130-2, 135, 138, 140, 143, 157-8, 163-5, 170-1, 173, 176-7, 179, 181, 183, 186-92, 196-99, 201-2, 206-10, 212-14, 217-18, 231, 237-42, 244-5, 247, 249-54, 256-9, 264-7, 269-70, 272-3, 275, 279, 282, 284, 286-7, 289, 291, 297, 301-3; Crossbench Peers ix, 3, 53, 82, 95, 134, 165, 171-2, 177, 190, 205, 229, 238, 247, 253-4; Engaging with Peers 78-86; Meetings with Peers 69-70; Non-affiliated Peers 95, 165, 171

Pepper v Hart 169

Personal Independent Payment 28

Petitions 21, 24, 51, 135, 229-37; Petitions Committee (House of Commons) 231-35, 237

'Policy asks' xii, 11, 13, 17, 25, 54, 60, 62-3, 66-9, 79, 84, 94, 96, 98, 120, 160, 201, 250, 266-7, 272, 274, 278, 280-4, 286, 289, 299, 301

Policy development xix-xx, 1, 7, 24, 61, 78, 83, 86-8, 94, 96, 101, 108, 259, 272, 278, 280, 283

Political parties Conferences 21, 24, 257-76; Influencing the political parties' manifestos 98-9, 134, 257; Influencing the political parties 87-100; Leaders 20, 22; The Party Whip (circular) xii, 3, 82, 164, 171, 175, 224-5, 253, 255; whips (party officers) xii, 97, 163, 174, 178, 223

Press Association 199

Prime Minister xii, xvii, 8-12, 19, 21-2, 60-1, 63, 66-8, 88, 283; Prime Minister's Question Time xii, 193-4, 294

Private Members' Bills xvii, 5, 21, 24, 27, 50, 54, 84, 114, 129-31, 184-92, 285-6, 299-300;

Private sector xviii, 8, 10

Public affairs strategy xviii-xix, 1, 4-6,

8-25, 27-8, 40, 43, 45, 47, 52-3, 57, 59-63, 65, 68-71, 77-8, 81, 85-7, 92-5, 98, 100-01, 117, 130-1, 135, 141-3, 158, 167, 170, 176, 195-6, 201-2, 207-8, 210, 213, 218, 221, 224-5, 233, 239, 244, 259-61, 263, 276-8, 283, 285-90, 298-302

Public Limited Company (PLC) xii, 9, 11

Public sector xviii, 8, 10-11

Queen's Speech xii, 16, 143

Salisbury Convention 143, 146, 151

Scotland 28-9, 35-7, 39, 114; Scottish Government 26-31; Scottish Parliament xvii, 26-31, 37, 145, 233; Scotland Office 37; Secretary of State for Scotland 36

Scotland Act (1998) 29

Scotland Act (2012) 29

Scotland Act (2016) 28, 30-1

Scottish Council for Voluntary Organisations 280

Shops Bill (1986) 144

Speaker xiii, 27, 114, 148-50, 173-4, 203-4, 230

Special advisers xiii, 2, 9, 40, 61-2, 66, 68, 74, 83, 88, 92-4, 122, 132-4, 138, 167, 178;

Statutory Guidance xiii, 37, 92, 179, 181-3, 285

Third sector xviii-xix, 10, 14, 36, 41, 248, 262, 291

Transparency of Lobbying, Non-Party Campaigning and Trade Union Administration Act 2014 xxii

'Two Chambers' approach 2-7, 301

United Kingdom (UK) 10-2, 29, 35-7, 70, 82-3, 87-8, 101, 130, 232, 285, 290-1

United Kingdom Government x, xvii-xx, 1-2, 4-6, 9-10, 12, 15-18, 23, 25-9, 31, 33-9, 49, 51, 60, 62-5, 67-8, 70-1, 73-8, 83-5, 87-90, 92-96, 99-105, 107-9, 111, 120-2, 126, 130-44, 157,

159-61, 163, 165-8, 172-3, 176-7, 179, 181, 183, 187-8, 190, 196-7, 199-203, 205, 207-9, 211-13, 215, 218-21, 228, 230-2, 235-7, 243, 245, 248, 256, 263, 265, 277, 281, 283, 285-7, 289, 294-5, 297-9; Budget Autumn Statement 16; Civil servants 2, 9, 40, 61, 66, 68, 74-5, 88, 91-3, 102, 121, 132-3, 138, 248; Engaging with the Government 87-94; Engagement with Government Ministers in the House of Lords 90-1; Government Ministers xvii, xix, 4, 8-10, 12, 14, 17, 19-22, 36, 39-40, 46, 61-2, 66, 72, 78, 80, 82-3, 88, 91, 121, 158, 163, 193-4, 198, 214, 223, 236, 252, 254, 256, 258, 263-5, 267, 270-2, 275, 282-3, 291-2, 301-2; Ministerial level 2; Ministerial visits 72-77, 80; Statements 2; Government Whips 223; Government Whips' Offices 172; Working groups 13, 77, 92, 102 'Usual channels' xiii, 114, 178;

Vacher's Quarterly 81, 252

Wales 28-9, 35-7, 39, 114; National Assembly for Wales xvii, 26-7, 29, 33, 38, 145, 233; Secretary of State for Wales 36, 38; Welsh Government 26, 29; Welsh Ministers 33, 35
Wales Act (2014) 34
Wales Act (2017) 35
Welfare Reform Act (2012) 285
Westminster 1-7, 24, 47, 80, 96, 134, 224, 272, 298
Whitehall departments 1, 234
White Papers xiii; Responding to White Papers 137-8

welsh academic press

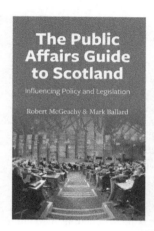

The Public Affairs Guide to
SCOTLAND

'[an excellent] guide for the newcomer and a 'memory stick' for the expert. It contains all a person needs to know to engage with the Parliament, the Government, local authorities and civic society in an effective and efficient way. This book shows how one can participate in that fast moving and interesting field and will become a tool for all who wish to get involved and achieve success in their endeavours.'
Michael P Clancy

'Effective and informed activity by MSPs, the Parliament, the Scottish Government and third sector bodies in taking forward legislation and promoting causes, whilst protecting the most vulnerable is the best way to ensure a truly participatory, power sharing democracy and that is why this guide will be so useful ... Mark Ballard and Robert McGeachy, through the pages of this important book, are therefore doing democracy a service.'

Michael Russell, MSP for Argyll & Bute Professor in Scottish Culture & Governance, The University of Glasgow

978-1-86057-126-8   224pp   £19.99   PB

The Financial Affairs of
DAVID LLOYD GEORGE

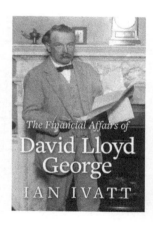

'In this important and pioneering study, Ian Ivatt has focussed his attention on a key theme rather neglected by historians and biographers of Lloyd George – his relationship with money and financial resources ... [these] compelling, engrossing themes, central to an understanding of Lloyd George's life, are dissected with a masterly touch by Mr. Ivatt. He has spared no effort to master the ever burgeoning published literature on David Lloyd George, has waded through the various scattered archival sources and scoured the newspaper columns too. He has also conducted personal interviews and undertaken research on the ground. All his enthralling discoveries have been deftly welded into a cohesive, absorbing account'
J. Graham Jones, from the Foreword

The Financial Affairs of David Lloyd George is the first serious and systematic study to examine, assess and analyse Lloyd George's attitude to money and finance, and compellingly illustrates how he accumulated great wealth by fair and more questionable methods.

978-1-86057-125-1   160pp   £19.99   PB

welsh academic press

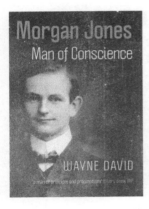

MORGAN JONES
Man of Conscience

Wayne David

'Wayne David deserves great credit for bringing Morgan Jones to life in this well-researched and very readable book.'
Nick Thomas-Symonds MP

'Wayne David writes of one of his predecessors as Labour MP for Caerphilly with the understanding of the political insider and the contextual knowledge of the historian.'
Professor Dai Smith

'Jones was a man of principle and pragmatism.'
Hilary Benn MP, from his Foreword

Imprisoned in Wormwood Scrubs for his pacifist beliefs during the First World War, Morgan Jones made history by becoming the first conscientious objector to be elected an MP when he won the Caerphilly by-election for Labour in 1921.

978-1-86057-141-1   128pp   £14.99   PB

POLITICAL CHAMELEON
In Search of George Thomas

Martin Shipton

'a very fair book and a very well researched book. The problem with George Thomas is that one can write a book that is very fair and very well researched yet he still comes out of it very badly.'
Vaughan Roderick, Welsh Affairs Editor, BBC Wales

'Compelling'
Kevin McGuire, New Statesman

'throws light on the career of its extremely complex, often disturbing and, ultimately, not-very-likable subject ... An unrelentingly hostile account ... [that] demolishes [Thomas'] reputation ... Shipton has fulfilled a necessary task'
Dr Martin Wright, Cardiff University, Parliamentary History

Award-winning journalist Martin Shipton reveals the real George Thomas, the complex character behind the carefully crafted facade of the devout Christian, and discovers a number of surprising and shocking personae - including the sexual predator - of this ultimate *Political Chameleon*.

978-1-86057-137-4   304pp   £16.99   PB

welsh academic press

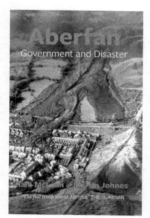

ABERFAN
Government and Disaster
(Second Edition)

Iain McLean & Martin Johnes

'The full truth about Aberfan'
The Guardian

'The research is outstanding...the investigation is substantial, balanced and authoritative...this is certainly the definitive book on the subject...Meticulous.'
John R. Davis, Journal of Contemporary British History

'Excellent...thorough and sympathetic.'
Headway 2000 (Aberfan Community Newspaper)

Aberfan - Government & Disaster is widely recognised as the definitive study of the disaster and, following meticulous research of previously unavailable public records - kept confidential by the UK Government's 30-year rule - the authors explain how and why the disaster happened and why nobody was held responsible.

978-1-86057-133-6   192pp   £19.99   PB

GARETH JONES
Eyewitness to the Holodomor

Ray Gamache

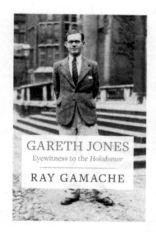

'Excellent ... serves as a warning to journalists not to be taken in by official sources and political ideology but to report what they actually learn through their own efforts.'
Prof. Maurine H. Beasley, Univ. of Maryland

'...meticulously researched book [that] returns Gareth Jones to his rightful status, as one of the most outstanding journalists of his generation'
Nigel Linsan Colley, www.garethjones.org

'Extraordinary ... Jones' articles ... caused a sensation ... Because [his] notebooks record immediate impressions and describe events as they were happening, they have an unusual freshness ... Jones' reputation has revived thanks to the Ukrainian government's broader efforts to tell the history of the famine.'
Anne Applebaum, The New York Review

Gareth Jones (1905-1934), the young Welsh investigative journalist, is revered in Ukraine as a national hero and is now rightly recognised as the first reporter to reveal the horror of the Holodomor, the Soviet Government-induced famine of the early 1930s, which killed millions of Ukrainians.

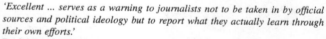

978-1-86057-122-0   256pp   £19.99   PB

Lightning Source UK Ltd.
Milton Keynes UK
UKHW022024220621
385966UK00004B/78

9 781860 571343